MOST REQUESTED

Taste *of* Home

RECIPES

TASTE OF HOME BOOKS • RDA ENTHUSIAST BRANDS, LLC • MILWAUKEE, WI

APPETIZERS, SNACKS & BEVERAGES

With these delish dips and spreads, hot bites, must-try drinks and other small-plate delights in your party-day repertoire, impressing guests has never been easier!

STEAK CROSTINI WITH CARROT-HORSERADISH MARMALADE

I've been making small tweaks to this family recipe for years. I suggest prepping everything ahead, then layering up the crostini right before serving.
—**Greg Fontenot** The Woodlands, TX

Prep: 1 hour • **Cook:** 30 min.
Makes: 3½ dozen

- 1 **French bread baguette (10½ ounces), cut into ¼-inch slices**
- ¼ **cup olive oil, divided**
- 1 **pound medium carrots, grated**
- 2 **cups water**
- 1½ **cups sugar**
- 1 **to 2 tablespoons prepared horseradish**
- 1 **tablespoon butter**
- 1 **cup chopped onion**
- 2 **cups shredded Swiss cheese**
- 1 **carton (8 ounces) mascarpone cheese**
- 2 **tablespoons mayonnaise**
- 1 **tablespoon sour cream**
- 1 **boneless beef top loin steak (12 to 14 ounces)**

1. Preheat the oven to 350°. Place baguette slices on baking sheets; brush with 2 tablespoons olive oil. Bake until toasted, about 10 minutes.

2. Place carrots and water in a large saucepan; bring to a boil over medium-high heat. Cook, uncovered, 10 minutes. Add sugar; cook on medium heat until thickened, about 15 minutes, stirring occasionally. Remove from heat; add desired amount of horseradish and mix well. Cool.

3. Meanwhile, in a small saucepan over medium-low heat, melt butter. Cook and stir onions until golden brown and tender, 10-12 minutes; cool. Stir in the cheeses, mayonnaise and sour cream.

4. In a large skillet, heat remaining olive oil over medium-high heat. Add steak; cook 4-6 minutes on each side until meat reaches desired doneness (for medium-rare, a thermometer should read 135°; medium, 140°; medium-well, 145°). Let stand 5 minutes; cut into thin slices.

5. To serve, spread cheese mixture on each baguette slice. Add a piece of steak; top with carrot mixture.

GARDEN-FRESH SEAFOOD COCKTAIL

For something cool on a hot day, we mix shrimp and crabmeat with crunchy veggies straight from the garden. Look for adobo seasoning in the international section of the grocery store.

—**Teri Rasey** Cadillac, MI

....

Prep: 15 min. + chilling
Makes: 6 cups

- ¾ pound peeled and deveined cooked shrimp (31-40 per pound), thawed
- 1 container (8 ounces) refrigerated jumbo lump crabmeat, drained
- 3 celery ribs, chopped
- 1 medium cucumber, peeled, seeded and chopped
- 1 medium sweet orange pepper, chopped
- 2 plum tomatoes, seeded and chopped
- ½ cup red onion, finely chopped
- 1 to 2 jalapeno peppers, seeded and finely chopped
- ¼ cup minced fresh cilantro
- 3 tablespoons lime juice
- 1 tablespoon olive oil
- 2¼ teaspoons adobo seasoning

Combine first nine ingredients. Whisk together the lime juice, oil and adobo seasoning; drizzle over shrimp mixture and toss gently to coat. Refrigerate at least 1 hour, tossing gently every 20 minutes. Place shrimp mixture in cocktail glasses.

RUSTIC TOMATO CHEESE TART

My fresh tomato tart is wonderful when you want a taste of summer, no matter the time of year. The crust stays nice and crisp.

—**Moji Dabney** Egg Harbor Township, NJ

....

Prep: 30 min. • **Bake:** 30 min.
Makes: 12 servings

- 7 sheets phyllo dough (14x9 inches)
- ⅓ cup olive oil
- 7 tablespoons crumbled goat cheese
- 1 cup thinly sliced sweet onion
- 1 cup shredded fontina cheese
- 4 plum tomatoes, thinly sliced
- 2 tablespoons minced chives
- 1 tablespoon minced fresh basil or 1 teaspoon dried basil
- ¼ teaspoon salt
- ¼ teaspoon pepper

1. Place one sheet of phyllo dough on a parchment-lined baking sheet. Brush with oil and sprinkle with 1 tablespoon goat cheese. (Keep remaining phyllo covered with plastic wrap and a damp towel to prevent it from drying out.) Repeat layers, brushing oil all the way to edges.
2. Sprinkle onion over top to within 1 in. of edges; sprinkle with fontina. Arrange tomato slices in a slightly overlapping pattern over cheese. Sprinkle with chives, basil, salt and pepper. Bring up edges of tart over filling.
3. Bake at 375° for 30-35 minutes or until crust is golden brown.

SPICY SWEET POTATO CHIPS & CILANTRO DIP

This cool, creamy dip tempers the heat in the spicy-sweet potato chips. Talk about a match made in heaven!

—Elizabeth Godecke Chicago, IL

Prep: 20 min. • **Bake:** 25 min./batch
Makes: 12 servings (1½ cups dip)

- 2 to 3 large sweet potatoes (1¾ pounds), peeled and cut into ⅛-inch slices
- 2 tablespoons canola oil
- 1 teaspoon chili powder
- ½ teaspoon garlic powder
- ½ teaspoon taco seasoning
- ¼ teaspoon salt
- ¼ teaspoon ground cumin
- ¼ teaspoon pepper
- ⅛ teaspoon cayenne pepper

DIP

- ¾ cup mayonnaise
- ½ cup sour cream
- 2 ounces cream cheese, softened
- 4½ teaspoons minced fresh cilantro
- 1½ teaspoons lemon juice
- ½ teaspoon celery salt
- ⅛ teaspoon pepper

1. Preheat oven to 400°. Place sweet potatoes in a large bowl. In a small bowl, mix oil and seasonings; drizzle over sweet potatoes and toss to coat.

2. Arrange half of the potatoes in a single layer in two ungreased 15x10x1-in. baking pans. Bake 25-30 minutes or until golden brown, turning once. Repeat with the remaining potatoes.

3. In a small bowl, beat dip ingredients until blended. Serve with chips.

GRILLED PEACH BBQ CHICKEN WINGS

I was proud to include the recipe for these moist and tender chicken wings in my cookbook, Cooking for Isaiah: Gluten-Free & Dairy-Free Recipes for Easy, Delicious Meals. *The sweet peach barbecue glaze makes them so yummy!*

—Silvana Nardone Brooklyn, NY

Prep: 20 min. + marinating • **Cook:** 30 min.
Makes: 4 servings

- 2 cups barbecue sauce
- 2 cloves garlic, finely chopped, divided
- 2 peaches, peeled, pitted and chopped Salt and pepper
- 24 chicken wings, separated at the joint and tips discarded
- 1 cup peach jam
- ¼ cup apple cider vinegar
- 2 tablespoons hot sauce, such as Frank's RedHot, or to taste Scallions, green parts only, thinly sliced

1. In a food processor, combine the barbecue sauce and half of the garlic. Add the peaches and process until finely chopped; season with about 1½ teaspoons salt and about ¼ teaspoon pepper. Reserve ½ cup for basting.

2. In a large bowl, toss together chicken wings and the remaining peach barbecue sauce; cover and refrigerate for about 30 minutes.

3. Meanwhile, combine the peach jam, vinegar, remaining garlic, hot sauce and ½ teaspoon salt in a small saucepan. Cook over medium heat until slightly thickened, about 5 minutes; let cool.

4. Drain and discard marinade. On a lightly greased grill rack, grill wings, covered, over medium heat or broil 4 in. from the heat for 12-16 minutes, turning occasionally.

5. Brush with reserved sauce. Grill or broil, uncovered, 8-10 minutes longer or until juices run clear, basting and turning several times. Top with scallions and serve with peach jam dipping sauce.

Note: Read all product ingredient labels for possible gluten and dairy content prior to use. Ingredient formulas can change, and production facilities vary among brands. If you're concerned your brand may contain gluten or dairy, contact the company.

GROUND BEEF TACO DIP

It's not a football party without taco dip. My version, made with spicy ground beef and fresh toppings, won't disappoint. It's full of classic flavors and is extra filling for those hearty game-day appetites.

—**Errika Perry** Green Bay, WI

Start to Finish: 25 min.
Makes: 24 servings

- 1 pound lean ground beef (90% lean)
- ¾ cup water
- 2 envelopes taco seasoning, divided
- 1 container (16 ounces) fat-free sour cream
- 1 package (8 ounces) cream cheese, softened
- 2 cups shredded iceberg lettuce
- 1 cup shredded cheddar cheese
- 3 medium tomatoes, finely chopped
- 1 medium green pepper, finely chopped
- 1 can (2¼ ounces) sliced ripe olives, drained

1. In a large skillet, cook and crumble beef over medium heat until no longer pink, 4-6 minutes; drain. Add the water and one envelope taco seasoning; cook until thickened. Cool slightly.
2. Beat sour cream, cream cheese and remaining taco seasoning until blended. Spread in a 3-qt. dish; add ground beef. Top with lettuce, cheddar, tomatoes, pepper and olives.

★ ★ ★ ★ ★ **READER REVIEW**

"Easy and delicious. I substituted one fresh jalapeno pepper in lieu of a green bell pepper. Good for a large crowd."

JANADELE TASTEOFHOME.COM

SPARKLING CRANBERRY KISS

Cranberry and orange juices are terrific with ginger ale. We like using cranberry juice cocktail for this punch, but other blends, like cranberry-apple, also sparkle.

—**Shannon Copley** Upper Arlington, OH

Start to Finish: 5 min.
Makes: 14 servings (¾ cup each)

- 6 cups cranberry juice
- 1½ cups orange juice
- 3 cups ginger ale
  Ice cubes
  Orange slices, optional

In a pitcher, combine cranberry juice and orange juice. Just before serving, stir in ginger ale; serve over ice. If desired, serve with orange slices.

BLIZZARD PARTY MIX

The sweet-salty combo of my snack mix is sure to be popular. It's perfect for a party, munching at home or giving away as a gift.

—**Kelley Scott** Parma, OH

Start to Finish: 30 min.
Makes: 6 cups

- 2 cups Corn Chex
- 2 cups miniature pretzels
- 1 cup dry roasted peanuts
- 20 caramels, coarsely chopped
- 1 package (10 to 12 ounces) white baking chips

1. In a large bowl, combine the first four ingredients. In a microwave, melt chips; stir until smooth. Pour over cereal mixture and toss to coat.
2. Immediately spread onto waxed paper-lined baking sheet; let stand until set, about 20 minutes.
3. Break into pieces. Store in an airtight container.

CAPRESE SALAD KABOBS

Trade in the usual veggie platter for these fun kabobs. I often make them for my family to snack on, and it's a great recipe for kids to help with.

—**Christine Mitchell** Glendora, CA

Start to Finish: 10 min.
Makes: 12 kabobs

- 24 **grape tomatoes**
- 12 **cherry-size fresh mozzarella cheese balls**
- 24 **fresh basil leaves**
- 2 **tablespoons olive oil**
- 2 **teaspoons balsamic vinegar**

On each of 12 appetizer skewers, alternately thread two tomatoes, one mozzarella ball and two basil leaves. To serve, whisk together oil and vinegar; drizzle over kabobs.

WHITE SANGRIA

Fruity, sweet and party-pretty, this light, refreshing beverage goes together in mere minutes.

—*Taste of Home* **Test Kitchen**

Prep: 15 min. + chilling
Makes: 7 servings

- 1 **cup unsweetened pineapple juice**
- ¼ **cup lemon juice**
- 2 **medium oranges, washed and sliced**
- 1 **medium lemon, washed and sliced**
- 1 **bottle (750 ml) Riesling or other sweet white wine**
- 1 **medium tart apple, thinly sliced**
- ¼ **cup Triple Sec**
- 2 **cups lemon-lime soda, chilled**
  Ice cubes

1. In a large pitcher, combine the pineapple juice, lemon juice and orange and lemon slices; mash gently with a wooden spoon until fruit is partially crushed. Add the wine, apple slices and triple sec. Refrigerate for 2-4 hours.
2. Just before serving, add soda. Serve sangria over ice.

BBQ CHICKEN PIZZA ROLL-UP

These appetizer slices make for fab, filling small bites with loads of sweet and tangy flavor. Refrigerated pizza crust and pantry staples keep prep easy and fast.
—**Tracey Birch** Queen Creek, AZ

Prep: 15 min. • **Bake:** 15 min. + cooling
Makes: 2 dozen

- 1 tube (13.8 ounces) refrigerated pizza crust
- ¼ cup honey barbecue sauce
- 1½ cups shredded part-skim mozzarella cheese
- 1½ cups shredded cooked chicken breast
- 1 small red onion, finely chopped
- ¼ cup minced fresh cilantro
- 1 teaspoon Italian seasoning, optional
- 1 large egg white
- 1 tablespoon water
- ¼ teaspoon garlic powder

1. On a lightly floured surface, roll crust into a 12x9-in. rectangle; brush with barbecue sauce. Layer with cheese, chicken, onion, cilantro and, if desired, Italian seasoning.

2. Roll up jelly-roll style, starting with a long side; pinch seams to seal. Place seam side down on a baking sheet coated with cooking spray.

3. Beat egg white and water; brush over top. Sprinkle with garlic powder. Bake at 400° for 15-20 minutes or until crust is lightly browned. Cool for 10 minutes before slicing.

TEST KITCHEN TIP
Save time by preparing this recipe with shredded rotisserie chicken from the supermarket deli.

5 INGREDIENTS FAST FIX
FLUFFY HOT CHOCOLATE

This is our daughter's favorite hot chocolate recipe. It may look like ordinary cocoa, but a touch of vanilla sets it apart. And the melted marshmallows give it a frothy texture you won't get from an instant cocoa packet.
—**Jo Ann Schimcek** Weimar, TX

Start to Finish: 15 min.
Makes: 4 servings

- 8 teaspoons sugar
- 4 teaspoons baking cocoa
- 4 cups 2% milk
- 1½ cups miniature marshmallows
- 1 teaspoon vanilla extract

In a small saucepan, combine the first four ingredients. Cook and stir over medium heat until marshmallows are melted, about 8 minutes. Remove from the heat; stir in vanilla. Ladle into mugs.

HOT WING DIP

Here is my go-to dip for entertaining friends and family. I usually have all the ingredients on hand, and folks love it!
—**Coleen Corner** Grove City, PA

Prep: 10 min. • **Cook:** 1 hour
Makes: 18 servings (¼ cup each)

- 2 cups shredded cooked chicken
- 1 package (8 ounces) cream cheese, cubed
- 2 cups shredded cheddar cheese
- 1 cup ranch salad dressing
- ½ cup Louisiana-style hot sauce
  Tortilla chips and celery sticks
  Minced fresh parsley, optional

In a 3-qt. slow cooker, mix the first five ingredients. Cook, covered, on low for 1-2 hours or until cheese is melted. Serve with chips and celery. If desired, sprinkle with parsley.

TUSCAN SAUSAGE & BEAN DIP

This is a spin-off of a Mexican dip I once had. The original was wicked good, but I was going through an "I'm-so-over-Mexican-dip" phase and decided to switch it up. Take it to a party—I bet you no one else will bring anything like it!

—**Mandy Rivers** Lexington, SC

Prep: 25 min. • **Bake:** 20 min.
Makes: 16 servings (¼ cup each)

- 1 pound bulk hot Italian sausage
- 1 medium onion, finely chopped
- 4 garlic cloves, minced
- ½ cup dry white wine or chicken broth
- ½ teaspoon dried oregano
- ¼ teaspoon salt
- ¼ teaspoon dried thyme
- 1 package (8 ounces) cream cheese, softened
- 1 package (6 ounces) fresh baby spinach, coarsely chopped
- 1 can (15 ounces) cannellini beans, rinsed and drained
- 1 cup chopped seeded tomatoes
- 1 cup shredded part-skim mozzarella cheese
- ½ cup shredded Parmesan cheese
       Assorted crackers or toasted French bread baguette slices

1. Preheat oven to 375°. In a large skillet, cook sausage, onion and garlic over medium heat until sausage is no longer pink, breaking up meat into crumbles; drain. Stir in wine, oregano, salt and thyme. Bring to a boil; cook until liquid is almost evaporated.
2. Add cream cheese; stir until melted. Stir in spinach, beans and tomatoes; cook and stir until spinach is wilted. Transfer to a greased 8-in. square baking dish; if using an ovenproof skillet, leave in skillet. Sprinkle with cheeses.
3. Bake until bubbly, 20-25 minutes. Serve with crackers.

FRESH FROM THE GARDEN WRAPS

We moved into a house with a garden that needed tending, so we made these fresh wraps using the herbs we found. What a lovely first dinner in our new home!
—**Chris Bugher** Asheville, NC

Prep: 20 min. + standing
Makes: 8 servings

- 1 medium ear sweet corn
- 1 medium cucumber, chopped
- 1 cup shredded cabbage
- 1 medium tomato, chopped
- 1 small red onion, chopped
- 1 jalapeno pepper, seeded and minced
- 1 tablespoon minced fresh basil
- 1 tablespoon minced fresh cilantro
- 1 tablespoon minced fresh mint
- ⅓ cup Thai chili sauce
- 3 tablespoons rice vinegar
- 2 teaspoons reduced-sodium soy sauce
- 2 teaspoons creamy peanut butter
- 8 Bibb or Boston lettuce leaves

1. Cut corn from cob and place in a large bowl. Add cucumber, cabbage, tomato, onion, jalapeno and herbs.
2. Whisk together chili sauce, vinegar, soy sauce and peanut butter. Pour over the vegetable mixture; toss to coat. Let stand 20 minutes.
3. Using a slotted spoon, place ½ cup salad in each lettuce leaf. Fold lettuce over the filling.
Note: Wear disposable gloves when cutting hot peppers; the oils can burn skin. Avoid touching your face.

SPICY BUTTERSCOTCH WINGS

We are die-hard fans of spicy chicken wings. My homemade butterscotch sauce balances the heat nicely. You could also glaze the wings with melted brown sugar.
—**Aaron Salazar** Westminster, CO

Prep: 25 min. • **Bake:** 25 min.
Makes: 10 servings

- 2 **pounds chicken wings**
- 2 **tablespoons soy sauce**
- 2 **tablespoons ketchup**
- 2 **tablespoons Sriracha Asian hot chili sauce**
- 1 **teaspoon pepper**
- 1 **teaspoon crushed red pepper flakes**
- 1 **teaspoon onion powder**
- ½ **teaspoon salt**

BUTTERSCOTCH SAUCE
- ½ **cup sugar**
- ½ **cup 2% milk, warmed**
- 2 **tablespoons butter**

CRUMB TOPPING
- 1 **tablespoon butter**
- ½ **cup panko (Japanese) bread crumbs**
- 2 **green onions, sliced diagonally, divided**
- 1 **garlic clove, minced**
- ½ **teaspoon salt**
- ½ **teaspoon pepper**
- 2 **red bird's eye chili peppers, minced, optional**

1. Preheat oven to 400°. Using a sharp knife, cut through the two wing joints; discard wing tips. Combine next seven ingredients; add wings and toss to coat.
2. Line a 15x10-in. pan with foil; grease with cooking spray. Bake wings in prepared pan 10 minutes; reduce heat to 350° and bake until juices run clear, 12-15 minutes. Remove from oven; keep warm.
3. Meanwhile, in a small skillet, spread sugar; cook, without stirring, over medium heat until it begins to melt. Gently drag melted sugar to center of pan so it melts evenly. Cook, without stirring, until melted sugar turns amber. Carefully stir in warm milk and butter. Simmer sauce, stirring frequently, until thickened, 5-7 minutes. Keep warm.
4. In a large skillet over medium heat, melt butter; add the bread crumbs, one green onion, garlic, salt and pepper. Cook and stir until bread crumbs are golden brown, about 2 minutes. Set aside.
5. To serve, toss wings in butterscotch sauce. Sprinkle with crumb topping, remaining green onion and, if desired, sliced peppers. Serve hot.

ROASTED VEGETABLE DIP

My children were always good at finishing their plates, but I wanted something to get them to eat more vegetables (and enjoy them). This dip did the trick!
—**Sarah Vasques** Milford, NH

Prep: 15 min. • **Bake:** 25 min. + cooling
Makes: 20 servings (2 tablespoons each)

- 2 large sweet red peppers
- 1 large zucchini
- 1 medium onion
- 1 tablespoon olive oil
- ½ teaspoon salt
- ¼ teaspoon pepper
- 1 package (8 ounces) reduced-fat cream cheese
  Assorted fresh vegetables or crackers

1. Preheat oven to 425°. Cut vegetables into 1-inch pieces. Place in a 15x10x1-in. baking pan coated with cooking spray; toss with oil, salt and pepper. Roast for 25-30 minutes or until tender, stirring occasionally. Cool completely.
2. Place vegetables and cream cheese in a food processor; process until blended. Transfer to a bowl; refrigerate, covered, until serving. Serve with vegetables.
Health tip: Roasted veggies account for more than half the volume of this blended dip, which means fewer calories, less saturated fat and more nutrients—not to mention amazing flavor.

CHEESE-TRIO ARTICHOKE & SPINACH DIP

No appetizer spread is complete without at least one amazing dip, and this is it. Creamy, cheesy and chock-full of fresh ingredients, it will become your new go-to party recipe.
—**Diane Speare** Kissimmee, FL

Prep: 20 min. • **Cook:** 2 hours
Makes: 4 cups

- 1 cup chopped fresh mushrooms
- 1 tablespoon butter
- 2 garlic cloves, minced
- 1½ cups mayonnaise
- 1 package (8 ounces) cream cheese, softened
- 1 cup plus 2 tablespoons grated Parmesan cheese, divided
- 1 cup shredded part-skim mozzarella cheese, divided
- 1 can (14 ounces) water-packed artichoke hearts, rinsed, drained and chopped
- 1 package (10 ounces) frozen chopped spinach, thawed and squeezed dry
- ¼ cup chopped sweet red pepper
  Toasted French bread baguette slices

1. In a large skillet, saute mushrooms in butter until tender. Add the garlic; cook 1 minute longer.
2. In a large bowl, combine mayonnaise, cream cheese, 1 cup Parmesan cheese and ¾ cup mozzarella cheese. Add the mushroom mixture, artichokes, spinach and red pepper.
3. Transfer to a 3-qt slow cooker. Sprinkle with remaining cheeses. Cover and cook on low for 2-3 hours or until heated through. Serve with baguette slices.

★ ★ ★ ★ ★ **READER REVIEW**
"I made this for a potluck dinner among friends and it was hit! Better than any found at any restaurant. I now make a large batch and freeze it in smaller portions."
TUSCALOOSO TASTEOFHOME.COM

MARGARITA CHICKEN QUESADILLAS

With the addition of sweet onions, peppers and lime butter, these quesadillas are the perfect balance of sweet and savory. We enjoy them during the warm summer months, but they're great any time of year.
—**Stephanie Bright** Simpsonville, SC

Prep: 35 min. + marinating • **Bake:** 10 min.
Makes: 16 wedges

- 4 boneless skinless chicken breast halves (5 ounces each)
- ¾ cup thawed frozen limeade concentrate
- 1 large onion, sliced
- 1 medium sweet orange pepper, julienned
- 1 medium sweet yellow pepper, julienned
- 1 tablespoon canola oil
- ¼ teaspoon salt
- ¼ teaspoon pepper
- 4 flour tortillas (10 inches)
- 1 cup shredded Monterey Jack cheese
- 1 cup shredded cheddar cheese
- 2 tablespoons butter, melted
- 1 tablespoon lime juice
- 1 tablespoon chopped fresh cilantro
  Lime wedges, optional

1. Place chicken in a large bowl. Add limeade concentrate and toss to coat. Cover; refrigerate 6 hours or overnight.
2. In a large nonstick skillet, saute the onion and sweet peppers in oil until tender; season with salt and pepper. Remove and set aside; wipe out skillet. Drain and discard marinade.
3. Grill chicken, covered, on a greased rack over medium heat or broil 4 in. from the heat for 5-8 minutes on each side or until a thermometer reads 170°. Cut chicken into ¼-in. strips; set aside. On half of each tortilla, layer Monterey Jack, chicken, pepper mixture and cheddar cheese; fold over. Combine butter and lime juice; brush over tortillas.
4. In same skillet used to cook vegetables, cook quesadillas over medium heat until cheese is melted, 2-3 minutes per side. Keep warm in oven while cooking the remaining quesadillas. Cut each quesadilla into four wedges. Sprinkle with cilantro; serve with lime wedges if desired.

BEST-EVER STUFFED MUSHROOMS

Every Christmas Eve, I bring out a big platter of my famous stuffed mushrooms. If you're in the mood for something lighter, skip the mushrooms and spread the filling over baguette slices or crackers.
—**Debby Beard** Eagle, CO

Prep: 20 min. • **Bake:** 15 min.
Makes: 2½ dozen

- 1 pound bulk pork sausage
- ¼ cup finely chopped onion
- 1 garlic clove, minced
- 1 package (8 ounces) reduced-fat cream cheese
- ¼ cup shredded Parmesan cheese
- ⅓ cup seasoned bread crumbs
- 3 teaspoons dried basil
- 1½ teaspoons dried parsley flakes
- 30 large fresh mushrooms (about 1½ pounds), stems removed
- 3 tablespoons butter, melted

1. Preheat oven to 400°. In a large skillet, cook the sausage, onion and garlic over medium heat 6-8 minutes or until meat is no longer pink and the onion is tender, breaking up sausage into crumbles; drain. Add cream cheese and Parmesan cheese; cook and stir until melted. Stir in bread crumbs, basil and parsley.
2. Meanwhile, place mushroom caps in a greased 15x10x1-in. baking pan, stem side up. Brush with butter. Spoon sausage mixture into mushroom caps and bake, uncovered, for 12-15 minutes or until mushrooms are tender.

1. In a large bowl, combine egg, cheese, bread crumbs and onion. Crumble beef over egg mixture and mix well. Shape into 1½-in. balls. Transfer meatballs to a 3-qt. slow cooker.

2. In a small bowl, combine the sauce ingredients; pour over meatballs. Cover and cook on low for 7-8 hours or until meat is no longer pink.

FAST FIX ▸
SPICED CHAI MIX
My sister-in-law mixed up this drink for a family gathering. I asked for the recipe and have been enjoying its warm, spicy flavor ever since.
—Dee Falk Stromsburg, NE

Start to Finish: 15 min.
Makes: about 5 cups mix (26 servings)

- 3   cups nonfat dry milk powder
- 1½ cups sugar
- 1   cup unsweetened instant tea
- ¾   cup vanilla powdered nondairy creamer
- 1½ teaspoons ground ginger
- 1½ teaspoons ground cinnamon
- ½   teaspoon ground cardamom
- ½   teaspoon ground cloves

OPTIONAL GARNISH
Whipped cream

1. In a food processor, combine all dry ingredients; cover and process until powdery. Store in an airtight container in a cool, dry place for up to 6 months.

2. To prepare one serving of chai, dissolve 3 tablespoons of mix in ¾ cup of boiling water; stir well. Dollop with whipped cream if desired.

DID YOU KNOW?

Chai is the word for tea in many cultures, but the hot beverage we think of as chai originated in India. It generally consists of black tea, milk, a sweetner and blend of seasonings, including cardamom, cinnamon, ginger and cloves.

⑤ INGREDIENTS FAST FIX ▸
PINA COLADA FRUIT DIP
A little taste of the tropics is welcome and refreshing. This cool and creamy dip makes a sweet appetizer or a fun dessert after a hearty meal.
—Shelly Bevington Hermiston, OR

Start to Finish: 15 min.
Makes: 2½ cups

- 1   package (8 ounces) cream cheese, softened
- 1   jar (7 ounces) marshmallow creme
- 1   can (8 ounces) crushed pineapple, drained
- ½   cup sweetened shredded coconut
     Assorted fresh fruit or cubed pound cake

In a small bowl, beat cream cheese and marshmallow creme until fluffy. Fold in pineapple and coconut. Cover and chill until serving. Serve with fruit, pound cake or both.

BBQ SAUCE MEATBALLS
I whipped these up for my son's first birthday so I could serve something savory alongside the cake and ice cream. They have just the right amount of zip, and using the slow cooker keeps them easy.
—Tara Reeder Mason, MI

Prep: 20 min. • **Cook:** 7 hours
Makes: 2 dozen

- 1   large egg, beaten
- ½   cup shredded Colby-Monterey Jack cheese
- ¼   cup seasoned bread crumbs
- ¼   cup finely chopped onion
- 2   pounds ground beef
SAUCE
- 2   cups ketchup
- 2   tablespoons prepared mustard
- 1   tablespoon brown sugar
- 1   tablespoon cider vinegar
- 1   tablespoon lemon juice
- 1   tablespoon soy sauce

⑤ INGREDIENTS FAST FIX ▶

BLUE CHEESE POTATO CHIPS

Game day calls for something bold! I top kettle potato chips with tomatoes, bacon and tangy blue cheese. I make two big pans, and they always disappear.

—Bonnie Hawkins Elkhorn, WI

....

Start to Finish: 15 min.
Makes: 10 servings

- 1 package (8½ ounces) kettle-cooked potato chips
- 2 medium tomatoes, seeded and chopped
- 8 bacon strips, cooked and crumbled
- 6 green onions, chopped
- 1 cup crumbled blue cheese

1. Preheat broiler. In a 15x10x1-in. baking pan, arrange potato chips in an even layer. Top with remaining ingredients.
2. Broil 4-5 in. from heat 2-3 minutes or until the cheese begins to melt. Serve chips immediately.

⑤ INGREDIENTS FAST FIX ▶

AUNT FRANCES' LEMONADE

My sister and I spent a week each summer with our Aunt Frances, who always had this thirst-quenching lemonade in a stoneware crock in the refrigerator. It makes a cool and refreshing drink after a hot day soaking up fresh air and sunshine.

—Debbie Reinhart New Cumberland, PA

....

Start to Finish: 15 min.
Makes: 12-16 servings (1 gallon)

- 5 lemons
- 5 limes
- 5 oranges
- 3 quarts water
- 1½ to 2 cups sugar

1. Squeeze the juice from four each of the lemons, limes and oranges; pour into a gallon container.
2. Thinly slice the remaining fruit and set aside for garnish. Add water and sugar; mix well. Store in the refrigerator. Serve over ice with fruit slices.

RAVIOLI APPETIZER POPS

Ravioli on a stick is simple, easy and fun. Use store-bought dipping sauces or make your own.

—**Erika Monroe-Williams** Scottsdale, AZ

Prep: 25 min. • **Cook:** 5 min./batch
Makes: 3½ dozen

- ½ cup dry bread crumbs
- 2 teaspoons pepper
- 1½ teaspoons dried oregano
- 1½ teaspoons dried parsley flakes
- 1 teaspoon salt
- 1 teaspoon crushed red pepper flakes
- ⅓ cup all-purpose flour
- 2 large eggs, lightly beaten
- 1 package (9 ounces) refrigerated cheese ravioli
- Oil for frying
- Grated Parmesan cheese, optional
- 42 lollipop sticks
- Warm marinara sauce and prepared pesto

1. In a shallow bowl, mix bread crumbs and seasonings. Place flour and eggs in separate shallow bowls. Dip ravioli in flour to coat both sides; shake off excess. Dip in egg, then in crumb mixture, patting to help coating adhere.

2. In a large electric or cast-iron skillet, heat ½ in. of oil to 375°. Fry ravioli, a few at a time, 1-2 minutes on each side or until golden brown. Drain on paper towels. If desired, immediately sprinkle with cheese. Carefully insert a lollipop stick into back of each ravioli. Serve warm with marinara sauce and pesto.

---

(5) INGREDIENTS FAST FIX

MEXICAN CHOCOLATE DIP

Chocolate, cinnamon and a touch of heat are a classic Mexican trio. Any fruit pairs well with this fudgy dip. And if you have churros...pure yum!

—*Taste of Home* Test Kitchen

Start to Finish: 10 min.
Makes: about ½ cup

- ¾ cup semisweet chocolate chips
- ⅓ cup heavy whipping cream
- ⅛ teaspoon ground cinnamon
- ⅛ teaspoon cayenne pepper
- Assorted fresh fruit

In a small heavy saucepan, combine the chocolate chips and cream. Heat and whisk over medium-low heat 4-5 minutes or until smooth. Remove from heat; stir in cinnamon and cayenne. Cool slightly. Serve with fruit.

Note: Dip will become firmer as it cools. If desired, warm gently in the microwave to soften.

TEST KITCHEN TIP

Before melting chocolate chips, be sure all of your equipment and utensils are completely dry. Any moisture may cause the chocolate to seize, or become thick and lumpy. Chocolate that has seized can sometimes be saved by immediately adding 1 tablespoon vegetable oil for each 6 ounces of chocolate. Slowly heat the mixture and stir until smooth.

in vinegar, brown sugar, salt and pepper. Bring to a boil. Reduce heat; simmer, uncovered, 15-20 minutes or until slightly thickened. Immediately stir in cilantro.

5. Carefully ladle the hot mixture into four hot 1-pint jars, leaving ½-in. headspace. Remove air bubbles and adjust headspace, if necessary, by adding hot mixture. Wipe rims. Center lids on jars; screw on bands until fingertip tight.

6. Place jars into canner with simmering water, ensuring that they are completely covered with water. Bring to a boil; process for 15 minutes. Remove jars and cool.

Note: Wear disposable gloves when cutting hot peppers; the oils can burn skin. Avoid touching your face.

⑤INGREDIENTS

KIDS' FAVORITE PUMPKIN SEEDS

My kids love these pumpkin seeds and ask for them every fall. Don't rinse the seeds... a bit of pulp in the mix adds to the flavor.
—**Gwyn Reiber** Spokane, WA

Prep: 5 min. • **Bake:** 45 min. + cooling
Makes: 2 cups

- 2 cups fresh pumpkin seeds
- ¼ cup butter, melted
- ½ teaspoon garlic salt
- ¼ teaspoon cayenne pepper
- ¼ teaspoon Worcestershire sauce

1. In a bowl, combine all ingredients; transfer to an ungreased 15x10x1-in. baking pan.

2. Bake at 250° for 45-50 minutes or until lightly browned and dry, stirring occasionally. Cool completely. Store in an airtight container.

SWEET & SMOKY SALSA

I love the roasted flavor that comes from grilling, so I decided to make a salsa from grilled vegetables. If you don't grill using wood chip charcoal, just add a little liquid smoke to the salsa while it cooks.
—**Shelly Bevington** Hermiston, OR

Prep: 1 hour • **Process:** 15 min.
Makes: 4 pints

- 1 cup soaked mesquite wood chips
- 2 medium onions
- 12 garlic cloves, peeled
- 3 teaspoons barbecue seasoning, divided
- 2 pounds tomatillos, husks removed (about 12)
- 2 pounds plum tomatoes (about 8)
- 6 jalapeno peppers
- 1½ cups cider vinegar
- 1¼ cups packed brown sugar
- 1½ teaspoons salt
- ½ teaspoon pepper
- ⅓ cup minced fresh cilantro

1. Add wood chips to grill according to manufacturer's directions.

2. Cut onions in quarters; place in a small bowl. Add the garlic and 1½ teaspoons barbecue seasoning; toss to coat. Arrange on grilling grid; place on greased grill rack. Grill, covered, over medium heat for 10-15 minutes or until tender, turning occasionally.

3. Meanwhile, cut tomatillos, tomatoes and jalapenos in half; place in a large bowl. Add remaining barbecue seasoning; toss to coat. Grill in batches, covered, over medium heat 4-6 minutes or until tender, turning occasionally.

4. When cool enough to handle, chop vegetables. Transfer to a Dutch oven; stir

⑤ INGREDIENTS
ROOT BEER PULLED PORK NACHOS

I count on my slow cooker to do the honors when I have a house full of summer guests. Teens especially love DIY nachos. Try cola, ginger ale or lemon-lime soda if you're not into root beer.

—James Schend Pleasant Prairie, WI

Prep: 20 min. • **Cook:** 8 hours
Makes: 12 servings

- 1 boneless pork shoulder butt roast (3 to 4 pounds)
- 1 can (12 ounces) root beer or cola
- 12 cups tortilla chips
- 2 cups shredded cheddar cheese
- 2 medium tomatoes, chopped
  Pico de gallo, chopped green onions and sliced jalapeno peppers, optional

1. In a 4- or 5-qt. slow cooker, combine pork roast and root beer. Cook, covered, on low until meat is tender, 8-9 hours.
2. Remove roast; cool slightly. When cool enough to handle, shred meat with two forks. Return to slow cooker; keep warm.
3. To serve, drain pork. Layer chips with pork, cheese, tomatoes and, if desired, optional toppings. Serve immediately.

TEST KITCHEN TIP
The cooked, cooled pork can be frozen in freezer containers for up to 4 months. Just be sure the cooking liquid covers the meat so it doesn't dry out. To use, partially thaw in refrigerator overnight, then reheat in the microwave or on the stovetop. We tested this recipe with regular root beer, not diet or low-calorie.

STEAK & BLUE CHEESE BRUSCHETTA WITH ONION & ROASTED TOMATO JAM

Some of my favorite steakhouse flavors—ribeye, tomato, sweet onion and blue cheese—inspired this bruschetta. Hearty and delicious, it's a must-have at all our parties and holiday gatherings.

—Debbie Reid Clearwater, FL

Prep: 45 min. • **Grill:** 10 min.
Makes: 16 appetizers

- 5 tablespoons olive oil, divided
- 1 large sweet onion, halved and thinly sliced
- 1 cup grape tomatoes, halved
- ½ teaspoon kosher salt, divided
- ¼ teaspoon freshly ground pepper, divided
- 6 ounces cream cheese, softened
- 3 ounces crumbled blue cheese
- 3 garlic cloves, minced
- 16 slices French bread baguette (½ inch thick)
- 2 beef ribeye steaks (¾ inch thick and 8 ounces each)
- 1½ teaspoons Montreal steak seasoning
- 2 tablespoons balsamic vinegar

1. Preheat oven to 400°. In large skillet, heat 2 tablespoons oil over medium-high heat; saute onion until softened. Reduce heat to medium-low; cook until onion is golden brown, 25-30 minutes, stirring occasionally.
2. Toss tomatoes with 1 tablespoon oil, ¼ teaspoon salt and ⅛ teaspoon pepper; spread in a 15x10x1-in. pan. Roast until softened, 10-15 minutes. Stir tomatoes into onion, mashing lightly. In small bowl, mix cream cheese, blue cheese, garlic and the remaining salt and pepper.
3. Brush bread slices with remaining oil; grill, covered, over medium heat until lightly toasted, 1-2 minutes per side. Sprinkle steaks with steak seasoning. Grill, covered, over medium heat until meat reaches desired doneness (for medium-rare, a thermometer should read 135°; medium, 140°; well-done, 145°), for 3-5 minutes per side. Let stand 5 minutes before slicing.
4. To serve, spread toasts with cheese mixture; top with steak and onion mixture. Drizzle with vinegar.

BREAKFAST & BRUNCH

Good mornings start with good food. Whether you're looking for a killer dish to prepare ahead of brunch with the family or something quick to whip up before you rush off to work, each of these sunny staples are worth waking up for!

GERMAN APPLE PANCAKE

If you're looking for a pretty dish to make when hosting guests for brunch, try this puffy pancake baked in a cast-iron skillet. Filled with apples and sprinkled with powdered sugar, it's so good you may want to eat it for dessert!
—**Judi Van Beek** Lynden, WA

Prep: 15 min. • **Bake:** 20 min.
Makes: 6 servings

PANCAKE
- 3 large eggs
- 1 cup whole milk
- ¾ cup all-purpose flour
- ½ teaspoon salt
- ⅛ teaspoon ground nutmeg
- 3 tablespoons butter

TOPPING
- 2 tart baking apples, peeled and sliced
- 3 to 4 tablespoons butter
- 2 tablespoons sugar
  Confectioners' sugar

1. Preheat a 10-in. cast-iron skillet in a 425° oven. Meanwhile, in a blender, combine the eggs, milk, flour, salt and nutmeg; cover and process until smooth.

2. Add butter to hot skillet; return to oven until butter bubbles. Pour batter into skillet. Bake, uncovered, 20 minutes or until pancake puffs and its edges are browned and crisp.

3. For topping, in a skillet, add the apples, butter and sugar; cook and stir over medium heat until apples are tender. Spoon into baked pancake. Sprinkle with confectioners' sugar. Cut and serve pancake immediately.

BREAKFAST SAUSAGE BREAD

This savory cheese- and sausage-filled bread goes over well whenever we take it to a party or potluck. My husband, who usually makes it, prides himself on the beautiful golden loaves.

—Shirley Caldwell Northwood, OH

Prep: 25 min. + rising • **Bake:** 25 min.
Makes: 2 loaves (16 slices each)

- 2 loaves (1 pound each) frozen white bread dough, thawed
- ½ pound mild pork sausage
- ½ pound bulk spicy pork sausage
- 1½ cups diced fresh mushrooms
- ½ cup chopped onion
- 3 large eggs, divided use
- 2½ cups shredded mozzarella cheese
- 1 teaspoon dried basil
- 1 teaspoon dried parsley flakes
- 1 teaspoon dried rosemary, crushed
- 1 teaspoon garlic powder

1. Cover dough and let rise in a warm place until doubled. Preheat oven to 350°. In a large skillet, cook sausage, mushrooms and onion over medium-high heat for 6-8 minutes or until sausage is no longer pink, breaking up sausage into crumbles. Drain. Transfer to a bowl; cool.

2. Stir in two eggs, cheese and seasonings. Roll each loaf of dough into a 16x12-in. rectangle. Spread half of the sausage mixture over each rectangle to within 1 in. of edges. Roll up jelly-roll style, starting with a short side; pinch seams to seal. Place on a greased baking sheet.

3. In a small bowl, whisk remaining egg. Brush over tops. Bake 25-30 minutes or until golden brown. Serve warm.

Freeze option: Securely wrap and freeze cooled loaves in foil and place in resealable plastic freezer bags. To use, place foil-wrapped loaf on a baking sheet and reheat in a 450° oven 10-15 minutes or until heated through. Carefully remove foil; return to oven a few minutes longer until crust is crisp.

FRENCH BANANA PANCAKES

These pancakes are a family favorite. Our daughters make them when they have friends spend the night. Now their friends' mothers are asking for the recipe!
—**Cheryl Sowers** Bakersfield, CA

Prep: 10 min. • **Cook:** 30 min.
Makes: 5-6 servings

PANCAKES
- 1 cup all-purpose flour
- ¼ cup confectioners' sugar
- 1 cup whole milk
- 2 large eggs
- 3 tablespoons butter, melted
- 1 teaspoon vanilla extract
- ¼ teaspoon salt

FILLING
- ¼ cup butter
- ¼ cup packed brown sugar
- ¼ teaspoon ground cinnamon
- ¼ teaspoon ground nutmeg
- ¼ cup half-and-half cream
- 5 to 6 firm bananas, halved lengthwise
  Whipped cream and additional cinnamon, optional

1. Sift flour and confectioners' sugar into a bowl. Add milk, eggs, butter, vanilla and salt; beat until smooth.
2. Heat a lightly greased 6-in. skillet; add about 3 tablespoons batter, spreading to almost cover bottom of skillet. Cook until lightly browned; turn and brown the other side. Remove to a wire rack. Repeat with remaining batter (make 10-12 pancakes), greasing skillet as needed.
3. For filling, melt butter in large skillet. Stir in brown sugar, cinnamon and nutmeg. Stir in half-and-half and cook until slightly thickened. Add half of the bananas at a time to the skillet; heat for 2-3 minutes, spooning sauce over them. Remove from the heat.
4. Roll a pancake around each banana half and place on a serving platter. Spoon sauce over pancakes. Top with whipped cream and dash of cinnamon if desired.

CALICO SCRAMBLED EGGS

When you're short on time and scrambling to get a meal on the table, this recipe is just what you need. There's a short ingredient list, and cooking is kept to a minimum. Plus, with green pepper and tomato, it makes a colorful addition to the table.
—*Taste of Home* Test Kitchen

Start to Finish: 15 min.
Makes: 4 servings

- 8 large eggs
- ¼ cup 2% milk
- ⅛ to ¼ teaspoon dill weed
- ⅛ to ¼ teaspoon salt
- ⅛ to ¼ teaspoon pepper
- 1 tablespoon butter
- ½ cup chopped green pepper
- ¼ cup chopped onion
- ½ cup chopped fresh tomato

1. In a bowl, whisk the first five ingredients until blended. In a 12-in. nonstick skillet, heat butter over medium-high heat. Add green pepper and onion; cook and stir until tender. Remove from pan.
2. In same pan, pour in egg mixture; cook and stir over medium heat until eggs begin to thicken. Add tomato and the pepper mixture; cook until heated through and no liquid egg remains, stirring gently.

NUTTY FRENCH TOAST

This sweet breakfast is a cross between caramel rolls and French toast. It's easy to begin making the night before.

—**Mavis Diment** Marcus, IA

....

Prep: 10 min. + chilling
Bake: 1 hour
Makes: 6 servings

- 12 slices French bread (1 inch thick)
- 8 large eggs
- 2 cups whole milk
- 2 teaspoons vanilla extract
- ½ teaspoon ground cinnamon
- ¾ cup butter, softened
- 1⅓ cups packed brown sugar
- 3 tablespoons dark corn syrup
- 1 cup chopped walnuts

1. Place bread in a greased 13x9-in. baking dish. In a large bowl, beat eggs, milk, vanilla and cinnamon; pour over the bread. Cover and refrigerate overnight. Remove from the refrigerator 30 minutes before baking.
2. Meanwhile, in a bowl, cream butter, brown sugar and syrup until smooth; spread over bread. Sprinkle with nuts. Bake, uncovered, at 350° for 1 hour or until golden brown.

SOUTHWEST BRUNCH CASSEROLE

My husband used to take this casserole, doubled, to office potlucks, and it was always a crowd-pleaser. I serve it at home as a special-occasion breakfast or even dinner for the two of us. Any leftovers taste just as good reheated the next day.

—**Linda Hinkley** Florence, OR

....

Prep: 15 min. + chilling • **Bake:** 20 min.
Makes: 4 servings

- 4 teaspoons butter, softened
- 2 English muffins, split
- ½ pound bulk pork sausage
- 4 large eggs
- ¼ cup sour cream
- ½ cup shredded sharp cheddar cheese
- ¼ cup canned chopped green chilies

1. Spread butter over cut sides of each muffin half. Place buttered side up in an 8-in. square baking dish coated with cooking spray; set aside.
2. In a small skillet, cook sausage over medium heat until no longer pink; drain. Spoon sausage over muffin halves. In a small bowl, whisk eggs and sour cream; pour over sausage. Sprinkle with cheese and chilies. Cover and refrigerate 3 hours or overnight.
3. Remove from refrigerator 30 minutes before baking. Preheat oven to 350°. Bake for 20-25 minutes or until a knife inserted in the center comes out clean. Let stand for 5 minutes before cutting.

★ ★ ★ ★ ★ **READER REVIEW**

"Super simple, can prep ahead, and a crowd-pleaser!"

KIMRC TASTEOFHOME.COM

BACON & EGGS CASSEROLE

This breakfast casserole is one of my favorites because prep is quick and easy and it's always a hit with family and friends. Attending a brunch after church? Serve alongside fruit salad, hot muffins and croissants for a meal to remember.
—**Deanna Durward-Orr** Windsor, ON

Prep: 20 min. • **Bake:** 40 min.
Makes: 10 servings

- 4 bacon strips
- 18 large eggs
- 1 cup whole milk
- 1 cup shredded cheddar cheese
- 1 cup sour cream
- ¼ cup sliced green onions
- 1 to 1½ teaspoons salt
- ½ teaspoon pepper

1. Preheat oven to at 325°. In a large skillet, cook bacon over medium heat until crisp. Remove to paper towel to drain.

2. In a large bowl, beat eggs. Add milk, cheddar cheese, sour cream, onions, salt and pepper.

3. Pour into a greased 13x9-in. baking dish. Crumble bacon and sprinkle on top. Bake, uncovered, 40-45 minutes or until a knife inserted in the center comes out clean. Let stand for 5 minutes.

CHEESY EGG PUFFS

My father loves to entertain, and these buttery egg bites are one of his favorite items to serve at brunch. The leftovers are great reheated in the microwave, so Dad always stashes a few aside for me to take home once the party is over.
—**Amy Soto** Winfield, KS

Prep: 15 min. • **Bake:** 35 min.
Makes: 2½ dozen

- ½ pound fresh mushrooms, sliced
- 4 green onions, chopped
- 1 tablespoon plus ½ cup butter, cubed, divided
- ½ cup all-purpose flour
- 1 teaspoon baking powder
- ½ teaspoon salt
- 10 large eggs, lightly beaten
- 4 cups shredded Monterey Jack cheese
- 2 cups 4% cottage cheese

1. In a skillet, saute the mushrooms and onions in 1 tablespoon butter until tender. In a large bowl, combine the flour, baking powder and salt.

2. In another bowl, combine eggs and cheeses. Melt remaining butter; add to egg mixture. Stir into dry ingredients along with mushroom mixture.

3. Fill greased muffin cups three-fourths full. Bake at 350° for 35-40 minutes or until a knife inserted in the center comes out clean. Carefully run the knife around edge of muffin cups before removing.

CINNAMON DOUGHNUT MUFFINS

Back when my children were youngsters, they loved these doughnut muffins as after-school treats or with Sunday brunch. Feel free to substitute your favorite kind of jam.

—Sharon Pullen Alvinston, ON

Prep: 15 min. • **Bake:** 20 min.
Makes: 10 standard-size muffins

- 1¾ cups all-purpose flour
- 1½ teaspoons baking powder
- ½ teaspoon salt
- ½ teaspoon ground nutmeg
- ¼ teaspoon ground cinnamon
- ¾ cups sugar
- ⅓ cup canola oil
- 1 large egg, lightly beaten
- ¾ cup whole milk
- 10 teaspoons seedless strawberry or other jam

TOPPING
- ¼ cup butter, melted
- ⅓ cup sugar
- 1 teaspoon ground cinnamon

1. In a large bowl, combine flour, baking powder, salt, nutmeg and cinnamon. In a small bowl, combine sugar, canola oil, egg and milk; stir into dry ingredients just until moistened.

2. Fill greased or paper-lined muffin cups half full; place 1 teaspoon jam on top. Cover jam with enough batter to fill muffin cups three-fourths full. Bake at 350° for 20-25 minutes or until a toothpick comes out clean.

3. Place melted butter in a small bowl; combine sugar and cinnamon in another bowl. Immediately after removing muffins from the oven, dip tops in butter, then in cinnamon sugar. Serve warm.

FLUFFY PUMPKIN PANCAKES

My daughters love these tender, fluffy pancakes served with butter, syrup and whipped cream. I freeze extras to pop in the toaster on busy mornings.

—Mindy Bauknecht Two Rivers, WI

Prep: 15 min. • **Cook:** 10 min./batch
Makes: 6 pancakes

- ⅓ cup all-purpose flour
- ⅓ cup whole wheat flour
- 2 tablespoons sugar
- ½ teaspoon baking powder
- ½ teaspoon baking soda
- ¼ teaspoon pumpkin pie spice
- ⅛ teaspoon ground cinnamon
  Dash salt
- 1 large egg
- ½ cup fat-free milk
- ⅓ cup vanilla yogurt
- ⅓ cup canned pumpkin
- 1 tablespoon canola oil
- ⅛ teaspoon vanilla extract
  Maple syrup

1. In a bowl, whisk together the first eight ingredients. In another bowl, whisk the next six ingredients until blended. Add to dry ingredients; stir just until moistened.

2. Lightly coat a griddle with cooking spray; preheat over medium heat. Pour batter by ⅓ cupfuls onto griddle. Cook until bubbles on top begin to pop. Turn; cook until golden brown. Serve with syrup.

DID YOU KNOW?

Homemade pumpkin pie spice may be used as a substitute for store-bought. Mix 4 teaspoons ground cinnamon, 2 teaspoons ground ginger, 1 teaspoon ground cloves and ½ teaspoon ground nutmeg. Store in an airtight container in a cool, dry place for up to 6 months.

BROCCOLI HAM QUICHE

This rich quiche is featured in a family cookbook I put together. My husband is proof that quiche can satisfy even the heartiest of appetites.

—**Marilyn Day** North Fort Myers, FL

Prep: 20 min. + cooling
Bake: 55 min. + standing
Makes: 8 servings

- 1 unbaked deep-dish pastry shell (9 inches)
- 1 cup shredded Swiss cheese
- 1 cup shredded part-skim mozzarella cheese
- 2 tablespoons all-purpose flour
- 4 large eggs, lightly beaten
- 1½ cups whole milk
- 2 tablespoons chopped green onion
- ¼ teaspoon salt
- ⅛ teaspoon pepper
- ⅛ teaspoon dried thyme
- ⅛ teaspoon dried rosemary, crushed
- ½ cup diced fully cooked ham
- ½ cup chopped fresh broccoli

1. Line unpricked pastry shell with a double thickness of heavy-duty foil. Bake at 450° for 8 minutes. Remove foil; bake 5 minutes longer. Cool on a wire rack while preparing filling.
2. Toss cheeses with flour; set aside. In a large bowl, combine the eggs, milk, onion and seasonings. Stir in the ham, broccoli and cheese mixture. Pour into prepared pie crust.
3. Bake at 350° for 55-60 minutes or until set. Let stand 10 minutes before cutting.

FAST FIX
BACON & CHEESE WAFFLES

Pancake mix gives a jump-start to this speedy recipe. Adding bacon and cheese to the waffle batter makes it a great all-in-one breakfast.

—**MarGenne Rowley** Oasis, UT

Start to Finish: 20 min.
Makes: 12 waffles (4-inch square)

- 2 cups pancake or biscuit/baking mix
- 1 large egg
- 1 cup 2% milk
- 1 cup (8 ounces) sour cream
- 1 tablespoon butter, melted
- 6 to 8 bacon strips, cooked and crumbled
- 1 cup shredded cheddar cheese

1. Place pancake mix in a large bowl. In another bowl, whisk the egg, milk, sour cream and butter. Stir into pancake mix until blended. Fold in bacon and cheese.
2. Bake in a preheated waffle iron according to manufacturer's directions until golden brown.

OVERNIGHT APPLE FRENCH TOAST

My in-laws own and operate an orchard, so we have an abundance of fruit fresh from the trees. This dish includes fresh apples, apple jelly and applesauce.
—**Debra Blazer** Hegins, PA

Prep: 25 min. + chilling • **Bake:** 35 min.
Makes: 9 servings

- 1 cup packed brown sugar
- ½ cup butter, cubed
- 2 tablespoons light corn syrup
- 2 large tart apples, peeled and cut into ¼-in. slices
- 3 large eggs
- 1 cup whole milk
- 1 teaspoon vanilla extract
- 9 slices day-old French bread (¾ inch thick)

SYRUP
- 1 jar (10 ounces) apple jelly
- 1 cup applesauce
- ½ teaspoon ground cinnamon
- ⅛ teaspoon ground cloves

1. In a small saucepan, combine the brown sugar, butter and corn syrup. Cook over medium heat for 5-7 minutes or until thickened. Pour into an ungreased 13x9-in. baking dish. Arrange apples over top.
2. In a large bowl, beat the eggs, milk and vanilla. Dip French bread slices into the egg mixture 1 minute; place over apples. Cover and refrigerate overnight.
3. Remove from refrigerator 30 minutes before baking. Preheat oven to 350°. Bake, uncovered, for 35-40 minutes. Meanwhile, in a small saucepan, combine the syrup ingredients; heat through. Serve with French toast.

EGGSQUISITE BREAKFAST CASSEROLE

My favorite things about this casserole is the rich, warm sauce. If you like, place a serving between two biscuit halves for an out-of-this world breakfast sandwich.
—**Bee Fischer** Jefferson, WI

Prep: 20 min. • **Bake:** 55 min.
Makes: 12-16 servings

- 1 pound sliced bacon, diced
- 2 packages (4½ ounces each) sliced dried beef, cut into thin strips
- 1 can (4 ounces) sliced mushrooms
- ½ cup all-purpose flour
- ⅛ teaspoon pepper
- 4 cups whole milk
- 16 large eggs
- 1 cup evaporated milk
- ¼ teaspoon salt
- ¼ cup butter, cubed
- Chopped fresh parsley, optional

1. In a large skillet, cook bacon until crisp. Remove bacon to paper towel to drain; discard all but ¼ cup drippings. In the same skillet, add the beef, mushrooms, flour and pepper to the drippings; cook until thoroughly combined. Gradually add milk; cook and stir until thickened. Stir in bacon; set aside.
2. In a large bowl, whisk eggs, evaporated milk and salt. In another large skillet, heat butter until hot. Add egg mixture; cook and stir over medium heat until eggs are completely set.
3. Place half of the eggs in a greased 13x9-in. baking dish; pour half of the sauce over the eggs. Repeat layers. Cover and bake at 350° for 55-65 minutes or until a knife inserted in the center comes out clean. Let stand 5 minutes before serving.

MAPLE SAUSAGE PATTIES

Maple syrup, sage and thyme give delightful flavor to these homemade sausage patties. It's a treat to have homemade sausage, especially alongside pancakes, waffles or French toast.

—**Margaret Eid** Huron, SD

Prep: 15 min. + chilling • **Cook:** 10 min.
Makes: 8 servings

- 1 tablespoon maple syrup
- ½ teaspoon salt
- ½ teaspoon onion powder
- ½ teaspoon rubbed sage
- ½ teaspoon dried thyme
- ½ teaspoon poultry seasoning
- ½ teaspoon ground nutmeg
- ¼ teaspoon cayenne pepper
- 1 to 2 teaspoons liquid smoke, optional
- 1 pound ground pork

1. In a large bowl, mix maple syrup, salt, spices and, if desired, liquid smoke. Add pork; mix lightly but thoroughly. Shape into eight 2½-in. patties. Refrigerate, covered, at least 1 hour.

2. In a large nonstick skillet coated with cooking spray, cook sausage patties over medium heat until a thermometer reads 160°, 4-6 minutes per side.

Health tip: Try these with lean ground turkey. The patties will be slightly more delicate to work with, but they will taste just as good.

ITALIAN SAUSAGE EGG BAKE

This comforting egg bake warms up any breakfast or brunch menu with its herb-seasoned flavor.

—**Darlene Markham** Rochester, NY

Prep: 20 min. + chilling • **Bake:** 50 min.
Makes: 12 servings

- 8 slices white bread, cubed
- 1 pound Italian sausage links, casings removed, sliced
- 2 cups shredded sharp cheddar cheese
- 2 cups shredded part-skim mozzarella cheese
- 9 large eggs, lightly beaten
- 3 cups 2% milk
- 1 teaspoon dried basil
- 1 teaspoon dried oregano
- 1 teaspoon fennel seed, crushed

1. Place bread cubes in a greased 13x9-in. baking dish; set aside. In a large skillet, cook sausage over medium heat until no longer pink; drain. Spoon sausage over bread; sprinkle with cheeses.

2. In a large bowl, whisk the eggs, milk and seasonings; pour over casserole. Cover and refrigerate overnight.

3. Remove from refrigerator 30 minutes before baking. Bake, uncovered, at 350° for 50-55 minutes or until a knife inserted in the center comes out clean. Let stand for 5 minutes before cutting.

TEST KITCHEN TIP
Dried herbs don't spoil, but they do lose flavor and potency over time. For maximum flavor in your cooking, replace herbs that are over a year old.

GRAN'S GRANOLA PARFAITS

My mother-in-law treats us to her yogurt parfaits whenever she has us over for brunch. They're refreshing, light and wholesome. I made a few changes to her recipe and came up with this sweet, crunchy and nutty variation. Yum!
—Angela Keller Newburgh, IN

Prep: 15 min. • **Bake:** 30 min. + cooling
Makes: 16 servings

- 2 cups old-fashioned oats
- 1 cup Wheaties
- 1 cup whole almonds
- 1 cup pecan halves
- 1 cup sweetened shredded coconut
- 4½ teaspoons toasted wheat germ
- 1 tablespoon sesame seeds, toasted
- 1 teaspoon ground cinnamon
- ¼ cup butter, melted
- 2 tablespoons maple syrup
- 2 tablespoons honey
- 1 can (20 ounces) pineapple tidbits, drained
- 1 can (15 ounces) mandarin oranges, drained
- 1 cup halved green grapes
- 2 to 3 medium firm bananas, sliced
- 1 cup sliced fresh strawberries
- 4 cups (32 ounces) vanilla yogurt

1. In a large bowl, combine the first eight ingredients. Combine the butter, syrup and honey; drizzle over oat mixture and stir until well coated. Pour into a greased 13x9-in. baking pan. Bake, uncovered, at 350° for 30 minutes, stirring every 10 minutes. Cool on a wire rack; crumble granola into pieces.

2. Combine the fruits in a large bowl. For each parfait, layer 2 tablespoons yogurt, 2 tablespoons granola and 3 rounded tablespoons fruit in a parfait glass or dessert bowl. Repeat layers. Sprinkle with remaining granola. Serve immediately.

GERMAN PANCAKE

Piping hot from the oven, this golden pancake made a lovely presentation for a skier's-themed breakfast I hosted. Served with my homemade buttermilk syrup, it's quite a treat. The syrup tastes great on waffles and French toast, too.
—**Renae Moncur** Burley, ID

Start to Finish: 30 min.
Makes: 8 servings (2 cups syrup)

- 6 **large eggs**
- 1 **cup 2% milk**
- 1 **cup all-purpose flour**
- ½ **teaspoon salt**
- 2 **tablespoons butter, melted**

BUTTERMILK SYRUP
- ½ **cup butter, cubed**
- 1½ **cups sugar**
- ¾ **cup buttermilk**
- 2 **tablespoons corn syrup**
- 1 **teaspoon baking soda**
- 2 **teaspoons vanilla extract**
  Confectioners' sugar
  Fresh blueberries, optional

1. Preheat the oven to 400°. Place first four ingredients in a blender; process just until smooth.
2. Pour melted butter into a 13x9-in. baking dish; tilt dish to coat. Add batter; bake, uncovered, until puffed and golden brown, about 20 minutes.
3. Meanwhile, place cubed butter, sugar, buttermilk, corn syrup and baking soda in a small saucepan; bring to a boil. Cook, uncovered, 7 minutes. Remove from heat; stir in vanilla.
4. Remove pancake from oven. Dust with confectioners' sugar; serve immediately with syrup and, if desired, fresh berries.
Health tip: The pancake by itself is just 150 calories and 7g fat. For a healthier spin, fill it with sauteed fresh fruit and a dusting of confectioners' sugar, or go savory with leftover cubed turkey, gravy and herbs.

SAUSAGE & HASHBROWN BREAKFAST PIZZA

Pizza for breakfast? Yes, please! Kids will love making—and eating—this hearty morning meal that's made with crescent roll dough and frozen hash browns.
—**Rae Truax** Mattawa, WA

Prep: 10 min. • **Bake:** 30 min. + standing
Makes: 6-8 servings

- 1 **tube (8 ounces) refrigerated crescent rolls**
- 1 **pound bulk pork sausage**
- 1 **cup frozen shredded hash brown potatoes, thawed**
- 1 **cup shredded cheddar cheese**
- 3 **large eggs**
- ¼ **cup whole milk**
- ¼ **teaspoon pepper**
- ¼ **cup grated Parmesan cheese**

1. Unroll crescent dough and place on a greased 12-in. pizza pan; press seams together and press up sides of pan to form a crust.
2. In a large skillet, brown sausage over medium heat; drain and cool slightly. Sprinkle the sausage, hash browns and cheddar cheese over crust.
3. In a small bowl, whisk the eggs, milk and pepper; pour over pizza. Sprinkle with Parmesan cheese. Bake at 375° for 28-30 minutes or until a knife inserted in the center comes out clean. Let stand for 10 minutes before cutting.

BREAKFAST BAKE

This light fluffy egg casserole, sprinkled with tasty bacon, retains its fresh flavor after freezing. While it's great for breakfast, it's easy to reheat for lunch or dinner, too. The recipe makes two casseroles, so you can serve one right away and freeze the second one for later.
—**Kim Weaver** Olathe, KS

Prep: 15 min. • **Bake:** 45 min.
Makes: 2 casseroles (8 servings each)

- 4½ cups seasoned croutons
- 2 cups shredded cheddar cheese
- 1 medium onion, chopped
- ¼ cup chopped sweet red pepper
- ¼ cup chopped green pepper
- 1 jar (4½ ounces) sliced mushrooms, drained
- 8 large eggs
- 4 cups whole milk
- 1 teaspoon salt
- 1 teaspoon ground mustard
- ⅛ teaspoon pepper
- 8 bacon strips, cooked and crumbled

1. Sprinkle the croutons, cheese, onion, peppers and mushrooms into two greased 8-in. square baking dishes. In a large bowl, whisk the eggs, milk, salt, mustard and pepper. Slowly pour over vegetables. Sprinkle with bacon.

2. Cover and freeze one casserole for up to 3 months. Bake the second casserole, uncovered, at 350° for 45-50 minutes or until a knife inserted in the center comes out clean.

To use frozen casserole: Completely thaw in the refrigerator for 24-36 hours. Remove from refrigerator 30 minutes before baking. Bake, uncovered, at 350° for 50-60 minutes or until a knife inserted in the center comes out clean.

SPINACH-EGG BREAKFAST PIZZAS

I like my food to look as good as it tastes, and these mini breakfast pizzas are eye-popping. Bring them to the table with a bowl of fresh fruit and coffee.
—**Lily Julow** Lawrenceville, GA

Prep: 20 min. • **Bake:** 15 min.
Makes: 4 servings

- Cornmeal
- 1 loaf (1 pound) frozen pizza dough, thawed
- 1 tablespoon plus additional extra virgin olive oil, divided
- 5 to 6 ounces fresh baby spinach
- ⅓ cup plus additional grated Parmesan cheese, divided
- 3 tablespoons sour cream
- 1 small garlic clove, minced
- ¼ teaspoon sea salt
- ⅛ teaspoon plus additional coarsely ground pepper, divided
- 4 large eggs

1. Preheat oven to 500°. Line two 15x10-in. baking pans with parchment paper; sprinkle lightly with cornmeal. Cut dough into four pieces; stretch and shape into 6- to 7-in. circles.

2. Meanwhile, in a large skillet, heat 1 tablespoon olive oil over medium-high heat. Add spinach; cook and stir until just starting to wilt, 1-2 minutes. Combine spinach with next five ingredients; spread mixture over each pizza. Leave a slight border of raised dough along edge. Bake on a lower oven rack for about 5 minutes.

3. Remove from oven; break an egg into center of each pizza. Return to lower oven rack, baking until egg whites are set but yolks are still runny, 6-10 minutes. Drizzle the additional olive oil over pizzas; top with additional Parmesan and pepper. Serve pizzas immediately.

SLOW COOKER CHORIZO BREAKFAST CASSEROLE

My kids ask for this slow-cooked casserole for breakfast and dinner. I like to serve it with white country gravy or salsa—it's fantastic either way.
—**Cindy Pruitt** Grove, OK

Prep: 25 min. • **Cook:** 4 hours + standing
Makes: 8 servings

- 1 pound fresh chorizo or bulk spicy pork sausage
- 1 medium onion, chopped
- 1 medium sweet red pepper, chopped
- 2 jalapeno peppers, seeded and chopped
- 1 package (30 ounces) frozen shredded hash brown potatoes, thawed
- 1½ cups shredded Mexican cheese blend
- 12 large eggs
- 1 cup 2% milk
- ½ teaspoon pepper

1. In a large skillet, cook chorizo, onion, red pepper and jalapenos over medium heat, 7-8 minutes or until cooked through and vegetables are tender, breaking the chorizo into crumbles; drain. Cool slightly.
2. In a greased 5-qt. slow cooker, layer a third each of the hash browns, chorizo mixture and cheese. Repeat layers twice. In a large bowl, whisk eggs, milk and pepper until blended; pour over top.
3. Cook, covered, on low, 4-4½ hours or until eggs are set and a thermometer reads 160°. Uncover and let stand 10 minutes before serving.
Note: Wear disposable gloves when cutting hot peppers; the oils can burn skin. Avoid touching your face.

BLUEBERRY OAT PANCAKES

I use ground oats in this recipe to boost the health value. But oats aren't the only power food in these fluffy pancakes. You get plenty of nutrient-packed blueberries in every bite, too!
—**Candy Summerhill** Alexander, AR

Prep: 20 min. • **Cook:** 5 min./batch
Makes: 10 pancakes

- ¾ cup quick-cooking oats, divided
- 3 tablespoons orange juice
- 1 large egg, lightly beaten
- ⅔ cup fat-free evaporated milk
- ¼ cup reduced-fat sour cream
- 2 tablespoons unsweetened applesauce
- ½ teaspoon vanilla extract
- ½ cup whole wheat flour
- ¼ cup all-purpose flour
- 3 tablespoons brown sugar
- 1 teaspoon baking powder
- ½ teaspoon ground cinnamon
- ¼ teaspoon salt
- ¼ teaspoon baking soda
- 1 cup fresh or frozen blueberries

1. In a small bowl, combine ¼ cup oats and orange juice; let stand for 5 minutes. Stir in the egg, evaporated milk, sour cream, applesauce and vanilla; set aside.
2. Place remaining oats in a small food processor; cover and process until ground. Transfer to a large bowl; add the flours, brown sugar, baking powder, cinnamon, salt and baking soda. Stir in the wet ingredients just until moistened.
3. Pour batter by ¼ cupfuls onto a hot griddle coated with cooking spray; sprinkle with blueberries. Turn pancakes when bubbles form on top; cook until second side is golden brown.

✳

TEST KITCHEN TIP
For best results, do not defrost frozen berries before adding them to pancakes, muffins and other baked items.

CHEESY VEGETABLE EGG DISH

I'm a cook at a Bible camp, and this is one of my most popular recipes with the youngsters. My heart melted when a 10-year-old boy asked me for the recipe so his mother could make it at home.
—Elsie Campbell Dulzura, CA

....

Prep: 20 min. • **Bake:** 35 min.
Makes: 8-10 servings

- 1 medium zucchini, diced
- 1 medium onion, chopped
- 1 can (4 ounces) mushroom stems and pieces, drained
- ¼ cup chopped green pepper
- ½ cup butter, cubed
- ½ cup all-purpose flour
- 1 teaspoon baking powder
- ½ teaspoon salt
- 10 large eggs, lightly beaten
- 2 cups 4% cottage cheese
- 4 cups shredded Monterey Jack cheese

1. In a large skillet, saute the zucchini, onion, mushrooms and green pepper in butter until tender. Stir in the flour, baking powder and salt until blended.
2. In a large bowl, combine the eggs and cottage cheese. Stir in vegetables and Monterey Jack cheese.
3. Transfer mixture to a greased 2½-qt. baking dish. Bake, uncovered, at 350° for 35-45 minutes or until a thermometer reads 160°.

★ ★ ★ ★ ★ READER REVIEW

"Awesome! I used a bunch of leftover sauteed peppers and onions for the veggies and totally omitted the butter. Tasted fantastic."

LURKY27 TASTEOFHOME.COM

FAST FIX
FAMILY-FAVORITE OATMEAL WAFFLES

My husband and I have a small herd of beef cattle and some pigs, so we need a hearty breakfast to get us going on early mornings. These nutritious and tasty waffles rank among our faves—our kids love them, too!
—Marna Heitz Farley, IA

....

Start to Finish: 30 min.
Makes: 6 waffles

- 1½ cups all-purpose flour
- 1 cup quick-cooking oats
- 3 teaspoons baking powder
- ½ teaspoon ground cinnamon
- ¼ teaspoon salt, optional
- 2 large eggs, lightly beaten
- 1½ cups whole milk
- 6 tablespoons butter, melted
- 2 tablespoons brown sugar
    Assorted fresh fruit
    Yogurt of your choice

1. In a large bowl, combine flour, oats, baking powder, cinnamon and, if desired, salt; set aside. In a small bowl, whisk eggs, milk, butter and brown sugar. Add to flour mixture; stir until blended.
2. Pour batter into a lightly greased waffle iron (amount will vary with size of waffle iron). Close lid quickly; do not open during baking. Use fork to remove baked waffle. Top with fresh fruit and yogurt.

ENERGIZING GRANOLA

Adding flaxseed to my granola is an easy way for me to add omega-3's to my diet, and the combination of nuts, grains and fruit packs a healthy and great-tasting punch! Enjoy it with milk or sprinkle over Greek yogurt.

—Janine Ann Weissmann Batavia, OH

Prep: 25 min. • **Bake:** 25 min. + cooling
Makes: 6 cups

- 2½ cups old-fashioned oats
- ¾ cup chopped walnuts
- ½ cup unsalted sunflower kernels
- ⅓ cup packed brown sugar
- ¼ cup sweetened shredded coconut
- ¼ cup toasted wheat germ
- 2 tablespoons sesame seeds
- 2 tablespoons ground flaxseed
- ⅓ cup water
- 2 tablespoons honey
- 2 tablespoons molasses
- 1 tablespoon canola oil
- ¾ teaspoon vanilla extract
- ½ teaspoon salt
- ½ teaspoon ground cinnamon
- ⅓ cup dried cranberries
- ⅓ cup golden raisins
- ¼ cup dried banana chips

1. In a large bowl, combine the first eight ingredients. In a small saucepan, combine the water, honey, molasses and oil. Heat for 3-4 minutes over medium until heated through. Remove from the heat; stir in the vanilla, salt and cinnamon. Pour over the oat mixture; stir to coat.

2. Transfer to a 15x10x1-in. baking pan coated with cooking spray. Bake at 350° for 25-30 minutes or until lightly browned, stirring every 10 minutes. Cool completely on a wire rack. Stir in dried fruits. Store in an airtight container.

---

⑤ INGREDIENTS FAST FIX

BISCUITS & SAUSAGE GRAVY

This is an old Southern recipe that I've adapted. It's the kind of traditional breakfast that will warm you right up.

—Sue Baker Jonesboro, AR

Start to Finish: 15 min.
Makes: 2 servings

- ¼ pound bulk pork sausage
- 2 tablespoons butter
- 2 to 3 tablespoons all-purpose flour
- ¼ teaspoon salt
- ⅛ teaspoon pepper
- 1¼ to 1⅓ cups whole milk
  Warm biscuits

In a small skillet, cook the sausage over medium heat until no longer pink; drain. Add butter and heat until melted. Add the flour, salt and pepper; cook and stir until blended. Gradually add the milk, stirring constantly. Bring to a boil; cook and stir for 2 minutes or until thickened. Serve sausage and gravy with biscuits.

---

⑤ INGREDIENTS FAST FIX

PANCAKE SYRUP

My husband has fond memories of this recipe. On Sunday mornings, his dad would get up early to make the family pancakes and syrup. They didn't have much money, but the kids never knew that. What they remember is that their dad always had time to make their Sunday breakfasts special.

—Lorrie McCurdy Farmington, NM

Start to Finish: 10 min.
Makes: 2 cups

- 1 cup packed brown sugar
- 1 cup sugar
- 1 cup water
- 1 teaspoon maple flavoring

In a small saucepan, combine the sugars and water. Bring to a boil; cook and stir for 2 minutes. Remove from the heat; stir in maple flavoring. Refrigerate leftovers.

PUFF PASTRY DANISHES

Even though they're simple to make, these danishes, filled with cream cheese and jam, add an elegant touch to a holiday brunch. They were my dad's favorite pastry, so the recipe will always be close to my heart.
—Chellie Richardson Sidney, OH

Prep: 30 min. • **Bake:** 15 min.
Makes: 1½ dozen

- 1 package (8 ounces) cream cheese, softened
- ¼ cup sugar
- 2 tablespoons all-purpose flour
- ½ teaspoon vanilla extract
- 2 large egg yolks, divided
- 1 tablespoon water
- 1 package (17.3 ounces) frozen puff pastry, thawed
- ⅔ cup seedless raspberry jam or jam of choice

1. Preheat oven to 425°. Beat the first four ingredients until smooth; beat in 1 egg yolk.

2. Mix water and remaining egg yolk. On a lightly floured surface, unfold each sheet of puff pastry; roll into a 12-in. square. Cut each into nine 4-in. squares; transfer to parchment paper-lined baking sheets.

3. Top each square with 1 tablespoon cream cheese mixture and 1 rounded teaspoon jam. Bring two opposite corners of pastry over filling, sealing with yolk mixture. Brush tops with the remaining yolk mixture.

4. Bake danishes until golden brown, 14-16 minutes. Serve warm. Refrigerate any leftovers.

DID YOU KNOW?

Puff pastry is a rich dough made by placing chilled butter between layers of pastry dough. It is then rolled out, folded into thirds and allowed to rest. This process is repeated six to eight times, producing a pastry made flaky by its many layers of dough and butter.

SOUPS & SANDWICHES

Soup's on! And grab a plate for a sandwich, too. The deliciously fun, creative flavor combinations in these recipes revolutionize what you thought could be simmered in a stockpot or piled high between two slices of bread. Yum!

CHICKEN PARMESAN SLIDER BAKE

Sliders are the perfect finger food for any get-together, and this flavorful chicken Parmesan version won't disappoint.
—**Nick Iverson** Denver, CO

....

Prep: 20 min. • **Bake:** 25 min.
Makes: 1 dozen

- 24 ounces frozen breaded chicken tenders
- 1 package (12 ounces) Hawaiian sweet rolls
- 1 package (7½ ounces) sliced provolone and mozzarella cheese blend
- 1 jar (24 ounces) marinara sauce

TOPPING

- ½ cup butter, cubed
- 1 teaspoon garlic powder
- 1 teaspoon crushed red pepper flakes
- ¼ cup grated Parmesan cheese
- 2 tablespoons minced fresh basil

1. Preheat oven to 375°. Prepare chicken tenders according to package directions. Meanwhile, without separating rolls, cut horizontally in half; arrange roll bottoms in a greased 13x9-in. baking dish. Spread half of cheese slices over roll bottoms. Bake until the cheese is melted, 3-5 minutes.
2. Layer rolls with half of sauce, chicken tenders, remaining sauce and remaining cheese slices. Replace top halves of rolls.
3. For topping, microwave butter, garlic powder and red pepper flakes, covered, on high, stirring occasionally, until butter is melted. Pour over rolls; sprinkle with Parmesan cheese. Bake, uncovered, until the sliders are golden brown and heated through, 20-25 minutes. Sprinkle with basil before serving.

TEST KITCHEN TIP
Bake-and-serve dinner rolls can be substituted for the Hawaiian sweet rolls and chicken nuggets can replace the tenders if desired. If you like, sneak a few slices of pepperoni or salami onto each roll to make it extra hearty.

SAVORY BEEF SANDWICHES

I put the chuck roast for these sammies in the slow cooker before I head to work in the morning, and it's ready to serve as soon as my husband and I walk in at the end of the day. When one of our kids moved out of state, I cut the beef roast in smaller portions, repackaged it and included seasonings to all go in a small slow cooker. I wanted him to have a little taste of home as a housewarming present.
—Lynn Williamson Hayward, WI

Prep: 15 min. • **Cook:** 6 hours
Makes: 10 servings

  1 tablespoon dried minced onion
  2 teaspoons salt
  2 teaspoons garlic powder
  2 teaspoons dried oregano
  1 teaspoon dried rosemary, crushed
  1 teaspoon caraway seeds
  1 teaspoon dried marjoram
  1 teaspoon celery seed
  ¼ teaspoon cayenne pepper
  1 boneless beef chuck roast
     (3 to 4 pounds), halved
 10 sandwich rolls, split

Combine seasonings; rub over roast. Place in a 5-qt. slow cooker. Cover and cook on low for 6-8 hours or until meat is tender. Shred with a fork. Serve on rolls.
Note: No liquid is added to the slow cooker. The moisture comes from the roast.

CALIFORNIA CHICKEN WRAPS

Hummus is a healthy alternative to mayo. The combination of hummus and feta makes these fresh-flavored wraps unbeatable.
—**Donna Munch** El Paso, TX

Start to Finish: 15 min.
Makes: 4 servings

- ⅓ cup prepared hummus
- 4 whole wheat tortillas (8 inches)
- 2 cups cubed cooked chicken breast
- ¼ cup chopped roasted sweet red peppers
- ¼ cup crumbled feta cheese
- ¼ cup thinly sliced fresh basil leaves

Spread hummus on tortillas; top with chicken, red peppers, cheese and basil. Roll up.

SIMPLE TOMATO SOUP

I created this recipe one day when we were stuck indoors due to bad weather. My family asks for it often. If I pack it in my daughter's lunch, I include some for her classmate, too. It's pure comfort food and worth sharing with a good friend.
—**Lanaee O'Neill** Chico, CA

Start to Finish: 30 min.
Makes: 8 servings (2 quarts)

- 2 cans (14.5 ounces each) diced tomatoes with basil, oregano and garlic, undrained
- ¼ cup butter
- ½ cup finely chopped red onion
- 2 garlic cloves, minced
- 6 tablespoons all-purpose flour
- 1 carton (48 ounces) chicken broth
  Grated Parmesan cheese, optional

1. Place tomatoes with juices in a blender; cover and process until pureed. In a large saucepan, heat butter over medium-high heat. Add onion; cook and stir until tender. Add garlic; cook 1 minute longer.
2. Remove from the heat; stir in flour until smooth. Cook for 1 minute. Gradually whisk in broth. Add pureed tomatoes; bring to a boil over medium heat, stirring occasionally. Reduce heat and simmer for 20-25 minutes to allow flavors to blend. If desired, sprinkle with cheese.

WHITE CHICKEN CHILI

Folks will enjoy the change of pace from traditional chili when they spoon into this zippy blend of tender chunks of chicken and white beans.
—*Taste of Home* Test Kitchen

Prep: 15 min. • **Cook:** 25 min.
Makes: 10 servings (2½ quarts)

- 1 pound boneless skinless chicken breasts, chopped
- 1 medium onion, chopped
- 1 tablespoon olive oil
- 2 garlic cloves, minced
- 2 cans (14 ounces each) chicken broth
- 1 can (4 ounces) chopped green chilies
- 2 teaspoons ground cumin
- 2 teaspoons dried oregano
- 1½ teaspoons cayenne pepper
- 3 cans (14½ ounces each) great northern beans, drained, divided
- 1 cup shredded Monterey Jack cheese
  Sliced jalapeno pepper, optional

1. In a Dutch oven over medium heat, cook chicken and onion in oil until lightly browned. Add garlic; cook 1 minute longer. Stir in the broth, chilies, cumin, oregano and cayenne; bring to a boil.
2. Reduce heat to low. With a potato masher, mash one can of beans until smooth. Add to saucepan. Add remaining beans to saucepan. Simmer 20-30 minutes or until chicken is no longer pink and onion is tender.
3. Top each serving with cheese and, if desired, jalapeno pepper.

TEST KITCHEN TIP
One of our favorite time-saving tricks is using shredded rotisserie chicken. We save the bones to make homemade broth in the slow cooker. Can't find great northern beans? Pinto, navy and cannellini all work well here. If you don't have a potato masher, no problem! Add all three cans of beans to the Dutch oven. Smush some of the beans against the sides of the pot with a ladle or wooden spoon until chili is slightly thickened.

HEARTY BUTTERNUT SQUASH SOUP

The comforting combination of squash, meat, beans and veggies makes this my go-to soup in fall. It's full of freshness.

—**Jaye Beeler** Grand Rapids, MI

Prep: 20 min. • **Cook:** 40 min.
Makes: 12 servings (4½ quarts)

- 1 pound bulk Italian sausage
- 1 medium onion, chopped
- 1 medium sweet red pepper, chopped
- 4 garlic cloves, minced
- 1 large butternut squash (about 5 pounds), peeled, seeded and cut into 1-inch pieces
- 1 package (16 ounces) frozen corn, divided
- 4 cups water
- 1 tablespoon chicken base
- 2 cans (15½ ounces each) great northern beans, rinsed and drained
- 2 cans (14½ ounces each) fire-roasted diced tomatoes, undrained
- 1 teaspoon salt
- ¼ teaspoon pepper
  Heavy whipping cream and minced fresh parsley, optional

1. In a stockpot, cook sausage, onion and red pepper over medium heat for 9-11 minutes or until sausage is no longer pink and onion is tender, breaking up the sausage into crumbles. Add garlic; cook 1 minute longer. Remove with a slotted spoon; discard drippings.

2. Add the squash, 1½ cups corn, water and chicken base to same pan; bring to a boil. Reduce heat; simmer, covered, for 15-20 minutes or until squash is tender.

3. Remove soup from heat; cool slightly. Process in batches in a blender until smooth. Return to pot. Add the beans, tomatoes, salt, pepper, sausage mixture and remaining corn; heat through. Drizzle servings with cream and sprinkle with parsley if desired.

Freeze option: Freeze cooled soup in freezer containers. To use, partially thaw in refrigerator overnight. Heat through in a saucepan, stirring occasionally and adding a little water if necessary.

ITALIAN MEATBALL SUBS

This is one of those recipes you always come back to. A flavorful tomato sauce and mildly spiced meatballs make a hearty sandwich filling, or they can be served over pasta. I broil the meatballs first to quickly brown them.

—**Jean Glacken** Elkton, MD

Prep: 25 min. • **Cook:** 4 hours
Makes: 6 servings

- 2 large eggs, lightly beaten
- ¼ cup whole milk
- ½ cup dry bread crumbs
- 2 tablespoons grated Parmesan cheese
- 1 teaspoon salt
- ¼ teaspoon pepper
- ⅛ teaspoon garlic powder
- 1 pound ground beef
- ½ pound bulk Italian sausage

SAUCE

- 1 can (15 ounces) tomato sauce
- 1 can (6 ounces) tomato paste
- 1 small onion, chopped
- ½ cup chopped green pepper
- ½ cup dry red wine or beef broth
- ⅓ cup water
- 2 garlic cloves, minced
- 1 teaspoon dried oregano
- 1 teaspoon salt
- ½ teaspoon sugar
- ½ teaspoon pepper
- 6 Italian rolls, split
  Shredded Parmesan cheese, optional

1. In a large bowl, combine eggs and milk; add the bread crumbs, Parmesan cheese, salt, pepper and garlic powder. Add beef and sausage; mix well. Shape into 1-in. balls. Preheat broiler. Place meatballs in a 15x10x1-in. baking pan. Broil 4 in. from the heat for 4 minutes; turn and broil for 3 minutes longer.

2. Transfer to a 5-qt. slow cooker. Combine the tomato sauce and paste, onion, green pepper, wine, water and seasonings; pour over meatballs. Cover and cook on low for 4-5 hours. Serve on rolls. Sprinkle with shredded cheese if desired.

ZIPPY CHICKEN & CORN CHOWDER

Gently spiced corn chowder is always a good choice for kids, but adults can rev up their serving with hot pepper sauce. It's my go-to on busy nights.
—**Andrea Early** Harrisonburg, VA

Prep: 15 min. • **Cook:** 25 min.
Makes: 8 servings (3 quarts)

- ¼ cup butter
- 1 large onion, chopped
- 1 medium green pepper, chopped
- ¼ cup all-purpose flour
- 1 tablespoon paprika
- 2 medium potatoes, peeled and chopped
- 1 carton (32 ounces) chicken broth
- 1 skinned rotisserie chicken, shredded
- 6 cups fresh or frozen corn
- 1 tablespoon Worcestershire sauce
- ½ to 1 teaspoon hot pepper sauce
- 1 teaspoon salt
- 1 cup 2% milk

1. In a stockpot, heat the butter over medium-high heat. Add onion and pepper; cook, stirring, until vegetables are crisp-tender, 3-4 minutes. Stir in flour and paprika until blended.
2. Add potatoes; stir in broth. Bring to a boil; reduce heat and simmer, covered, until tender, 12-15 minutes.
3. Stir in shredded chicken, corn, sauces and salt; bring to a boil. Reduce heat and cook, uncovered, until corn is tender, 4-6 minutes. Add milk; heat through (do not boil).

★ ★ ★ ★ ★ **READER REVIEW**

"We made this potato soup at work for one of our weekly lunches. Two full crockpots and there was nothing left! We also added some mined garlic and a bit more pepper, to give it some more spice."
LDKELLY TASTEOFHOME.COM

SLOW-COOKED LOADED POTATO SOUP

I like to put a twist on my grandmother's recipes, as I did with this one. I look forward to passing my own delicious comfort food recipes down to my kids.
—**Jamie Chase** Rising Sun, IN

Prep: 30 min. • **Cook:** 8¼ hours
Makes: 12 servings (4 quarts)

- 5 pounds potatoes, peeled and cubed (about 10 cups)
- 1 medium onion, finely chopped
- 5 cans (14½ ounces each) chicken broth
- 1 garlic clove, minced
- 1½ teaspoons salt
- ¼ teaspoon pepper
- 2 packages (8 ounces each) cream cheese, softened and cubed
- 1 cup half-and-half cream
- ¼ cup butter, cubed

TOPPINGS
- 1 pound bacon strips, cooked and crumbled
- ¾ cup shredded sharp cheddar cheese
- ¼ cup minced chives

1. Place potatoes and onion in a 6-qt. slow cooker; add broth, garlic, salt and pepper. Cook, covered, on low 8-10 hours or until potatoes are tender.
2. Mash potatoes to desired consistency. Stir in cream cheese, cream and butter. Cook, covered, 15 minutes longer or until heated through.
3. Just before serving, whisk soup to combine. Top servings with bacon, cheese and chives.

4 cups water
1 cup reduced-sodium chicken broth
1 whole garlic bulb, loose paper removed, cut in half crosswise
5 whole cloves
2 bay leaves
2 boneless skinless chicken breast halves (6 ounces each)
1 pound uncooked chorizo or bulk spicy pork sausage
2 cans (15 ounces each) hominy, rinsed and drained
3 teaspoons lime juice, divided
1 teaspoon dried oregano
1 teaspoon ground cumin
½ teaspoon salt, divided
1 cup minced fresh cilantro, divided

SALSA
1 medium mango, peeled and cubed
1 medium ripe avocado, peeled and cubed
5 radishes, chopped

GARNISH
6 cups tortilla chips

1. Place the tomatillos, onion, jalapenos and garlic cloves on a greased baking sheet. Bake at 425° for 25-30 minutes or until tomatillos are tender. Cool slightly. Transfer to a food processor; cover and process until blended.
2. In a Dutch oven, bring the water, broth, garlic bulb, cloves and bay leaves to a boil. Reduce heat; add chicken breasts and poach, uncovered, for 15-20 minutes or until no longer pink.
3. Remove chicken from broth and shred. Strain the broth, discarding seasonings. Crumble chorizo into Dutch oven; cook over medium heat for 6-8 minutes or until fully cooked. Drain. Return broth to Dutch oven. Stir in the hominy, 2 teaspoons lime juice, oregano, cumin, ¼ teaspoon salt, tomatillo mixture and shredded chicken; heat through. Stir in ½ cup cilantro.
4. For salsa, in a small bowl, combine the mango, avocado and radishes with the remaining cilantro, lime juice and salt. Serve with soup. Garnish with chips.
Freeze option: Freeze cooled soup in freezer containers. To use, partially thaw in refrigerator overnight. Heat through in a saucepan, stirring occasionally and adding a little broth if necessary. Prepare salsa and serve with soup.
Note: Wear disposable gloves when cutting hot peppers; the oils can burn skin. Avoid touching your face.

HERB & CHEESE-STUFFED BURGERS

Tired of the same old ground beef burgers? Try this quick-fix alternative, with its creamy cheese filling, at your next barbecue. It will wake up taste buds.
—**Sherri Cox** Lucasville, OH

Start to Finish: 30 min.
Makes: 4 servings

¼ cup shredded cheddar cheese
2 tablespoons cream cheese, softened
2 tablespoons minced fresh parsley
3 teaspoons Dijon mustard, divided
2 green onions, thinly sliced
3 tablespoons dry bread crumbs
2 tablespoons ketchup
½ teaspoon salt
½ teaspoon dried rosemary, crushed
¼ teaspoon dried sage leaves
1 pound lean ground beef (90% lean)
4 hamburger buns, split
 Optional toppings: lettuce leaves and tomato slices

1. In a small bowl, mix cheddar cheese, cream cheese, parsley and 1 teaspoon mustard. In another bowl, mix sliced green onions, bread crumbs, ketchup, seasonings and remaining mustard. Add beef; mix lightly but thoroughly.
2. Shape mixture into eight thin patties. Spoon cheese mixture onto the center of four patties; top with remaining patties, pressing edges firmly to seal.
3. Grill burgers, covered, over medium heat or broil 4 in. from heat 4-5 minutes on each side or until a thermometer reads 160°. Serve on hamburger buns and top as desired.

CHICKEN CHORIZO POSOLE

I first tasted posole while visiting a friend in Santa Fe. It was a revelation! I have since been experimenting with many versions, and this one has become a much-loved tradition for my family.
—**Jennifer Beckman** Falls Church, VA

Prep: 40 min. • **Cook:** 40 min.
Makes: 9 servings

1 pound tomatillos, husked and cut in half
1 large onion, quartered
2 jalapeno peppers, halved and seeded
4 garlic cloves, peeled

FAVORITE MEAT LOAF GYROS

I always wanted to make Greek gyros but was intimidated. Then I tried this recipe, and they turned out great. I slice leftover meat into individual portions and freeze them for when I'm craving a gyro.
—**Sharon Rawlings** Tampa, FL

Prep: 30 min. • **Bake:** 1 hour + chilling
Makes: 8 servings

- 1 **large egg, lightly beaten**
- 6 **garlic cloves, minced**
- 3 **tablespoons dried oregano**
- 1½ **teaspoons kosher salt**
- 1 **teaspoon pepper**
- 1 **pound ground lamb**
- 1 **pound ground beef**

TZATZIKI SAUCE
- 1 **cup (8 ounces) plain yogurt**
- 1 **medium cucumber, peeled, seeded and chopped**
- 2 **tablespoons lemon juice**
- 2 **garlic cloves, minced**
- ½ **teaspoon salt**
- ¼ **teaspoon pepper**

GYROS
- 8 **whole pita breads**
- 3 **tablespoons olive oil, divided**
- 16 **slices tomato**
- 8 **slices sweet onion, halved**

1. In a large bowl, combine the egg, garlic, oregano, kosher salt and pepper. Crumble lamb and beef over mixture; mix well.
2. Pat into an ungreased 9x5-in. loaf pan.

Bake at 350°, uncovered, 60-70 minutes or until no pink remains and a thermometer reads 160°. Cool completely on a wire rack. Refrigerate for 1-2 hours.
3. For sauce, in a small bowl, combine the yogurt, cucumber, lemon juice, garlic, salt and pepper. Cover and refrigerate until serving.
4. Brush pita breads with 1 tablespoon oil; heat on a lightly greased griddle for 1 minute on each side. Keep warm. Cut meat loaf into very thin slices. In a large skillet, fry meat loaf in remaining oil in batches until crisp.
5. On each pita bread, layer the tomato, onion and meat loaf slices; top with some tzatziki sauce. Carefully fold pitas in half. Serve with remaining sauce.

CHEDDAR, CORN & POTATO CHOWDER

Curry powder gives this chowder just the right amount of zip without being overpowering. I especially like all the veggies. I make a double or triple batch so we have plenty of leftovers.

—**Becky Ruff** McGregor, IA

Prep: 15 min. • **Cook:** 35 min.
Makes: 6 servings

- ¼ cup butter, cubed
- 2 celery ribs, chopped
- 2 medium carrots, sliced
- 1 medium green pepper, finely chopped
- 1 medium onion, chopped
- ¼ cup all-purpose flour
- 1 teaspoon curry powder
- ½ teaspoon salt
- ¼ teaspoon pepper
- 1 cup 2% milk
- 1 carton (32 ounces) chicken broth
- 1 pound potatoes (about 2 medium), peeled and cubed
- 1 can (8¾ ounces) whole kernel corn, drained
- 2 cups shredded cheddar cheese
- 1 tablespoon minced fresh parsley

1. In a 6-qt. stockpot, heat the butter over medium heat. Add celery, carrots, green pepper and onion; cook and stir 3-4 minutes or until onion is tender. Stir in flour and seasonings until blended.

2. Gradually stir in the milk. Add broth, potatoes and corn; bring to a boil. Reduce heat; simmer, covered, 15-20 minutes or until potatoes are tender.

3. Stir in cheese until melted; remove from heat. Puree soup using an immersion blender. Or, cool slightly and puree in batches in a blender; return to pot and heat through. Stir in parsley.

THAI SHRIMP SOUP

This tasty, crowd-pleasing soup comes together in minutes, and I like the fact that the ingredients are available in my little local grocery store.

—**Jessie Grearson-Sapat** Falmouth, ME

Prep: 20 min. • **Cook:** 20 min.
Makes: 8 servings (2 quarts)

- 1 medium onion, chopped
- 1 tablespoon olive oil
- 3 cups reduced-sodium chicken broth
- 1 cup water
- 1 tablespoon brown sugar
- 1 tablespoon minced fresh gingerroot
- 1 tablespoon fish sauce or soy sauce
- 1 tablespoon red curry paste
- 1 lemongrass stalk
- 1 pound uncooked large shrimp, peeled and deveined
- 1½ cups frozen shelled edamame
- 1 can (13.66 ounces) light coconut milk
- 1 can (8¾ ounces) whole baby corn, drained and cut in half
- ½ cup bamboo shoots
- ¼ cup fresh basil leaves, torn
- ¼ cup minced fresh cilantro
- 2 tablespoons lime juice
- 1½ teaspoons grated lime peel
- 1 teaspoon curry powder

1. In a Dutch oven, saute onion in oil until tender. Add the broth, water, brown sugar, ginger, fish sauce, curry paste and lemongrass. Bring to a boil. Reduce heat; carefully stir in shrimp and edamame. Cook, uncovered, for 5-6 minutes or until shrimp turn pink.

2. Add the coconut milk, corn, bamboo shoots, basil, cilantro, lime juice, lime peel and curry powder; heat through. Discard the lemongrass.

ROASTED POBLANO BEEF STEW

My wife is Hispanic, and I like to celebrate her heritage through cooking. She gave this stew high praise when I presented it!
—**Greg Fontenot** The Woodlands, TX

Prep: 40 min. + standing • **Cook:** 2 hours
Makes: 8 servings (3 quarts)

- 5 poblano peppers
- 1 boneless beef chuck roast (2 to 3 pounds), cut into 1-inch cubes
- 2 tablespoons olive oil
- 1 medium onion, chopped
- 3 garlic cloves, minced
- 1 carton (32 ounces) beef broth
- 2 medium tomatoes, chopped
- ⅓ cup minced fresh cilantro
- 1 tablespoon chili powder
- 1 teaspoon salt
- 1 teaspoon ground cumin
- ½ teaspoon pepper
- 2 large potatoes, peeled and cut into 1-inch cubes

1. Broil poblano peppers 4 in. from the heat until skins blister, about 5 minutes. With tongs, rotate peppers a quarter turn. Broil and rotate until all sides are blistered and blackened. Immediately place the poblanos in a small bowl; cover and let stand for 20 minutes.
2. Peel off and discard charred poblano skins. Remove stems and seeds. Coarsely chop poblanos.
3. In a Dutch oven, brown beef in oil in batches. Remove and keep warm. In the same pan, saute onion until tender. Add garlic; cook 1 minute longer.
4. Gradually add beef broth; stir in the tomatoes, cilantro, chili powder, salt, cumin, pepper, poblanos and beef. Bring to a boil. Reduce heat; cover and simmer 1½ hours or until beef is tender. Add potatoes; cook 10-15 minutes longer or until potatoes are tender. Skim fat.

BBQ CHICKEN SLIDERS

Brining the chicken overnight helps it taste exceptionally good. It becomes so tender, it melts in your mouth when you take a bite of one of these sandwiches.
—**Rachel Kunkel** Schell City, MO

Prep: 25 min. + brining • **Cook:** 4 hours
Makes: 8 servings (2 sliders each)

BRINE
- 1½ quarts water
- ¼ cup packed brown sugar
- 2 tablespoons salt
- 1 tablespoon liquid smoke
- 2 garlic cloves, minced
- ½ teaspoon dried thyme

CHICKEN
- 2 pounds boneless skinless chicken breasts
- ⅓ cup liquid smoke
- 1½ cups hickory smoke-flavored barbecue sauce
- 16 slider buns or dinner rolls, split and warmed

1. In a large bowl, mix brine ingredients, stirring to dissolve brown sugar. Reserve 1 cup brine for cooking chicken; cover and refrigerate.
2. Place chicken in a large resealable bag; add remaining brine. Seal bag, pressing out as much air as possible; turn to coat chicken. Place in a large bowl; refrigerate 18-24 hours, turning occasionally.
3. Remove chicken from brine. Transfer to a 3-qt. slow cooker; discard brine in bag. Add reserved 1 cup brine and ⅓ cup liquid smoke to chicken. Cook, covered, on low 4-5 hours or until chicken is tender.
4. Remove chicken; cool slightly. Discard cooking juices. Shred chicken with two forks and return to slow cooker. Stir in barbecue sauce; heat through. Serve the chicken on buns.

PUMPKIN BISQUE WITH SMOKED GOUDA

I love the smell of this rich, cheesy soup as it bubbles on the stove. The Gouda cheese adds a delightful smokiness that is perfect for a cool autumn day.

—**Kerry Dingwall** Wimington, NC

....

Prep: 20 min. • **Cook:** 35 min.
Makes: 9 servings (2¼ quarts)

- 4 bacon strips, chopped
- 1 medium onion, chopped
- 3 garlic cloves, minced
- 6 cups chicken broth
- 1 can (29 ounces) solid-pack pumpkin
- ½ teaspoon salt
- ¼ teaspoon ground nutmeg
- ⅛ teaspoon pepper
- 1 cup heavy whipping cream
- 1 cup shredded Gouda cheese
- 2 tablespoons minced fresh parsley
  Additional shredded Gouda cheese, optional

1. In a Dutch oven, cook bacon over medium heat until crisp. Remove to paper towels with a slotted spoon; drain pan, reserving 1 tablespoon drippings. Saute onion in drippings until tender. Add garlic; cook 1 minute longer.
2. Stir in the broth, pumpkin, salt, nutmeg and pepper. Bring to a boil. Reduce heat; simmer, uncovered, for 10 minutes. Cool soup slightly.
3. In a blender, process soup in batches until smooth. Return all to pan. Stir in cream; heat through. Add cheese; stir until melted. Sprinkle each serving with parsley, bacon and, if desired, additional cheese.

BLACK BEAN CHIP & DIP BURGERS

I wanted to create a healthy veggie burger that wasn't dry or crumbly. These amazing burgers taste like chips and dip. Who can resist that? Even my grandkids prefer them over regular burgers!

—**KT Rehrig** Allentown, PA

....

Prep: 30 min. • **Grill:** 10 min.
Makes: 8 servings

- ⅔ cup water
- ⅓ cup quinoa, rinsed
- 1 can (15 ounces) black beans, rinsed and drained
- 1 jar (16 ounces) salsa, divided
- 1 cup crushed baked tortilla chip scoops
- 2 tablespoons reduced-sodium taco seasoning
- 8 whole wheat hamburger buns, split
- 8 lettuce leaves
- 8 slices tomato
- 8 slices red onion

1. In a small saucepan, bring water to a boil. Add quinoa. Reduce heat; simmer, covered, 12-15 minutes or until liquid is absorbed. Remove from heat; fluff with a fork.
2. In a large bowl, mash black beans. Add 1 cup salsa, tortilla chips, taco seasoning and cooked quinoa; mix well. Shape into eight ¼-in.-thick patties.
3. Grill, covered, over medium heat 5-6 minutes on each side or until heated through. Serve on buns with lettuce, tomato, onion and remaining salsa.
To bake patties: Preheat oven to 350°. Place patties on a baking sheet coated with cooking spray. Bake 25-30 minutes or until heated through, turning once.

CREAMY EGG SALAD

I love this egg salad's versatility—serve it on a nest of mixed greens, tucked into a sandwich or with your favorite crackers.

—Cynthia Kolberg Syracuse, IN

....

Start to Finish: 10 min.
Makes: 3 cups

- 3 ounces cream cheese, softened
- ¼ cup mayonnaise
- ½ teaspoon salt
- ⅛ teaspoon pepper
- ¼ cup finely chopped green or sweet red pepper
- ¼ cup finely chopped celery
- ¼ cup sweet pickle relish
- 2 tablespoons minced fresh parsley
- 8 hard-boiled large eggs, chopped

In a bowl, mix cream cheese, mayonnaise, salt and pepper until smooth. Stir in green pepper, celery, relish and parsley. Fold in eggs. Refrigerate, covered, until serving.

TEST KITCHEN TIP

For a heartier egg salad, substitute a 4-ounce jar of pimientos for the finely chopped pepper and add ½ cup of finely grated sharp cheddar cheese. Add extra flavor and freshness by using dill from the garden instead of (or in addition to) the parsley. Remember, dill is an herb that packs a punch, so 2 teaspoons instead of 2 tablespoons should do it.

MUSHROOM-STUFFED CHEESEBURGERS

No need to call my family twice when these burgers are on the menu. Get ahead of the game and stuff them in advance, then toss them on the grill when ready to eat.

—**Joyce Guth** Mohnton, PA

Prep: 30 min. • **Grill:** 10 min.
Makes: 8 servings

- 2 bacon strips, finely chopped
- 2 cups chopped fresh mushrooms
- ¼ cup chopped onion
- ¼ cup chopped sweet red pepper
- ¼ cup chopped green pepper
- 2 pounds lean ground beef (90% lean)
- 2 tablespoons steak sauce
- ½ teaspoon seasoned salt
- 4 slices provolone cheese, halved
- 8 kaiser rolls, split

1. In a large skillet, cook the bacon over medium heat until crisp, stirring occasionally. Remove with a slotted spoon; drain on paper towels. Cook and stir mushrooms, onion and peppers in bacon drippings until tender. Using slotted spoon, remove to a small bowl; cool completely. Stir in bacon.

2. In a large bowl, combine beef, steak sauce and seasoned salt, mixing lightly but thoroughly. Shape into 16 thin patties. Top eight of the patties with provolone, folding cheese to fit within ¾ inch of edge. Spread with mushroom mixture. Top with remaining patties, pressing edges to enclose filling.

3. Grill the burgers, uncovered, over medium-high heat or broil 4 in. from heat for 5-6 minutes on each side or until a thermometer inserted in meat portion reads 160°. Serve on rolls.

FAST FIX ▶
FIESTA TURKEY TORTILLA SOUP

I'm always amazed when I can pull together such a tasty soup in less than half an hour. It's a great way to use up leftover turkey.

—**Amy Mcfadden** Chelsea, AL

Start to Finish: 25 min.
Makes: 8 servings

- 4 cans (14½ ounces each) chicken broth
- 3 cups shredded cooked turkey or rotisserie chicken
- 1 can (15 ounces) black beans, rinsed and drained
- 1 can (15¼ ounces) whole kernel corn, drained
- ½ cup medium salsa
- 5 corn tortillas (6 inches), cut into ¼-inch strips
- ¼ cup chopped fresh cilantro
    Additional salsa, optional

1. In a Dutch oven, combine first five ingredients; bring to a boil. Reduce the heat; simmer mixture for 10 minutes, stirring occasionally.

2. Meanwhile, spread tortilla strips in a single layer on a baking sheet. Bake at 400° 4-6 minutes or until golden brown and crisp.

3. Stir cilantro into soup. Top servings with tortilla strips. If desired, serve with additional salsa.

Freeze option: Reserving tortillas for later, freeze cooled soup in freezer containers. To use, partially thaw in refrigerator overnight. Heat in a saucepan, stirring occasionally and adding a little broth or water if necessary. Meanwhile, bake tortillas as directed and sprinkle over each serving. If desired, serve with additional salsa.

ANYTHING GOES SAUSAGE SOUP

I call this Anything Goes Soup, because you can add or take out a variety of ingredients and it still turns out delicious. The broth is extra creamy and decadant thanks to the evaporated milk.

—**Sheena Wellard** Nampa, ID

Prep: 40 min. • **Cook:** 9½ hours
Makes: 15 servings (about 4 quarts)

- 1 pound bulk pork sausage
- 4 cups water
- 1 can (10¾ ounces) condensed cream of mushroom soup, undiluted
- 1 can (10¾ ounces) condensed cheddar cheese soup, undiluted
- 5 medium red potatoes, cubed
- 4 cups chopped cabbage
- 3 large carrots, thinly sliced
- 4 celery ribs, chopped
- 1 medium zucchini, chopped
- 1 large onion, chopped
- 5 chicken bouillon cubes
- 1 tablespoon dried parsley flakes
- ¾ teaspoon pepper
- 1 can (12 ounces) evaporated milk

1. In a large skillet, cook sausage over medium heat until no longer pink; drain. Transfer to a 6-qt. slow cooker. Stir in the water and soups until blended. Add the vegetables, bouillon, parsley and pepper.
2. Cover and cook on low for 9-10 hours or until vegetables are tender. Stir in milk; cover and cook 30 minutes longer.

★ ★ ★ ★ ★ **READER REVIEW**

"Made this soup the other night and my family loved it! I swiched out the cream of mushroom for cream of chicken and the cabbage for a bag of baby spinach. So yummy."

MKPD777 TASTEOFHOME.COM

MOZZARELLA BEEF ROLL-UPS

The kids will love these pepperoni and beef wraps. They're easy to assemble because each tortilla is simply wrapped around a portion of hearty meat filling and a piece of string cheese.

—*Taste of Home* Test Kitchen

Start to Finish: 30 min.
Makes: 6 servings

- 1 pound ground beef
- 1 medium green pepper, chopped
- ⅓ cup chopped onion
- 1 can (8 ounces) pizza sauce
- 2 ounces sliced pepperoni (about ⅔ cup)
- ½ teaspoon dried oregano
- 6 flour tortillas (10 inches), warmed
- 6 pieces string cheese (about 6 ounces)

1. Preheat oven to 350°. In a large skillet, cook and crumble beef with pepper and onion over medium-high heat until no longer pink, 5-7 minutes; drain. Stir in pizza sauce, pepperoni and oregano.
2. Spoon ½ cup mixture across center of each tortilla; top with a string cheese. Fold bottom and sides of tortilla over filling and roll up.
3. Place on an ungreased baking sheet, seam side down. Bake until heated through, about 10 minutes.
Freeze option: Cool beef mixture before assembly. Individually wrap roll-ups in foil and freeze in a resealable plastic freezer bag. To use, partially thaw overnight in refrigerator. Reheat foil-wrapped roll-ups on a baking sheet in a preheated 350° oven until heated through. To reheat roll-ups individually, remove foil and rewrap in paper towel; place on a microwave-safe plate. Microwave on high until heated through, turning once. Let stand 15 seconds.

BLACK BEAN & PUMPKIN CHILI

My family is crazy about this slow cooker recipe because it uses ingredients you don't usually find in chili, such as pumpkin. Cook up a big batch and freeze some for later; it tastes even better reheated.
—**Deborah Vliet** Holland, MI

Prep: 20 min. • **Cook:** 4 hours
Makes: 10 servings (2½ quarts)

- 2 tablespoons olive oil
- 1 medium onion, chopped
- 1 medium sweet yellow pepper, chopped
- 3 garlic cloves, minced
- 2 cans (15 ounces each) black beans, rinsed and drained
- 1 can (15 ounces) solid-pack pumpkin
- 1 can (14½ ounces) diced tomatoes, undrained
- 3 cups chicken broth
- 2½ cups cubed cooked turkey
- 2 teaspoons dried parsley flakes
- 2 teaspoons chili powder
- 1½ teaspoons ground cumin
- 1½ teaspoons dried oregano
- ½ teaspoon salt
  Cubed avocado and thinly sliced green onions, optional

1. In a large skillet, heat oil over medium-high heat. Add onion and pepper; cook and stir until tender. Add the garlic; cook 1 minute longer.

2. Transfer to a 5-qt. slow cooker; stir in the next 10 ingredients. Cook, covered, on low 4-5 hours. If desired, top with avocado and green onions.

TEST KITCHEN TIP

For a clever way to serve this chili, make bowls with fresh pumpkins. Purchase pie pumpkins; wash and dry. Cut wide circles around the stems, making lids. Scrape out each pumpkin. Place the pumpkins and lids in a large shallow roasting pan. Cover with foil and bake at 350° for 30-50 minutes or just until tender (do not overbake). Cool slightly; fill with chili.

LAYERED PICNIC LOAVES

This big sandwich is inspired by one I fell in love with at a New York deli. It's easy to make ahead of time and cart to any party. Kids and adults alike say it's super.
—**Marion Lowery** Medford, OR

Prep: 15 min. + chilling
Makes: 2 loaves (12 servings each)

- 2 unsliced loaves (1 pound each) Italian bread
- ¼ cup olive oil
- 3 garlic cloves, minced
- 2 teaspoons Italian seasoning, divided
- ½ pound deli roast beef
- 12 slices part-skim mozzarella cheese (1 ounce each)
- 16 fresh basil leaves
- 3 medium tomatoes, thinly sliced
- ¼ pound thinly sliced salami
- 1 jar (6½ ounces) marinated artichoke hearts, drained and sliced
- 1 package (10 ounces) ready-to-serve salad greens
- 8 ounces thinly sliced deli chicken
- 1 medium onion, thinly sliced
- ¼ teaspoon salt
- ⅛ teaspoon pepper

1. Cut loaves in half horizontally; hollow out tops and bottoms, leaving ½-in. shells (discard removed bread or save for another use).

2. Combine oil and garlic; brush inside bread shells. Sprinkle with 1 teaspoon Italian seasoning. Layer bottom of each loaf with a fourth each of the roast beef, mozzarella, basil, tomatoes, salami, artichokes, salad greens, chicken and onion. Repeat layers. Season with salt, pepper and remaining Italian seasoning.

3. Drizzle with remaining oil mixture if desired. Replace bread tops; wrap tightly in plastic. Refrigerate for at least 1 hour before slicing.

(5) INGREDIENTS

SPICY FRENCH DIP

When I'm cooking for a party or a family get-together, I put this beef in the slow cooker in the morning and then turn my attention to other party preparations. It's a great time-saver, and the tender meat never fails to get rave reviews.
—**Ginny Koeppen** Winnfield, LA

Prep: 10 min. • **Cook:** 8 hours
Makes: 12 servings

- 1 beef sirloin tip roast (3 pounds), cut in half
- ½ cup water
- 1 can (4 ounces) diced jalapeno peppers, drained
- 1 envelope Italian salad dressing mix
- 12 crusty rolls (5 inches)

1. Place beef in a 5-qt. slow cooker. In a small bowl, combine the water, jalapenos and dressing mix; pour over beef. Cover and cook on low for 8-10 hours or until meat is tender.

2. Remove beef and shred with two forks. Skim fat from cooking juices. Serve beef on rolls with juice.

UPSTATE MINESTRONE SOUP

Veggie lovers will find this minestrone especially satisfying. Keep the recipe in mind when you have a bounty of fresh garden produce to use up.
—**Yvonne Krantz** Mount Upton, NY

Prep: 25 min. • **Cook:** 1½ hours
Makes: 8 servings

- 1 pound Italian sausage links, cut into ½-inch slices
- 1 tablespoon olive oil
- 1 cup finely chopped onion
- 1 cup sliced fresh carrots
- 1 garlic clove, finely minced
- 1 teaspoon dried basil
- 2 cups shredded cabbage
- 2 small zucchini, sliced
- 2 cans (10½ ounces each) condensed beef broth, undiluted or 3 beef bouillon cubes plus 1½ cups water
- 1 can (14½ ounces) diced tomatoes, undrained
- 1 teaspoon salt
- ¼ teaspoon pepper
- 1 can (15½ ounces) great northern beans, rinsed and drained
  Minced fresh parsley

1. In a Dutch oven, brown sausage in oil. Add the onion, carrots, garlic and basil; cook for 5 minutes. Stir in the cabbage, zucchini, broth, tomatoes, salt and pepper.
2. Bring to a boil. Reduce heat; cover and simmer for 1 hour. Add beans; cook 20 minutes longer. Garnish with parsley.
Freeze option: Freeze cooled soup in freezer containers. To use, partially thaw in refrigerator overnight. Heat through in a saucepan, stirring occasionally and adding a little broth or water if necessary.

THE BEST CHICKEN & DUMPLINGS

Chicken and dumplings harken back to my childhood days when we devoured those comforting balls of dough swimming in a hot, rich broth. This soup is especially good on a chilly day.
—**Erika Monroe-Williams** Scottsdale, AZ

Prep: 25 min. • **Cook:** 1 hour 10 min.
Makes: 8 servings (3 quarts)

- ¾ cup all-purpose flour, divided
- ½ teaspoon salt
- ½ teaspoon freshly ground pepper
- 1 broiler/fryer chicken (about 3 pounds), cut up
- 2 tablespoons canola oil
- 1 large onion, chopped
- 2 medium carrots, chopped
- 2 celery ribs, chopped
- 3 garlic cloves, minced
- 6 cups chicken stock
- ½ cup white wine or apple cider
- 2 teaspoons sugar
- 2 bay leaves
- 5 whole peppercorns

DUMPLINGS
- 1⅓ cups all-purpose flour
- 2 teaspoons baking powder
- ¾ teaspoon salt
- ⅔ cup 2% milk
- 1 tablespoon butter, melted

SOUP
- ½ cup heavy whipping cream
- 2 teaspoons minced fresh parsley
- 2 teaspoons minced fresh thyme
  Additional salt and pepper to taste

1. In a shallow bowl, mix ½ cup flour, salt and pepper. Add chicken, one piece at a time, and toss to coat; shake off excess. In a 6-qt. stockpot, heat oil over medium-high heat. Brown chicken in batches on all sides; remove from pan.

2. Add onion, carrots and celery to same pan; cook and stir 6-8 minutes or until onion is tender. Add garlic; cook and stir 1 minute longer. Stir in ¼ cup flour until blended. Gradually add stock, stirring constantly. Stir in wine, sugar, bay leaves and peppercorns. Return chicken to pan; bring to a boil. Reduce heat; simmer, covered, 20-25 minutes or until chicken juices run clear.

3. Meanwhile, in a bowl, whisk flour, baking powder and salt. In another bowl, whisk the milk and melted butter until blended. Add to flour mixture; stir just until moistened (do not overmix). Drop by rounded tablespoonfuls onto a parchment paper-lined baking sheet; set aside.

4. Remove chicken from stockpot; cool slightly. Discard bay leaves and skim fat from soup. Remove skin and bones from chicken and discard. Using two forks, coarsely shred meat into 1- to 1½-in. pieces; return to soup. Cook, covered, on high until mixture reaches a simmer.

5. Drop dumplings on top of simmering soup, a few at a time. Reduce heat to low; cook, covered, 15-18 minutes or until a toothpick inserted in center of dumplings comes out clean (do not lift cover while simmering). Gently stir in cream, parsley and thyme. Season with additional salt and pepper to taste.

SLOW-COOKED SLOPPY JOES

Slow cook your way to a crowd-pleasing entree. Ground beef is transformed into a classic sandwich filling with just a few pantry staples.
—**Joeanne Steras** Garrett, PA

Prep: 15 min. • **Cook:** 4 hours
Makes: 12 servings

- 2 pounds ground beef
- 1 cup chopped green pepper
- ⅔ cup chopped onion
- 2 cups ketchup
- 2 envelopes sloppy joe mix
- 2 tablespoons brown sugar
- 1 teaspoon prepared mustard
- 12 hamburger buns, split

1. In a large skillet, cook the beef, pepper and onion over medium heat until meat is no longer pink; drain. Stir in the ketchup, sloppy joe mix, brown sugar and mustard.

2. Transfer to a 3-qt. slow cooker. Cover and cook on low for 4-5 hours or until flavors are blended. Spoon ½ cup onto each bun.

SIDES, SALADS & MORE

The perfect menu simply isn't complete without sensational sides to complement the main course. From picnic pleasers to speedy weeknight favorites, find the best in classic sidekicks right here.

DILLY POTATO & EGG SALAD

Everyone has a favorite potato salad, and this is mine. As a young bride, I was eager to learn how to cook and make things that my husband would love. I combined my mom's and his mom's recipes, and this is the delicious result.

—**Angela Leinenbach** Mechanicsvlle, VA

Prep: 20 min. + chilling
Cook: 20 min. + cooling
Makes: 12 servings (¾ cup each)

- 4 pounds medium red potatoes (about 14), peeled and halved
- 5 hard-boiled large eggs
- 1 cup chopped dill pickles
- 1 small onion, chopped
- 1½ cups mayonnaise
- 1 teaspoon celery seed
- ½ teaspoon salt
- ¼ teaspoon pepper
  Paprika

1. Place potatoes in a large saucepan; add water to cover. Bring to a boil. Reduce heat; cook, uncovered, until potatoes are tender, 15-20 minutes. Drain; cool completely.
2. Cut potatoes into ¾-in. cubes; place in a large bowl. Peel and chop four eggs. Peel and slice the remaining egg; set aside. Add chopped eggs, pickles and onion to potatoes. Mix mayonnaise, celery seed, salt and pepper; stir gently into potato mixture.
3. Top with sliced egg; sprinkle with paprika. Refrigerate, covered, at least 2 hours before serving.

TEST KITCHEN TIP
To make hard-boiled eggs, place a single layer of eggs in a saucepan. Add enough water to cover by 1 inch. Cover and bring to a boil, then turn off heat, remove from the burner and let stand (15 minutes for large eggs; for smaller eggs, 12 minutes). Rinse with cold water and cover with ice water until completely cool. Unpeeled hard-boiled eggs will stay fresh in the refrigerator up to 1 week. Once shelled, they should be used right away.

GRANDMA'S SPINACH SALAD

With all its fresh and flavorful ingredients, this pretty salad was my grandmother's favorite. Even my little ones like it. I love that it's good for them.
—**Shelley Riebel** Armada, MI

Start to Finish: 20 min.
Makes: 8 servings

- ½ cup sugar
- ½ cup canola oil
- ¼ cup white vinegar
- ½ teaspoon celery seed
- 10 ounces fresh baby spinach (about 13 cups)
- 1 small red onion, thinly sliced
- ½ pound sliced fresh mushrooms
- 5 hard-boiled large eggs, sliced
- 8 bacon strips, cooked and crumbled

1. Whisk first four ingredients until sugar is dissolved.

2. In a 13x9-in. dish, layer half of each of the following: spinach, onion, mushrooms and eggs. Repeat layers. Drizzle with dressing; top with bacon.
Health tip: Skip the bacon to make this a meat-free, gluten-free, dairy-free potluck dish or side salad.

CREAMY STUFFED BAKED POTATOES

My mom gave me her recipe for twice-baked potatoes, and I altered it by adding garlic, bacon and green onions. The spuds are perfect for a casual potluck or an elegant meal. We can't get enough!
—**Kristyn Drews** Omaha, NE

Prep: 15 min. • **Bake:** 1¼ hours
Makes: 10 servings

- 5 medium baking potatoes
- ¼ cup butter, softened
- 2 cups shredded cheddar cheese, divided
- ¾ cup sour cream
- 1 envelope ranch salad dressing mix
- 1 tablespoon minced chives
- 1 garlic clove, minced
  Crumbled cooked bacon and chopped green onion

1. Scrub and pierce potatoes. Bake at 375° for 1 hour or until tender. When cool enough to handle, cut a thin slice off the top of each potato and discard. Cut each potato in half lengthwise. Scoop out the pulp, leaving thin shells.
2. In a large bowl, beat the pulp with butter. Stir in 1 cup cheese, sour cream, salad dressing mix, chives and garlic. Spoon into potato shells. Sprinkle with remaining cheese.
3. Place on a baking sheet. Bake at 375° for 15-20 minutes or until heated through. Top with bacon and green onion.

MAPLE-GLAZED ACORN SQUASH

With a maple syrup and brown sugar glaze, this squash becomes pleasantly sweet. This is comfort food—easy to prepare and a tasty pairing for a pork entree.
—**Nancy Mueller** Menomonee Falls, WI

Prep: 10 min. • **Bake:** 55 min.
Makes: 2 servings

- 1 medium acorn squash, halved
- ¾ cup water
- ¼ cup maple syrup
- 2 tablespoons brown sugar
- ½ teaspoon ground cinnamon
- ¼ teaspoon ground ginger
- ¼ teaspoon salt

1. Preheat oven to 350°. Scoop out and discard seeds from squash. Place cut side down in a 13x9-in. baking dish; add water. Bake, uncovered, for 45 minutes.

2. If necessary, drain water from pan; turn squash cut side up. Combine maple syrup, brown sugar, cinnamon, ginger and salt; pour into squash halves. Bake, uncovered, 10 minutes or until glaze is heated through.

QUICK AMBROSIA FRUIT SALAD

I mix in a little shredded coconut and just enough marshmallows so it tastes like the creamy ambrosia I grew up with. Now everyone in my home loves it, too.
—**Trisha Kruse** Eagle, ID

Start to Finish: 10 min.
Makes: 6 servings

- 1 can (8¼ ounces) fruit cocktail, drained
- 1 can (8 ounces) unsweetened pineapple chunks, drained
- 1 cup green grapes
- 1 cup seedless red grapes
- 1 cup miniature marshmallows
- 1 medium banana, sliced
- ¾ cup vanilla yogurt
- ½ cup sweetened shredded coconut

In a large bowl, combine all ingredients. Chill until serving.

FRESH BROCCOLI MANDARIN SALAD

I write a food column for our local newspaper, and I consider myself a pretty good judge of recipes. But I'll admit I was surprised by this one—I didn't think the unusual ingredients would go together as well as they do. Take it from me...this one's a keeper!
—**Connie Blommers** Pella, IA

Prep: 30 min. + chilling
Makes: 12 servings

CUSTARD DRESSING
- ½ cups sugar
- 1½ teaspoons cornstarch
- 1 teaspoon ground mustard
- ¼ cup white vinegar
- ¼ cup water
- 1 large egg plus 1 large egg yolk, lightly beaten
- ½ cup mayonnaise
- 3 tablespoons butter, softened

SALAD
- 4 cups fresh broccoli florets, 1-inch cuts
- 2 cups sliced fresh mushrooms
- ½ medium red onion, sliced in ⅛-inch-thick rings
- 1 can (11 ounces) mandarin oranges, drained
- 6 slices bacon, cooked and crumbled
- ½ cup slivered almonds, toasted
- ½ cup golden raisins

1. In a large saucepan, combine the sugar, cornstarch and mustard. Combine vinegar and water. Stir into sugar mixture until smooth. Cook and stir over medium-high heat until thickened and bubbly. Reduce heat; cook and stir 2 minutes longer. Remove from the heat.

2. Stir a small amount of hot filling into egg and yolk; return all to pan, stirring constantly. Bring to a gentle boil; cook and stir 2 minutes longer. Remove from the heat. Gently stir in mayonnaise and butter. Cool to room temperature without stirring. Chill.

3. In a large salad bowl, combine the broccoli, mushrooms, onion, oranges, bacon, almonds and raisins. Pour dressing over salad; toss to coat. Refrigerate.

CHEESY CORN SPOON BREAD

Homey and comforting, this custard-like side dish is a much-requested recipe at potlucks and holiday dinners. The jalapeno pepper adds just the right amount of bite. Seconds helpings of this tasty casserole are common—leftovers aren't.

—**Katherine Franklin** Carbondale, IL

Prep: 15 min. • **Bake:** 35 min.
Makes: 15 servings

- ¼ cup butter, cubed
- 1 medium onion, chopped
- 2 large eggs
- 2 cups (16 ounces) sour cream
- 1 can (15¼ ounces) whole kernel corn, drained
- 1 can (14¾ ounces) cream-style corn
- ¼ teaspoon salt
- ¼ teaspoon pepper
- 1 package (8½ ounces) corn bread/ muffin mix
- 2 medium jalapeno peppers, divided
- 2 cups shredded cheddar cheese, divided

1. Preheat oven to 375°. In a large skillet, heat butter over medium-high heat. Add onion; saute until tender. Set aside.
2. Beat eggs; add sour cream, both cans of corn, salt and pepper. Stir in corn bread mix just until blended. Mince 1 jalapeno pepper; fold into corn mixture with sauteed onion and 1½ cups of cheese.
3. Transfer to a greased shallow 3-qt. baking dish. Sprinkle with the remaining cheese. Bake, uncovered, until a toothpick inserted in the center comes out clean, 35-40 minutes; cool slightly. Slice remaining jalapeno; sprinkle over dish.
Note: Wear disposable gloves when cutting hot peppers; the oils can burn skin. Avoid touching your face.

DIJON VEGGIES WITH COUSCOUS

Coated in a tangy Dijon sauce, these tasty veggies and fluffy couscous make for a delightful side.

—**Juliana Dumitru** Fairview Park, OH

Prep: 20 min. • **Bake:** 20 min.
Makes: 6 servings

- ½ pound medium fresh mushrooms, quartered
- 1 medium zucchini, halved lengthwise and cut into ¼-inch slices
- 1 medium sweet red pepper, cut into 1-inch pieces
- ¼ cup dry red wine or reduced-sodium chicken broth
- 3 tablespoons Dijon mustard
- 2 tablespoons olive oil
- 2 garlic cloves, minced
- 1 teaspoon prepared horseradish
- ½ teaspoon salt
- ¼ teaspoon pepper
- 1 cup water
- 1 cup uncooked couscous

1. Place an 18x12-in. piece of heavy-duty foil on a large baking sheet; set aside.
2. In a large bowl, combine mushrooms, zucchini and red pepper. Combine wine, mustard, oil, garlic, horseradish, salt and pepper; drizzle over vegetables. Toss to coat; transfer to baking sheet. Top with a second large piece of foil. Bring edges of foil pieces together; crimp to seal, forming a large packet.
3. Bake at 350° for 20-25 minutes or until vegetables are tender. Open foil carefully to allow steam to escape.
4. Meanwhile, in a small saucepan, bring water to a boil. Stir in couscous. Remove from the heat; cover and let stand for 5-10 minutes or until water is absorbed. Fluff with a fork. Transfer the couscous and vegetables to a large serving bowl; toss to combine.
Freeze option: Freeze cooled mixture in a freezer container. To use, partially thaw in the refrigerator overnight. Microwave, covered, on high in a microwave-safe dish until heated, adding 2-3 tablespoons water to moisten.

CAULIFLOWER CASSEROLE

To dress up cauliflower, my mom used a delightful mixture of cheesy sauce, bright red and green pepper pieces and crushed cornflakes. We enjoyed this so much growing up that leftovers were rare.
—Linda McGinty Parma, OH

Prep: 15 min. • **Bake:** 30 min.
Makes: 8 servings

- 1 medium head cauliflower, broken into florets
- 1 cup (8 ounces) sour cream
- 1 cup shredded cheddar cheese
- ½ cup crushed cornflakes
- ¼ cup chopped green pepper
- ¼ cup chopped sweet red pepper
- 1 teaspoon salt
- ¼ cup grated Parmesan cheese Paprika

1. Place 1 in. of water in a saucepan; add cauliflower. Bring to a boil. Reduce heat; cover and simmer for 5-10 minutes or until crisp-tender. Drain.

2. In a large bowl, combine cauliflower, sour cream, cheddar cheese, cornflakes, peppers and salt; transfer to a greased 2-qt. baking dish. Sprinkle with Parmesan cheese and paprika.

3. Bake casserole, uncovered, at 325° for 30-35 minutes or until heated through.

★ ★ ★ ★ ★ READER REVIEW

"Who asks for a cauliflower recipe? I did, because this one was worth asking for. I got this recipe from my friend Laura, and now I can actually say that my kids love cauliflower!"

JASCHNEIDER1 TASTEOFHOME.COM

BAKED GERMAN POTATO SALAD

What makes this German potato salad so unique is that it's sweet instead of tangy. I prepare this for my family's annual holiday ham dinner. It pairs perfectly with the savory main dish and other special dishes.
—**Julie Myers** Lexington, OH

Prep: 50 min. • **Bake:** 30 min.
Makes: 10 servings

- 12 medium red potatoes (about 3 pounds)
- 8 bacon strips
- 2 medium onions, chopped
- ¾ cup packed brown sugar
- ⅔ cup water, divided
- ⅓ cup white vinegar
- ⅓ cup sweet pickle juice
- 2 teaspoons dried parsley flakes
- 1 teaspoon salt
- ½ to ¾ teaspoon celery seed
- 4½ teaspoons all-purpose flour

1. In a saucepan, cook potatoes until just tender; drain. Peel and slice into an ungreased 2-qt. baking dish; set aside.

2. In a skillet, cook bacon until crisp; drain, reserving 2 tablespoons drippings. Crumble bacon and set aside. Saute onions in drippings until tender. Stir in the brown sugar, ½ cup water, vinegar, pickle juice, parsley, salt and celery seed. Simmer, uncovered, for 5-10 minutes.

3. Meanwhile, combine flour and the remaining water until smooth; stir into onion mixture. Bring to a boil. Cook and stir 2 minutes or until thickened. Pour over potatoes. Add bacon; gently stir to coat. Bake, uncovered, at 350° for 30 minutes or until heated through.

SPECTACULAR OVERNIGHT SLAW

To come up with this dish, I used a number of different recipes, plus some ideas of my own. It's great for a potluck because it gets made the night before and the flavor keeps getting better. Whenever I serve it, I'm inundated with recipe requests.
—**Ruth Lovett** Bay City, TX

Prep: 15 min. + chilling
Makes: 16 servings

- 1 medium head cabbage, shredded
- 1 medium red onion, thinly sliced
- ½ cup chopped green pepper
- ½ cup chopped sweet red pepper
- ½ cup sliced pimiento-stuffed olives
- ½ cup white wine vinegar
- ½ cup canola oil
- ½ cup sugar
- 2 teaspoons Dijon mustard
- 1 teaspoon salt
- 1 teaspoon celery seed
- 1 teaspoon mustard seed

Combine cabbage, onion, peppers and olives. In a large saucepan, mix remaining ingredients; bring to a boil. Cook and stir 1 minute. Pour over vegetables; stir gently. Cover and refrigerate overnight. Mix well before serving.

(5) INGREDIENTS

CREAMED CORN

Five ingredients are all you'll need for my popular dinner accompaniment. Try it on a barbecue buffet or holiday menu.
—**Barbara Brizendine** Harrisonville, MO

Prep: 10 min. • **Cook:** 3 hours
Makes: 5 servings

- 2 packages (one 16 ounces, one 10 ounces) frozen corn
- 1 package (8 ounces) cream cheese, softened and cubed
- ¼ cup butter, cubed
- 1 tablespoon sugar
- ½ teaspoon salt

In a 3-qt. slow cooker coated with cooking spray, combine all ingredients. Cover and cook on low for 3-3½ hours or until the cheese is melted and corn is tender. Stir just before serving.

(5) INGREDIENTS FAST FIX

PARMESAN ROASTED ASPARAGUS

Need a fast, upscale side? Just a few staples make fresh asparagus amazing. Say hello to flavor!
—**Mar Brown** Pooler, GA

Start to Finish: 30 min.
Makes: 4 servings

- 1 pound fresh asparagus, trimmed
- 3 tablespoons olive oil
- ⅓ cup shredded Parmesan cheese
- 1 teaspoon lemon-pepper seasoning
- ¼ teaspoon salt

1. Preheat oven to 400°. Place asparagus in an ungreased 15x10x1-in. baking pan. Drizzle with oil; toss to coat. Sprinkle with cheese, lemon pepper and salt.
2. Bake 20-25 minutes or until tender, stirring occasionally.

FAST FIX

PEA & PEANUT SALAD

A friend gave me this easy salad recipe. Even folks who normally push away their peas devour this by the bowlful.
—**Laurinda Nelson** Phoenix, AZ

Start to Finish: 15 min.
Makes: 4 servings

- 2½ cups frozen peas (about 10 ounces), thawed
- 1 cup dry roasted peanuts
- 1 cup chopped celery
- 6 bacon strips, cooked and crumbled
- ¼ cup chopped red onion
- ½ cup mayonnaise
- ¼ cup prepared zesty Italian salad dressing

In a large bowl, combine the first five ingredients. In a small bowl, mix the mayonnaise and salad dressing; stir into salad. Refrigerate, covered, until serving.

FAST FIX ▶
SOBA NOODLES WITH GINGER-SESAME DRESSING

We love it when opposite flavors attract. Here, a sweet-and-sour gingery dressing complements soba noodles, edamame and crunchy slaw. Add grilled shrimp or chicken for a protein-packed finish.

—Mandy Rivers Lexington, SC

Start to Finish: 30 min.
Makes: 6 servings

- ½ cup reduced-sodium soy sauce
- ¼ cup packed brown sugar
- 2 tablespoons rice vinegar
- 2 tablespoons canola oil
- 2 tablespoons orange juice
- 1 tablespoon minced fresh gingerroot
- 1 teaspoon sesame oil
- 1 garlic clove, minced
- 1 teaspoon Sriracha Asian hot chili sauce or ½ teaspoon hot pepper sauce

SALAD
- 2 cups frozen shelled edamame, thawed
- ½ pound uncooked Japanese soba noodles or whole wheat linguini
- 1 package (14 ounces) coleslaw mix
- 1 cup shredded carrots
- 1 cup thinly sliced green onions
- 3 tablespoons sesame seeds, toasted

1. In a small bowl, whisk the first nine ingredients; set aside. Cook edamame and soba noodles according to package directions; drain. Rinse noodles in cold water; drain again.
2. Just before serving, combine the coleslaw mix, carrots, green onions, noodles and edamame in a large bowl. Add dressing; toss to coat. Garnish with sesame seeds.

FAST FIX ▶
GARLIC-ROASTED BRUSSELS SPROUTS WITH MUSTARD SAUCE

Don't be afraid to bring out the Brussels sprouts. Mellowed by roasting and tossed with mustard sauce, they may just delight even the most skeptical folks.

—Becky Walch Orland, CA

Start to Finish: 20 min.
Makes: 6 servings

- 1½ pounds fresh Brussels sprouts, halved
- 2 tablespoons olive oil
- 3 garlic cloves, minced
- ½ cup heavy whipping cream
- 3 tablespoons Dijon mustard
- ⅛ teaspoon white pepper
- Dash salt

1. Preheat oven to 450°. Place Brussels sprouts in an ungreased 15x10x1-in. baking pan. Combine olive oil and garlic; drizzle over sprouts and toss to coat.
2. Bake, uncovered, 10-15 minutes or until sprouts are tender, stirring occasionally.
3. Meanwhile, in a saucepan, combine the whipping cream, mustard, pepper and salt. Bring to a gentle boil; cook for 1-2 minutes or until slightly thickened. Spoon over the Brussels sprouts.

DID YOU KNOW?

Brussels sprouts are at their peak from September to February. Store unwashed sprouts in an airtight container in the refrigerator for 3-4 days.

BAKED PARMESAN BROCCOLI

I began making this creamy side dish years ago as a way to get my kids to eat broccoli. They've since grown up but still request this satisfying casserole.
—**Barbara Uhl** Wesley Chapel, FL

Prep: 30 min. • **Bake:** 15 min.
Makes: 12 servings (¾ cup each)

- 4   bunches broccoli, cut into florets
- 6   tablespoons butter, divided
- 1   small onion, finely chopped
- 1   garlic clove, minced
- ¼   cup all-purpose flour
- 2   cups 2% milk
- 1   large egg yolk, beaten
- 1   cup grated Parmesan cheese
- ½   teaspoon salt
- ⅛   teaspoon pepper
- ½   cup seasoned bread crumbs

1.   Preheat oven to 400°. Place half of broccoli in a steamer basket; place in a large saucepan over 1 in. of water. Bring to a boil; cover and steam 3-4 minutes or until crisp-tender. Place in a greased 13x9-in. baking dish; repeat with remaining broccoli florets.
2.   Meanwhile, in a small saucepan over medium heat, melt 4 tablespoons butter. Add onion; cook and stir until tender. Add garlic; cook 1 minute longer.
3.   Stir in flour until blended; gradually add milk. Bring to a boil; cook and stir for 2 minutes or until thickened. Stir a small amount of hot mixture into egg yolk; return all to the pan, stirring constantly. Cook and stir 1 minute longer. Remove from heat; stir in cheese, salt and pepper.
4.   Pour over broccoli. In a small skillet, cook bread crumbs in remaining butter until golden brown; sprinkle over the top.
5.   Bake, uncovered, 15-18 minutes or until heated through.

(5)INGREDIENTS FAST FIX
CHERRY TOMATO MOZZARELLA SAUTE

This side dish is fast to fix and full of flavor. The mix of cherry tomatoes and mozzarella make it the perfect pair for almost any main dish.
—**Summer Jones** Pleasant Grove, UT

Start to Finish: 25 min.
Makes: 4 servings

- 2   teaspoons olive oil
- ¼   cup chopped shallots
- 1   teaspoon minced fresh thyme
- 1   garlic clove, minced
- 2½ cups cherry tomatoes, halved
- ¼   teaspoon salt
- ¼   teaspoon pepper
- 4   ounces fresh mozzarella cheese, cut into ½-inch cubes

In a large skillet, heat oil over medium-high heat; saute shallots with thyme until tender. Add garlic; cook and stir 1 minute. Stir in tomatoes, salt and pepper; heat through. Remove from heat; stir in cheese.

FAST FIX
FABULOUS GREEN BEANS

My family loves this buttery sauce over fresh or frozen green beans. I've made this easy recipe with sugar snap peas, as well.
—**Lori Daniels** Beverly, WV

Start to Finish: 20 min.
Makes: 4 servings

- 1   pound fresh green beans, trimmed
- ¼   cup butter, cubed
- 1   tablespoon olive oil
- ½   teaspoon salt
- ½   teaspoon Italian seasoning
- ½   teaspoon lemon juice
- ¼   teaspoon grated lemon peel

1.   Place beans in a steamer basket; place in a large saucepan over 1 in. water. Bring to a boil; cover and steam for 8-10 minutes or until crisp-tender.
2.   Meanwhile, in a small saucepan, heat the remaining ingredients until butter is melted. Transfer beans to a serving bowl; drizzle with butter mixture and toss to coat.

PARMESAN POTATO WEDGES

I recommend serving these seasoned wedges alongside a salad for a light lunch or serving them as a side dish with a chicken or beef entree.

—**Beth Ask** Ulster, PA

....

Prep: 10 min. • **Bake:** 30 min.
Makes: 8 servings

- ¼ cup grated Parmesan cheese
- 1 teaspoon garlic salt
- ½ teaspoon garlic powder
- ½ teaspoon dried oregano
- ½ teaspoon paprika
- 4 medium baking potatoes (about 8 ounces each)
  Cooking spray

1. Preheat oven to 400°. Mix the first five ingredients.
2. Cut each potato lengthwise into eight wedges; place in a parchment paper-lined 15x10x1-in. pan. Spritz with cooking spray; sprinkle with cheese mixture. Bake until tender, about 30 minutes.

⑤INGREDIENTS

GERMAN RED CABBAGE

Sunday afternoons were a time for family gatherings when I was a kid. While my uncles played cards, my aunts had fun in the kitchen making traditional German recipes like this red cabbage.

—**Jeannette Heim** Dunlap, TN

....

Prep: 10 min. • **Cook:** 65 min.
Makes: 10 servings

- 1 medium onion, halved and sliced
- 1 medium apple, sliced
- 1 medium head red cabbage, shredded (about 8 cups)
- ⅓ cup sugar
- ⅓ cup white vinegar
- ¾ teaspoon salt, optional
- ¼ teaspoon pepper

In a large Dutch oven coated with cooking spray, cook and stir onion and apple over medium heat until onion is tender, about 5 minutes. Stir in remaining ingredients; cook, covered, until cabbage is tender, about 1 hour, stirring occasionally. Serve warm or cold.

MAKE-AHEAD HEARTY SIX-LAYER SALAD

This salad is an all-time favorite. I reach for the recipe whenever I need a dish to pass. It's easy to make, can be assembled ahead of time and looks great.

—**Noreen Meyer** Madison, WI

....

Prep: 20 min. + chilling
Makes: 12 servings

- 1½ cups uncooked small pasta shells
- 1 tablespoon vegetable oil
- 3 cups shredded lettuce
- 3 large hard-boiled large eggs, sliced
- ¼ teaspoon salt
- ⅛ teaspoon pepper
- 2 cups shredded cooked chicken breast
- 1 package (10 ounces) frozen peas, thawed

DRESSING
- 1 cup mayonnaise
- ¼ cup sour cream
- 2 green onions, chopped
- 2 teaspoons Dijon mustard

TOPPINGS
- 1 cup shredded Colby or Monterey Jack cheese
- 2 tablespoons minced fresh parsley

1. Cook pasta according to package directions; drain and rinse with cold water. Drizzle with oil and toss to coat.
2. Place the lettuce in a 2½-qt. glass serving bowl; top with pasta and eggs. Sprinkle with salt and pepper. Layer with chicken and peas. In a small bowl, mix dressing ingredients until blended; spread over top. Refrigerate, covered, for several hours or overnight.
3. Just before serving, sprinkle with cheese and parsley.

✱
TEST KITCHEN TIP
Use other greens in place of the lettuce if you prefer. Baby spinach and peppery arugula are great choices. Lighten things up by using low-fat sour cream and mayonnaise.

FAST FIX ▶

SHRIMP & NECTARINE SALAD

For a cool salad on a hot summer day, I combine shrimp, corn, tomatoes and nectarines with a drizzle of tarragon dressing. We love it chilled, but it's great warm, too.
—**Mary Ann Lee** Clifton Park, NY

Start to Finish: 30 min.
Makes: 4 servings

- ⅓ cup orange juice
- 3 tablespoons cider vinegar
- 1½ teaspoons Dijon mustard
- 1½ teaspoons honey
- 1 tablespoon minced fresh tarragon

SALAD
- 4 teaspoons canola oil, divided
- 1 cup fresh or frozen corn
- 1 pound uncooked shrimp (26-30 per pound), peeled and deveined
- ½ teaspoon lemon-pepper seasoning
- ¼ teaspoon salt
- 8 cups torn mixed salad greens
- 2 medium nectarines, cut into 1-inch pieces
- 1 cup grape tomatoes, halved
- ½ cup finely chopped red onion

1. In a small bowl, whisk orange juice, vinegar, mustard and honey until blended. Stir in tarragon.

2. In a large skillet, heat 1 teaspoon oil over medium-high heat. Add corn; cook and stir 1-2 minutes or until crisp-tender. Remove from pan.

3. Sprinkle shrimp with lemon pepper and salt. In same skillet, heat remaining oil over medium-high heat. Add shrimp; cook and stir 3-4 minutes or until shrimp turn pink. Stir in corn.

4. In a large bowl, combine remaining ingredients. Drizzle with ⅓ cup dressing and toss to coat. Divide mixture among four plates. Top with shrimp mixture; drizzle with remaining dressing. Serve salad immediately.

FAST FIX ▶

TEQUILA-LIME FRUIT SALAD

Looking for a fast, colorful side to round out any meal? This refreshing fruit salad is pure perfection!
—**Angela Howland** Haynesville, ME

Start to Finish: 20 min.
Makes: 10 servings

- ¾ cup sugar
- ¼ cup water
- ¼ cup lime juice
- 3 tablespoons tequila or additional lime juice
- 2 cups cubed fresh pineapple
- 2 cups sliced fresh strawberries
- 2 cups chopped peeled kiwifruit
- 2 cups seedless red grapes, halved

1. In a small saucepan, bring sugar and water to a boil over medium heat. Remove from the heat; cool completely. Stir in lime juice and tequila.

2. In a large bowl, combine the fruit. Drizzle with syrup and toss gently to coat.

ORANGE SPICE CARROTS

In order to get my son to eat veggies, I mix and match flavors and spices that have kid appeal. My slow cooker carrots with orange and cinnamon have him hooked.

—**Christina Addison** Blanchester, OH

....

Prep: 10 min. • **Cook:** 4 hours
Makes: 6 servings

- 2 pounds medium carrots or baby carrots, cut into 1-inch pieces
- ½ cup packed brown sugar
- ½ cup orange juice
- 2 tablespoons butter
- ¾ teaspoon ground cinnamon
- ½ teaspoon salt
- ¼ teaspoon ground nutmeg
- 4 teaspoons cornstarch
- ¼ cup cold water

1. In a 3-qt. slow cooker, combine the first seven ingredients. Cook, covered, on low 4-5 hours or until carrots are tender.
2. In a small bowl, mix cornstarch and water until smooth; gradually stir into carrot mixture until sauce is thickened, 1-2 minutes.

TEST KITCHEN TIP
For extra zing, top this recipe with a sprinkling of orange zest.

THREE-BEAN BAKED BEANS

I got this recipe from an aunt and made a few changes to suit our tastes. With ground beef and bacon mixed in, these satisfying beans are a big hit at backyard barbecues and church picnics.

—**Julie Currington** Gahanna, OH

....

Prep: 20 min. • **Bake:** 1 hour
Makes: 12 servings (¾ cup each)

- ½ pound ground beef
- 5 bacon strips, diced
- ½ cup chopped onion
- ⅓ cup packed brown sugar
- ¼ cup sugar
- ¼ cup ketchup
- ¼ cup barbecue sauce
- 2 tablespoons molasses
- 2 tablespoons prepared mustard
- ½ teaspoon chili powder
- ½ teaspoon salt
- 2 cans (16 ounces each) pork and beans, undrained
- 1 can (16 ounces) butter beans, rinsed and drained
- 1 can (16 ounces) kidney beans, rinsed and drained

1. Preheat oven to 350°. In a large skillet, cook and crumble beef with bacon and onion over medium heat until no longer pink; drain.
2. Stir in sugars, ketchup, barbecue sauce, molasses, mustard, chili powder and salt until blended. Stir in beans. Transfer to a greased 2½-qt. baking dish. Bake, covered, until beans reach desired thickness, about 1 hour.

Freeze option: Freeze cooled bean mixture in freezer containers. To use, partially thaw in refrigerator overnight. Heat through in a saucepan, stirring occasionally and adding a little water if necessary.

OVERNIGHT LAYERED LETTUCE SALAD

This salad is a family favorite adapted from a church cookbook I've had for many years. The bacon adds a fabulous crunch.

—**Mary Brehm** Cape Coral, FL

Prep: 20 min. + chilling
Makes: 16 servings (1 cup each)

- 1 medium head iceberg lettuce, torn
- 1 medium green pepper, chopped
- 1 small sweet red pepper, chopped
- 1 medium onion, sliced and separated into rings
- 2 cups frozen peas (about 10 ounces)
- 1 cup mayonnaise
- 2 tablespoons sugar
- 1 cup shredded cheddar cheese
- 12 bacon strips, cooked and crumbled
- ¾ cup dried cranberries

1. In a 4-qt. or 13x9-in. glass dish, layer the first five ingredients. In a small bowl, mix mayonnaise and sugar; spoon over salad, spreading to cover.
2. Sprinkle the top with cheese, bacon and dried cranberries. Refrigerate salad, covered, overnight.

POTLUCK MACARONI & CHEESE

Here's a no-fuss way to make America's most popular comfort food. The dish turns out cheesy, rich and extra creamy.

—**Jennifer Babcock** Chicopee, MA

Prep: 25 min. • **Cook:** 2 hours
Makes: 16 servings (¾ cup each)

- 3 cups uncooked elbow macaroni
- 1 package (16 ounces) process cheese (Velveeta), cubed
- 2 cups shredded Mexican cheese blend
- 2 cups shredded white cheddar cheese
- 1¾ cups whole milk
- 1 can (12 ounces) evaporated milk
- ¾ cup butter, melted
- 3 large eggs, lightly beaten

1. Cook macaroni according to package directions for al dente; drain. Transfer to a greased 5-qt. slow cooker. Stir in the remaining ingredients.
2. Cook macaroni and cheese, covered, on low until a thermometer reads at least 160°, 2-2½ hours, stirring once.

FAST FIX

ALMOND VEGETABLE STIR-FRY

While broccoli florets and chunks of red pepper give this dish plenty of color, it's the fresh gingerroot, garlic, soy sauce and sesame oil that round out the flavor.

—**Mary Relyea** Canastota, NY

Start to Finish: 20 min.
Makes: 5 servings

- 1 teaspoon cornstarch
- 1 teaspoon sugar
- 3 tablespoons cold water
- 2 tablespoons reduced-sodium soy sauce
- 1 teaspoon sesame oil
- 4 cups fresh broccoli florets
- 2 tablespoons canola oil
- 1 large sweet red pepper, cut into 1-inch chunks
- 1 small onion, cut into thin wedges
- 2 garlic cloves, minced
- 1 tablespoon minced fresh gingerroot
- ¼ cup slivered almonds, toasted

1. In a small bowl, combine cornstarch and sugar. Stir in water, soy sauce and sesame oil until smooth; set aside.
2. In a large nonstick wok or skillet, stir-fry broccoli in hot oil 3 minutes. Add pepper, onion, garlic and ginger; stir-fry 2 minutes. Reduce heat. Stir soy sauce mixture; stir into vegetables with nuts. Cook and stir 2 minutes or until thickened.

PRETZEL-TOPPED SWEET POTATOES

I've shared this recipe with a lot of people, and everyone says it's the tastiest way to serve sweet potatoes. I like to make it for special dinners and even for brunch as a colorful accompaniment. The sweet, tart and salty flavors are a fabulous treat.
—**Sue Mallory** Lancaster, PA

....

Prep: 20 min. • **Bake:** 25 min.
Makes: 12 servings

- 2 cups chopped pretzel rods (about 13)
- 1 cup chopped pecans
- 1 cup fresh or frozen cranberries
- 1 cup packed brown sugar
- 1 cup butter, melted, divided
- 1 can (2½ pounds) sweet potatoes, drained
- 1 can (5 ounces) evaporated milk
- ½ cup sugar
- 1 teaspoon vanilla extract

1. In a large bowl, combine the pretzels, pecans, cranberries, brown sugar and ½ cup butter; set aside.
2. In a large bowl, beat the potatoes until smooth. Add the milk, sugar, vanilla and remaining butter; beat until well blended.
3. Spoon sweet potato mixture into a greased shallow 2-qt. baking dish; sprinkle with pretzel mixture. Bake, uncovered, at 350° for 25-30 minutes or until the edges are bubbly.

★ ★ ★ ★ ★ **READER REVIEW**

"This looks fabulous and tastes awesome. The cranberries add a sweet, tangy surprise and the pretzel rods, pecans and brown sugar all add to the taste and presentation."

MUFFIE_SUZ TASTEOFHOME.COM

FAST FIX ▶

GARDEN CHICKPEA SALAD

Looking for something different that won't heat up the kichen on a hot day? This refreshing salad makes a terrific cold side dish or even an entree.

—**Sally Sibthorpe** Shelby Township, MI

....

Start to Finish: 25 min.
Makes: 2 servings

- ½ teaspoon cumin seeds
- ¼ cup chopped tomato
- ¼ cup lemon juice
- ¼ cup olive oil
- 1 garlic clove, minced
- ¼ teaspoon salt
- ¼ teaspoon cayenne pepper

SALAD

- ¾ cup canned garbanzo beans or chickpeas, rinsed and drained
- 1 medium carrot, julienned
- 1 small zucchini, julienned
- 2 green onions, thinly sliced
- ½ cup coarsely chopped fresh parsley
- ¼ cup thinly sliced radishes
- ¼ cup crumbled feta cheese
- 3 tablespoons chopped walnuts
- 3 cups spring mix salad greens

1. For the dressing, in a dry small skillet, toast cumin seeds over medium heat until aromatic, stirring frequently. Transfer to a small bowl. Stir in tomato, lemon juice, oil, garlic, salt and cayenne pepper.
2. In a bowl, combine chickpeas, carrot, zucchini, green onions, parsley, radishes, cheese and walnuts. Stir in ⅓ cup dressing.
3. To serve, divide greens between two plates; top with chickpea mixture. Drizzle with remaining dressing.

ITALIAN MUSHROOMS

Only four ingredients create this rich and flavorful side dish that goes great with beef and mashed potatoes.
—**Kim Reichert** Fargo, ND

....

Prep: 10 min. • **Cook:** 4 hours
Makes: 6 servings

- 1 **pound medium fresh mushrooms**
- 1 **large onion, sliced**
- ½ **cup butter, melted**
- 1 **envelope Italian salad dressing mix**

In a 3-qt. slow cooker, layer mushrooms and onion slices. Combine butter and salad dressing mix; pour over vegetables. Cover and cook on low for 4-5 hours or until the vegetables are tender. Serve mushrooms with a slotted spoon.

SAUTEED APPLES

Here's a sweet dish my family loves. It's wonderful as a side, but you can also use it to top pancakes, French toast or a scoop of vanilla ice cream.
—**Shirley Heston** Pickerington, OH

....

Start to Finish: 30 min.
Makes: 6 servings

- ¼ **cup butter, cubed**
- 5 **medium Golden Delicious apples, peeled and thinly sliced**
- ¼ **cup water**
- ½ **cup sugar**
- ½ **teaspoon ground cinnamon**

In a large skillet, heat butter over medium-high heat; saute apples for 1 minute. Add water; bring to a boil. Stir in sugar and cinnamon. Reduce heat; simmer, covered, until apples are tender, 10-12 minutes, stirring occasionally.

COBB SALAD

Made on the fly by Hollywood restaurateur Bob Cobb in 1937, this salad has become a world-famous American dish. Here's a fresh take, with all the original appeal and an extra-special presentation.
—***Taste of Home*** Test Kitchen

....

Prep: 40 min.
Makes: 6 servings (1¼ cups dressing)

- ¼ **cup red wine vinegar**
- 2 **teaspoons salt**
- 1 **teaspoon lemon juice**
- 1 **small garlic clove, minced**
- ¾ **teaspoon coarsely ground pepper**
- ¾ **teaspoon Worcestershire sauce**
- ¼ **teaspoon sugar**
- ¼ **teaspoon ground mustard**
- ¾ **cup canola oil**
- ¼ **cup olive oil**

SALAD

- 6½ **cups torn romaine**
- 2½ **cups torn curly endive**
- 1 **bunch watercress (4 ounces), trimmed, divided**
- 2 **cooked chicken breasts, chopped**
- 2 **medium tomatoes, seeded and chopped**
- 1 **medium ripe avocado, peeled and chopped**
- 3 **hard-boiled large eggs, chopped**
- ½ **cup crumbled blue or Roquefort cheese**
- 6 **bacon strips, cooked and crumbled**
- 2 **tablespoons minced fresh chives**

1. In a blender, combine the first eight ingredients. While processing, gradually add the oils in a steady stream.
2. In a large bowl, combine the romaine, endive and half of the watercress; toss lightly. Transfer to a serving platter. Arrange the chicken, tomatoes, avocado, eggs, cheese and bacon over the greens; sprinkle with chives. Top with remaining watercress. Cover and chill until serving.
3. To serve, drizzle 1 cup dressing over salad. Serve with the remaining dressing if desired.

HEARTY MAIN DISHES

The centerpiece for any great meal is the main course. Whether you're reviving the Sunday dinner tradition or just in need of something easy and delish for a busy weeknight, these celebrated family favorites will earn a place in the keeper file.

JERK CHICKEN WITH TROPICAL COUSCOUS

Caribbean cuisine brightens up our usual weekday dinner rotation thanks to its bold colors and flavors. Done in less than 30 minutes, this sensational skillet is one of my go-to meals.
—**Jeanne Holt** Mendota Heights, MN

....

Start to Finish: 25 min.
Makes: 4 servings

- 1 can (15.25 ounces) mixed tropical fruit
- 1 pound boneless skinless chicken breasts, cut into 2½-in. strips
- 3 teaspoons Caribbean jerk seasoning
- 1 tablespoon olive oil
- ½ cup chopped sweet red pepper
- 1 tablespoon finely chopped seeded jalapeno pepper
- ⅓ cup thinly sliced green onions (green portion only)
- 1½ cups reduced-sodium chicken broth
- 3 tablespoons chopped fresh cilantro, divided
- 1 tablespoon lime juice
- ¼ teaspoon salt
- 1 cup uncooked whole-wheat couscous
  Lime wedges

1. Drain mixed fruit, reserving ¼ cup syrup. Chop fruit.

2. Toss chicken with jerk seasoning. In a large skillet, heat oil over medium-high heat; saute chicken until no longer pink, 4-5 minutes. Remove from pan, reserving the drippings.

3. In same pan, saute peppers and green onions in drippings 2 minutes. Add the broth, 1 tablespoon cilantro, lime juice, salt, reserved syrup and chopped fruit; bring to a boil. Stir in couscous; reduce heat to low. Place chicken on top; cook, covered, until the liquid is absorbed and chicken is heated through, 3-4 minutes. Sprinkle with remaining cilantro. Serve with lime wedges.

BAKED CHICKEN CHALUPAS

I wanted an easy alternative to deep-fried chalupas. I decided to bake them in the oven with the filling on top. They're both quick to fix and healthier!

—Magdalena Flores Abilene, TX

....

Prep: 20 min. • **Bake:** 15 min.
Makes: 6 servings

- 6   corn tortillas (6 inches)
- 2   teaspoons olive oil
- ¾   cup shredded part-skim mozzarella cheese
- 2   cups chopped cooked chicken breast
- 1   can (14½ ounces) diced tomatoes with mild green chilies, undrained
- 1   teaspoon garlic powder
- 1   teaspoon onion powder
- 1   teaspoon ground cumin
- ¼   teaspoon salt
- ¼   teaspoon pepper
- ½   cup finely shredded cabbage

1. Preheat oven to 350°. Place tortillas on an ungreased baking sheet. Brush each tortilla with oil; sprinkle with cheese.

2. Place the chicken, tomatoes and seasonings in a large skillet; cook and stir over medium heat 6-8 minutes or until most of the liquid is evaporated. Spoon over tortillas. Bake 15-18 minutes or until tortillas are crisp and cheese is melted. Top with cabbage.

MAPLE-SAGE BRINED TURKEY

When the leaves start turning color, we know it will soon be turkey time at our house. We use a homemade maple-sage brine to help brown the bird and make the meat incredibly juicy.
—**Kimberly Forni** Laconia, NH

Prep: 40 min. + brining
Bake: 2½ hours + standing
Makes: 20 servings

- 4 quarts water
- 1½ cups packed brown sugar
- 1 cup sea salt
- 1 cup maple syrup
- 1 cup cider vinegar
- 24 fresh sage leaves
- 6 bay leaves
- 2 tablespoons yellow prepared mustard
- 2 tablespoons coarsely ground pepper
- 1 teaspoon ground cloves
- 4 quarts ice water
- 2 turkey-size oven roasting bags
- 1 turkey (14 to 16 pounds)

TURKEY
- 2 tablespoons olive oil
- ½ teaspoon pepper
- ½ teaspoon salt, optional

1. In a large stockpot, combine first 10 ingredients; bring to a boil. Cook and stir until sugar and salt are dissolved. Remove from heat. Add 4 quarts ice water to cool the brine to room temperature.
2. Put one turkey-sized oven roasting bag inside the other; place in a large stockpot. Place turkey inside both bags; pour in the cooled brine. Seal the bags, pressing out as much air as possible. Refrigerate for 18-24 hours.
3. Preheat oven to 350°. Remove turkey from brine; rinse and pat dry. Discard brine. Place turkey on a rack in a shallow roasting pan, breast side up. Tuck wings under turkey; tie drumsticks together. Rub oil over outside of turkey; sprinkle with pepper and, if desired, salt.
4. Roast, uncovered, until a thermometer inserted in thickest part of thigh reads 170°-175°, 2½ to 3 hours. (Cover loosely with foil if turkey browns too quickly.)
5. Remove turkey from oven; tent with foil. Let stand 20 minutes before carving.

PORK CHOPS WITH SCALLOPED POTATOES

Mom always managed to put a hearty meal on the table for our family and our crew of farmhands. This all-in-one main dish reminds me of all the comforts of home.
—**Bernice Morris** Marshfield, MO

Prep: 25 min. • **Bake:** 1½ hours
Makes: 6 servings

- 3 tablespoons butter
- 3 tablespoons all-purpose flour
- 1½ teaspoons salt
- ¼ teaspoon pepper
- 1 can (14½ ounces) chicken broth
- 6 pork rib or loin chops (¾ inch thick)
- 2 tablespoons canola oil
  Additional salt and pepper, optional
- 6 cups thinly sliced peeled potatoes
- 1 medium onion, sliced
  Paprika and minced fresh parsley, optional

1. In a small saucepan, melt butter; stir in the flour, salt and pepper until smooth. Add broth. Bring to a boil; cook and stir for 1 minute or until thickened. Remove from heat and set aside. In a large skillet, brown pork chops on both sides in oil; sprinkle with additional salt and pepper if desired.
2. In a greased 13x9-in. baking dish, layer potatoes and onion. Pour broth mixture over layers. Place pork chops on top.
3. Cover and bake at 350° for 1 hour; uncover and bake 30 minutes longer or until meat and potatoes are tender. If desired, sprinkle with paprika and parsley.

TEST KITCHEN TIP

We recommend rib chops for this recipe because they have a slightly higher fat content than leaner loin chops. Even with longer cooking times, they tend to stay juicy and flavorful. Bonus: They're usually less expensive!

BUTTERNUT SQUASH & SAUSAGE STUFFED SHELLS

This comforting casserole is one of my standbys for dinner parties with friends. The sweet squash complements the spicy sausage, and the melted goat cheese makes it over-the-top creamy. Feel free to substitute manicotti or even rolled lasagna noodles for the shells. The stuffed shells and sauce can be prepared a day ahead and assembled just before baking.

—**Taylor Hale** Sonoma, CA

Prep: 55 min. • **Bake:** 30 min. + standing
Makes: 10 servings

- 5 cups peeled butternut squash, cut into 1-inch cubes
- 3 tablespoons extra virgin olive oil, divided
- 32 uncooked jumbo pasta shells
- ¾ pound bulk hot Italian sausage
- 2 cups finely chopped sweet onion, divided
- 1 package (5 ounces) baby kale salad blend, chopped
- 8 ounces crumbled goat cheese, divided
- 4 garlic cloves, minced
- 1 carton (26.46 ounces) chopped tomatoes, undrained
- 2 tablespoons fresh sage
- 1 tablespoon sugar
- ½ cup fat-free half-and-half

1. Preheat the oven to 400°. Using a foil-lined baking sheet, toss the squash with 1 tablespoon olive oil. Roast squash, stirring halfway through, until tender and starting to caramelize, about 40 minutes. Transfer to a large bowl; roughly mash. Reduce heat to 350°.

2. Cook pasta according to the package directions. Drain.

3. In a large nonstick skillet over medium-high heat, cook sausage and 1 cup onion, crumbling meat, until no longer pink. Add the baby kale; cook until the kale is tender, 3-5 minutes. Mix with the squash. Stir in 4 ounces goat cheese.

4. In same skillet, heat remaining olive oil. Add remaining onion; cook until softened, 3-5 minutes. Add garlic; cook, stirring, for 1 minute more. Add the tomatoes, sage and sugar; bring to a boil. Reduce the heat; simmer, stirring occasionally, until sauce is thickened, about 15 minutes. Cool about 5 minutes. Pulse in blender until combined. Add the half-and-half; pulse until smooth. Pour about half of the sauce into a greased 13x9-in. baking dish.

5. Stuff each of the shells with about 2 tablespoons squash mixture; arrange in the baking dish. Pour remaining tomato sauce over shells; top with the remaining goat cheese. Bake, covered, until sauce mixture begins to bubble, 20 minutes. Remove cover; bake another 10 minutes. Let stand 10 minutes before serving.

CLASSIC BEEF STEW

Here's a good old-fashioned stew with lots of veggies swimming in a rich beef gravy. It's perfect for a blustery winter day.
—**Alberta McKay** Bartlesville, OK

Prep: 15 min. • **Bake:** 2½ hours
Makes: 6-8 servings

- 2 pounds beef stew meat, cut into 1-inch cubes
- 1 to 2 tablespoons canola oil
- 1½ cups chopped onions
- 1 can (14½ ounces) diced tomatoes, undrained
- 1 can (10½ ounces) condensed beef broth, undiluted
- 3 tablespoons quick-cooking tapioca
- 1 garlic clove, minced
- 1 tablespoon dried parsley flakes
- 1 teaspoon salt
- ¼ teaspoon pepper
- 1 bay leaf
- 6 medium carrots, cut into 2-inch pieces
- 3 medium potatoes, peeled and cut into 2-inch pieces
- 1 cup sliced celery (1-inch lengths)

1. In a Dutch oven, brown beef in batches in oil; drain. Return all meat to the pan. Add onions, tomatoes, broth, tapioca, garlic, parsley, salt, pepper and bay leaf. Bring to a boil.

2. Cover the stew and bake at 350° for 1 hour. Stir in carrots, potatoes and celery. Bake, covered, 1 hour longer or until meat and vegetables are tender. Discard bay leaf.

GRILLED FAJITAS

Make tonight Mexican night! A special marinade gives the beef in these fajitas outstanding flavor. The recipe is a fun way to use up garden-fresh peppers and onions in the summer. But don't let that stop you from making it all year long.
—**Cheryl Smith** The Dalles, OR

Prep: 20 min. + marinating • **Grill:** 10 min.
Makes: 4 servings

- 1 beef flank steak (about 1 pound)
- 1 envelope onion soup mix
- ¼ cup canola oil
- ¼ cup lime juice
- ¼ cup water
- 2 garlic cloves, minced
- 1 teaspoon grated lime peel
- 1 teaspoon ground cumin
- ½ teaspoon dried oregano
- ¼ teaspoon pepper
- 1 medium onion, thinly sliced
  Green, sweet red and/or yellow peppers, julienned
- 1 tablespoon canola oil
- 8 flour tortillas (8 inches), warmed
  Sour cream and lime wedges, optional

1. In a large resealable plastic bag, combine the first nine ingredients; add steak. Seal bag; turn to coat. Cover and refrigerate 4 hours or overnight.

2. Drain and discard marinade. Grill steak over high heat until the meat reaches desired doneness (for medium-rare, a thermometer should read 145°; medium, 160°; well-done, 170°).

3. Meanwhile, in a small skillet, saute onion and peppers if desired in oil for 3-4 minutes or until crisp-tender. Slice meat into thin strips across the grain; place on tortillas. Top with vegetables; roll up. Serve with sour cream and lime wedges if desired.

FAST FIX

SKILLET SHEPHERD'S PIE

This is the best shepherd's pie I've ever tasted. It's quick to make on the stovetop and the recipe calls for pantry staples.
—**Tirzah Sandt** San Diego, CA

Start to Finish: 30 min.
Makes: 6 servings

- 1 pound ground beef
- 1 cup chopped onion
- 2 cups frozen corn, thawed
- 2 cups frozen peas, thawed
- 2 tablespoons ketchup
- 1 tablespoon Worcestershire sauce
- 2 teaspoons minced garlic
- 1 tablespoon cornstarch
- 1 teaspoon beef bouillon granules
- ½ cup cold water
- ½ cup sour cream
- 3½ cups mashed potatoes (prepared with milk and butter)
- ¾ cup shredded cheddar cheese

1. In a large skillet, cook beef and onion over medium heat until meat is no longer pink; drain. Stir in the corn, peas, ketchup, Worcestershire sauce and garlic. Reduce the heat to medium-low; cover and cook for 5 minutes.
2. Combine the cornstarch, bouillon and water until well blended; stir intothe beef mixture. Bring to a boil over medium heat; cook and stir 2 minutes or until thickened. Stir in the sour cream and heat through (do not boil).
3. Spread mashed potatoes over the top; sprinkle with cheese. Cover and cook until potatoes are heated through and cheese is melted.
Freeze option: Prepare beef mixture as directed but do not add sour cream. Freeze cooled meat mixture in a freezer container. To use, partially thaw pie in the refrigerator overnight. Heat through in a large skillet, stirring occasionally and adding a little water if necessary. Stir in sour cream and proceed as directed.

✳
TEST KITCHEN TIP
For a colorful and healthy take on this recipe, substitute mashed butternut squash or sweet potato in place of regular mashed potatoes. Ground lamb can also be used in place of ground beef.

FAST FIX

BEEF & BACON GNOCCHI SKILLET

This gnocchi dish tastes like bacon cheeseburgers. Go ahead and top it as you would a burger—with ketchup, mustard, pickles and all your favorite ingredients.
—**Ashley Lecker** Green Bay, WI

Start to Finish: 30 min.
Makes: 6 servings

- 1 package (16 ounces) potato gnocchi
- 1¼ pounds lean ground beef (90% lean)
- 1 medium onion, chopped
- 8 cooked bacon strips, crumbled and divided
- 1 cup water
- ½ cup heavy whipping cream
- 1 tablespoon ketchup
- ¼ teaspoon salt
- ¼ teaspoon pepper
- 1½ cups shredded cheddar cheese
- ½ cup chopped tomatoes
- 2 green onions, sliced

1. Preheat the broiler. Cook the gnocchi according to package directions; drain.
2. Meanwhile, in a large ovenproof skillet, cook beef and onion, crumbling beef over medium heat until no longer pink, about 4-6 minutes. Drain.
3. Stir in half of the bacon; add gnocchi, water, cream and ketchup. Bring to a boil. Cook, stirring, over medium heat until sauce has thickened, 3-4 minutes. Add seasonings. Sprinkle with cheese.
4. Broil 3-4 in. from heat until cheese has melted, 1-2 minutes. Top with tomatoes, green onions and remaining bacon.
Note: Look for potato gnocchi in the pasta or frozen foods section.

FAST FIX ▶

WHITE CHEDDAR MAC & CHEESE

My white mac and cheese is simple and has lots of flavor from the cheeses and ground chipotle chile. I prefer conchiglie pasta because its large openings allow more melted cheese to pool inside. Yum!
—**Colleen Delawder** Herndon, VA

Start to Finish: 25 min.
Makes: 8 servings

- 1 package (16 ounces) small pasta shells
- ½ cup butter, cubed
- ½ cup all-purpose flour
- ½ teaspoon onion powder
- ½ teaspoon ground chipotle pepper
- ½ teaspoon pepper
- ¼ teaspoon salt
- 4 cups 2% milk
- 2 cups shredded sharp white cheddar cheese
- 2 cups shredded manchego or additional white cheddar cheese (about 8 ounces)

1. In a 6-qt. stockpot, cook the pasta according to package directions. Drain; return to pot.
2. Meanwhile, in a large saucepan, melt butter over medium heat. Stir in flour and seasonings until smooth; gradually whisk in milk. Bring to a boil, stirring constantly; cook and stir until thickened, 6-8 minutes. Remove from heat; stir in cheeses until melted. Add to pasta; toss to coat.

RICE-STUFFED PEPPERS

My mother used to fix this dish when we had company. The cheese sauce sets these stuffed peppers apart.
—**Lisa Easley** Longview, TX

Prep: 40 min. • **Bake:** 1 hour
Makes: 8 servings

- 2 pounds ground beef
- 1 medium onion, chopped
- 1 small green pepper, chopped
- 2 garlic cloves, minced
- 1½ teaspoons salt
- ½ teaspoon pepper
- 3¾ cup water
- 1 can (14½ ounces) diced tomatoes, undrained
- 1 can (10 ounces) diced tomatoes and green chilies, undrained
- 1 can (15 ounces) tomato sauce
- 1 tablespoon ground cumin
- 4 medium green peppers

CHEESE SAUCE
- 1½ pounds process American cheese, cubed
- 1 can (10 ounces) diced tomatoes and green chilies, undrained

1. In a Dutch oven, cook beef, onion, chopped green pepper, garlic, salt and pepper over medium heat until the beef is no longer pink; drain. Add the water, tomatoes, tomato sauce and cumin. Bring to a boil. Reduce heat; simmer, uncovered, for 10 minutes.
2. Stir in rice; simmer, uncovered, for 5 minutes. Remove from the heat; cover and let stand for 5 minutes.
3. Remove tops and seeds from the peppers; cut in half widthwise. Place pepper halves in a large pan of boiling water; boil for 4 minutes.
4. Drain peppers and stuff with meat mixture. Place remaining meat mixture in an ungreased 13x9-in. baking dish; top with stuffed peppers, pressing down gently. Cover and bake at 350° for 1 hour. In a saucepan, heat sauce ingredients until cheese is melted. Serve over peppers.

BEST MEAT LOAF

My husband loves meat loaf. Everyone who's tried this one agrees that it lives up to its name.
—**Dorothy Pritchett** Wills Point, TX

Prep: 15 min. + chilling • **Bake:** 1½ hours
Makes: 8 servings

- ⅓ cup chopped onion
- ⅓ cup chopped sweet red pepper
- ⅓ cup chopped green pepper
- 3 tablespoons minced fresh parsley
- 3 garlic cloves, minced
- 1¼ teaspoons chili powder
- 1¼ teaspoons dried sage
- 1¼ teaspoons salt
- 1 teaspoon pepper
- 2 pounds ground beef
- ¾ cup whole milk
- 2 large eggs, beaten
- ¼ cup Worcestershire sauce
- ⅔ cup dry bread crumbs
- 4 bacon strips

SAUCE
- ¼ cup canned diced tomatoes
- ¼ cup ketchup
- 2 tablespoons brown sugar
- 1 teaspoon salt
- 1 teaspoon ground mustard
- ½ teaspoon pepper

1. In a large bowl, combine the first nine ingredients. Crumble beef over mixture; mix well. Combine the milk, eggs and Worcestershire sauce; mix into the beef mixture. Add crumbs.

2. Grease a large sheet of foil. Place bacon on foil. Mold meat mixture into a loaf and place over bacon. Seal foil tightly around loaf. Refrigerate for 2 hours or overnight.

3. Place wrapped loaf on a baking sheet. Bake at 350° for 1 hour. Open foil; drain juices. Combine sauce ingredients and spoon over loaf. Bake, uncovered, 30 minutes longer or until no pink remains and a thermometer reads 160°.

FAST FIX ▶
FAJITA-STYLE SHRIMP & GRITS

I combined two of my favorite dishes—shrimp with cheesy grits, and fajitas—into this spicy one-dish meal. For more heat, use pepper jack cheese instead of Mexican cheese blend.
—**Arlene Erlbach** Morton Grove, IL

Start to Finish: 30 min.
Makes: 4 servings

- 1 pound uncooked shrimp (16-20 per pound), peeled and deveined
- 2 tablespoons fajita seasoning mix
- 1 cup quick-cooking grits
- 4 cups boiling water
- 1½ cups shredded Mexican cheese blend
- 3 tablespoons 2% milk
- 2 tablespoons canola oil
- 3 medium sweet peppers, seeded and cut into 1-inch strips
- 1 medium sweet onion, cut into 1-inch strips
- 1 jar (15½ to 16 ounces) medium chunky salsa
- ¼ cup orange juice
- ¼ cup plus 1 tablespoon fresh cilantro leaves, divided

1. Sprinkle shrimp with fajita seasoning; toss to coat. Set aside.

2. Slowly stir grits into boiling water. Reduce heat to medium; cook, covered, stirring occasionally, until thickened, 5-7 minutes. Remove from heat. Stir in cheese until melted; stir in milk. Keep warm.

3. In a large skillet, heat oil over medium-high heat. Add peppers and onion; cook and stir until tender and pepper edges are slightly charred. Add salsa, orange juice and shrimp. Cook, stirring constantly, until shrimp turn pink, 4-6 minutes. Stir in ¼ cup cilantro. Remove from heat.

4. Spoon the grits into serving bowls; top with the shrimp mixture. Sprinkle with the remaining cilantro.

✳

TEST KITCHEN TIP

This recipe is a great for people who may not have tried grits before. The grits' creamy, soft texture balances the rest of the chunkier ingredients and lets them shine. Don't skip the orange juice—even though it's a small amount, it adds a lot of flavor. Be sure to watch the shrimp while they're cooking and remove them from the heat as soon as they're done. Shrimp can become tough and rubbery if overcooked.

CHEDDAR BEAN BURRITOS

My family goes meatless several nights a week, and these burritos are one of our favorites. My fast-fix trick is to puree a can or two of chipotles in adobo and freeze in ice cube trays so I can use a small amount whenever I need it.

—**Amy Bravo** Ames, IA

Start to Finish: 25 min.
Makes: 6 servings

- 2 teaspoons canola oil
- 1 tablespoon minced chipotle pepper in adobo sauce
- 2 garlic cloves, minced
- 2 teaspoons chili powder
- 1 teaspoon ground cumin
- ⅛ teaspoon salt
- 2 cans (15 ounces each) black beans, rinsed and drained
- 2 tablespoons water
- ½ cup pico de gallo
- 6 flour tortillas (8 inches), warmed
- 1 cup shredded cheddar or Monterey Jack cheese
- ½ cup sour cream
  Additional pico de gallo and sour cream, optional

1. In a large skillet, heat oil over medium heat; saute chipotle pepper, garlic and seasonings 2 minutes. Stir in beans and water; bring to a boil. Reduce the heat; simmer, uncovered, until the flavors are blended, 5-7 minutes, stirring occasionally.

2. Coarsely mash bean mixture; stir in the pico de gallo. Spoon onto the tortillas; top with cheese and sour cream and roll up. If desired, serve with additional pico de gallo and sour cream.

Freeze option: Let the filling cool before making burritos. Individually wrap burritos in paper towels and foil; freeze in resealable plastic freezer bag. To use, remove the foil; place a paper towel-wrapped burrito on a microwave-safe plate. Microwave on high until heated through, 4-6 minutes, turning once. Let stand 2 minutes.

BAVARIAN POT ROAST

All of my grandparents were German, so it's no wonder so many Bavarian recipes have been handed down to me. But no matter your heritage, you're going to love this pot roast.

—Susan Robertson Hamilton, OH

Prep: 15 min. • **Cook:** 2¾ hours
Makes: 10 servings

- 1 boneless beef chuck pot roast (about 3 pounds)
- 2 tablespoons canola oil
- 1¼ cups water
- ¾ cup beer or beef broth
- 1 can (8 ounces) tomato sauce
- ½ cup chopped onion
- 2 tablespoons sugar
- 1 tablespoon vinegar
- 2 teaspoons salt
- 1 teaspoon ground cinnamon
- 1 bay leaf
- ½ teaspoon pepper
- ½ teaspoon ground ginger
  Cornstarch and water, optional

1. In a Dutch oven, brown roast in hot oil. Combine the water, beer, tomato sauce, onion, sugar, vinegar, salt, cinnamon, bay leaf, pepper and ginger. Pour over meat and bring to a boil. Reduce the heat; cover and simmer until the meat is tender, about 2½-3 hours.

2. Remove the meat. Discard bay leaf. If desired, thicken the juices with cornstarch and water.

Freeze option: Place sliced pot roast in freezer containers; top with cooking juices. Cool and freeze. To use, partially thaw in the refrigerator overnight. Microwave, covered, on high in a microwave-safe dish until heated through, gently stirring and adding a little broth to pot roast if needed.

FAST FIX
EASY SALISBURY STEAK

Looking for a quick comfort food? This can be made in 25 minutes or made ahead and reheated with the gravy in the microwave. I often double the recipe and freeze one batch of cooked steaks and gravy for an even faster meal on a hectic night.

—Carol Callahan Rome, GA

Start to Finish: 25 min.
Makes: 4 servings

- ⅓ cup chopped onion
- ¼ cup crushed saltines
- 1 large egg white, lightly beaten
- 2 tablespoons 2% milk
- 1 tablespoon prepared horseradish
- ¼ teaspoon salt, optional
- ⅛ teaspoon pepper
- 1 pound lean ground beef (90% lean)
- 1 jar (12 ounces) beef gravy
- 1¼ to 1½ cups sliced fresh mushrooms
- 2 tablespoons water
  Hot cooked noodles, optional

1. In a large bowl, combine the onion, saltines, egg white, milk, horseradish, salt if desired, and pepper. Crumble beef over mixture. Shape into four oval patties.

2. In a large skillet over medium heat, cook patties for 5-6 minutes on each side or until no pink remains and thermometer reads 160°.

3. Remove patties and keep warm. Add the gravy, mushrooms and water to skillet; cook for 3-5 minutes or until they are heated through. Serve with patties and noodles if desired.

★ ★ ★ ★ ★ **READER REVIEW**

"Delicious! I make extra and freeze for those busy nights during the holidays when there's not enough time in the day to get everything done. My family loves it."

RRHARDING TASTEOFHOME.COM

CHICKEN VERDE QUESADILLAS

I tossed together ingredients I had in my fridge—corn, peppers and zucchini—to create these quick quesadillas. Dollop with sour cream and you're good to go!
—**Julie Merriman** Seattle, WA

Start to Finish: 30 min.
Makes: 4 servings

- 2 tablespoons olive oil, divided
- 1 large sweet onion, halved and thinly sliced
- 1½ cups (about 7½ ounces) frozen corn
- 1 small zucchini, chopped
- 1 poblano pepper, thinly sliced
- 2 cups frozen grilled chicken breast strips, thawed and chopped
- ¾ cup green enchilada sauce
- ¼ cup minced fresh cilantro
- ¼ teaspoon salt
- ⅛ teaspoon pepper
- 8 flour tortillas (10 inches)
- 4 cups shredded Monterey Jack cheese
  Pico de gallo, optional
  Sour cream, optional

1. Preheat oven to 400°. In a large skillet, heat 1 tablespoon oil over medium-high heat. Add the onion, corn, zucchini and poblano pepper; cook and stir for 8-10 minutes or until tender. Add the chicken, enchilada sauce, cilantro, salt and pepper; heat through.

2. Brush remaining oil over one side of each tortilla. Place half of the tortillas on two baking sheets, with oiled side down. Sprinkle each with ½ cup cheese and top with 1 cup chicken mixture, remaining cheese and remaining tortillas, oiled side up. Bake until golden brown and cheese is melted, 7-9 minutes. If desired, serve with pico de gallo and sour cream.

DID YOU KNOW?

With its slightly sharp flavor, cilantro—also known as Chinese parsley—gives a distinctive taste to Mexican, Latin American and Asian dishes. Like other fresh herbs, it should be used as soon as possible. For short-term storage, immerse the freshly cut stems in water about 2 inches deep. Cover leaves loosely with a plastic bag and refrigerate for several days. Wash just before using.

GARLIC & HERB STEAK PIZZA

We crave pizza that is super fast, cheesy and original. This one featuring steak and veggies is for folks who like their pie with everything on top.
—**Jade Fears** Grand Ridge, FL

Start to Finish: 30 min.
Makes: 6 servings

- 1 beef top sirloin steak (¾ inch thick and 1 pound)
- ¾ teaspoon salt
- ¾ teaspoon pepper
- 1 tablespoon olive oil
- 1 prebaked 12-inch thin pizza crust
- ½ cup garlic-herb spreadable cheese (about 3 ounces)
- 2 cups chopped fresh spinach
- 1 cup sliced red onion
- 1 cup sliced fresh mushrooms
- 1½ cups shredded part-skim mozzarella cheese

1. Preheat oven to 450°. Season the steak with salt and pepper. In a large skillet, heat oil over medium heat. Add steak; cook 5-6 minutes on each side or until thermometer reads 145° for medium-rare doneness. Remove from pan.

2. Meanwhile, place the pizza crust on an ungreased baking sheet; spread it with garlic-herb cheese. Top with the spinach and onion.

3. Cut steak into slices; arrange on pizza. Top with mushrooms and cheese. Bake 8-10 minutes or until cheese is melted. Cut into 12 pieces.

FAST FIX ▶

GINGER HALIBUT WITH BRUSSELS SPROUTS

I moved to the United States from Russia and love cooking Russian food for family and friends. Halibut with soy sauce, ginger and pepper is a favorite.
—**Margarita Parker** New Bern, NC

Start to Finish: 25 min.
Makes: 4 servings

- 4 teaspoons lemon juice
- 4 halibut fillets (4 to 6 ounces each)
- 1 teaspoon minced fresh gingerroot
- ¼ to ¾ teaspoon salt, divided
- ¼ teaspoon pepper
- ½ cup water
- 10 ounces (about 2½ cups) fresh Brussels sprouts, halved
  Crushed red pepper flakes
- 1 tablespoon canola oil
- 5 garlic cloves, sliced lengthwise
- 2 tablespoons sesame oil
- 2 tablespoons soy sauce
  Lemon slices, optional

1. Brush lemon juice over halibut fillets. Sprinkle with minced ginger, ¼ teaspoon salt and pepper.

2. Place fish on an oiled grill rack, skin side down. Grill, covered, over medium heat (or broil 6 in. from heat) until the fish just begins to flake easily with a fork, 6-8 minutes.

3. In a large skillet, bring water to a boil over medium-high heat. Add the Brussels sprouts, pepper flakes and, if desired, the remaining salt. Cook, covered, until tender, 5-7 minutes. Meanwhile, in a small skillet, heat the oil over medium heat. Add the garlic; cook until golden brown. Drain on paper towels.

4. Drizzle the sesame oil and soy sauce over halibut. Serve with Brussels sprouts; sprinkle with fried garlic. If desired, serve with lemon slices.

FAST FIX ▶

TURKEY CURRY

I'm always looking for new and interesting ways to use leftover turkey—especially around the holidays. This is a zesty entree you can make as spicy as you like by varying the amount of curry powder.
—**Martha Balser** Cincinnati, OH

Start to Finish: 20 min.
Makes: 4 servings

- 1 cup sliced celery
- ½ cup sliced carrots
- 1 cup fat-free milk, divided
- 2 tablespoons cornstarch
- ¾ cup reduced-sodium chicken broth
- 2 cups diced cooked turkey or chicken
- 2 tablespoons dried minced onion
- ½ teaspoon garlic powder
- 1 to 4 teaspoons curry powder
  Hot cooked rice, optional

1. Lightly coat a skillet with cooking spray; saute celery and carrots until tender. In a bowl, mix ¼ cup milk and cornstarch until smooth. Add broth and remaining milk; mix until smooth.

2. Pour over the vegetables. Bring to a boil; cook and stir for 2 minutes or until thickened. Add the turkey, onion, garlic powder and curry powder; heat through, stirring occasionally. Serve the dish with rice if desired.

OVEN-FRIED FISH & CHIPS

My baked dish is a winner when you want classic fish and chips without the mess of frying. Find more of my recipes on my blog, cinnamonspiceandeverythingnice.com.
—**Reeni Pisano** Wappingers Falls, NY

Prep: 15 min. • **Bake:** 55 min.
Makes: 4 servings

- ⅓ cup mayonnaise
- 2 tablespoons dill pickle relish or chopped dill pickle
- 2 teaspoons grated lemon zest

FISH AND POTATOES

- 1½ pounds baking potatoes (about 3 medium)
- 2 teaspoons olive oil
- ¾ teaspoon kosher salt, divided
- ½ teaspoon coarsely ground pepper, divided
- ½ cup panko (Japanese) bread crumbs
- ¼ cup seasoned bread crumbs
- 4 cod fillets (4 ounces each)
- 2 tablespoons mayonnaise
- 2 tablespoons grated Parmesan cheese
- 2 teaspoons chopped fresh parsley
  Malt vinegar, optional

1. For tartar sauce, in a small bowl, mix the mayonnaise, relish and lemon zest. Refrigerate until serving.

2. Preheat oven to 400°. Cut potatoes lengthwise into 1-in.-thick wedges; toss with oil, ½ teaspoon salt and ¼ teaspoon pepper. Spread evenly inside a greased 15x10x1-in. baking pan. Roast for 40-45 minutes or until the potatoes are golden brown, stirring occasionally.

3. Meanwhile, in a small skillet, toast panko bread crumbs over medium-low heat 5-7 minutes or until lightly browned, stirring occasionally. Transfer to a shallow bowl; stir in seasoned bread crumbs.

4. Sprinkle cod with the remaining salt and pepper; spread top and sides of fish with mayonnaise. Dip in the crumb mixture to cover mayonnaise, pressing firmly to help it adhere. Place in a greased 15x10x1-in. baking pan, crumb side up. Sprinkle with any remaining crumb mixture. Bake 12-15 minutes or until fish just begins to flake easily with a fork.

5. Toss potatoes with cheese and parsley. Serve fish and potatoes with tartar sauce and, if desired, vinegar.

MEXICAN TURKEY ROLL-UPS

I whip up these fun and tasty roll-ups when we're craving Mexican food. They're a great way to use up leftover turkey or chicken.

—Marlene Muckenhirn Delano, MN

Prep: 10 min. • **Bake:** 30 min.
Makes: 5 servings

- 2½ cups cubed cooked turkey
- 1½ cups (12 ounces) sour cream, divided
- 3 teaspoons taco seasoning, divided
- 1 can (10¾ ounces) condensed cream of mushroom soup, undiluted, divided
- 1½ cups shredded cheddar cheese, divided
- 1 small onion, chopped
- ½ cup salsa
- ¼ cup sliced ripe olives
- 10 flour tortillas (6 inches)
  Shredded lettuce
  Chopped tomatoes
  Additional salsa and sliced ripe olives, optional

In a bowl, combine turkey, ½ cup sour cream, 1½ teaspoons taco seasoning, half of the soup, 1 cup cheese, onion, salsa and olives. Place ⅓ cup filling on each tortilla. Roll up and place, seam side down, in a greased 13x9-in. baking dish. Combine remaining sour cream, taco seasoning and soup; pour over tortillas. Cover and bake at 350° for 30 minutes or until heated through. Sprinkle with remaining cheese. Serve with shredded lettuce and chopped tomatoes. Top with additional salsa and sliced ripe olives if desired.

GRILLED HAM BURGERS

My family loves my ham loaf, so I decided to make the ham loaf mixture into patties and grill them—it was an instant hit. Adding the arugula gives these burgers a peppery bite, and honey mustard dressing adds just the right sweet and sour flavor.

—Susan Bickta Kutztown, PA

Prep: 20 min. + chilling • **Grill:** 10 min.
Makes: 8 servings

- 1½ pounds fully cooked boneless ham
- ¾ pound ground pork
- 2 large eggs
- ⅔ cup graham cracker crumbs
- ⅓ cup packed brown sugar
- ⅓ cup unsweetened crushed pineapple plus 3 tablespoons juice
- 1 tablespoon spicy brown mustard
- ¼ teaspoon ground cloves
- 8 slices Swiss cheese (1 ounce each)
- 8 kaiser rolls, split
- 2 large tomatoes, cut in sixteen ¼-inch slices
- ½ cup honey mustard salad dressing
- 1½ cups fresh baby arugula, packed
  Additional honey mustard salad dressing, optional

1. Pulse ham in food processor until finely ground. Combine with pork, eggs, cracker crumbs, brown sugar, pineapple and juice, mustard and cloves. Mix it lightly but thoroughly. Shape into eight patties. Using fingertips, make a shallow indentation in center of each patty so it remains flat while grilling. Refrigerate 1 hour.

2. Grill burgers, covered, on a greased rack over medium-high direct heat for 5-6 minutes; turn and grill for another 3-4 minutes. Add a slice of cheese to each burger; grill, covered, until cheese melts, 1-2 minutes more. Remove from heat when a thermometer reads 160°.

3. Place a burger on bottom half of each roll; add two tomato slices. Drizzle with 1 tablespoon of honey mustard dressing. Divide the arugula evenly among rolls; top each burger with a few sprigs. Replace the top half of the roll. If desired, serve with additional dressing.

✳
TEST KITCHEN TIP
Make a double batch of burgers and freeze what you don't eat. Reheat a minute or two in the microwave, and they will taste just like they came hot off the grill.

SWEET HORSERADISH GLAZED RIBS

Go beyond hot dogs for your next camping trip. Roast and wrap these ribs at home before you leave, then finish them with a sweet, savory sauce over the campfire.
—**Ralph Jones** San Diego, CA

Prep: 10 min. + chilling • **Cook:** 2 ¼ hours
Makes: 8 servings

- 3 racks pork baby back ribs (about 8 pounds)
- 1½ teaspoons salt, divided
- 1½ teaspoons coarsely ground pepper, divided
- 2 bottles (12 ounces each) beer or 3 cups unsweetened apple juice
- 1 jar (12 ounces) apricot preserves
- ¼ cup prepared horseradish, drained
- 2 tablespoons honey or maple syrup
- 1 teaspoon liquid smoke, optional

1. Preheat oven to 325°. If necessary, remove thin membrane from ribs and discard. Sprinkle 1 teaspoon each salt and pepper over ribs. Transfer to a large shallow roasting pan, bone side down; add beer or juice. Bake, covered, until tender, 2-3 hours.

2. Meanwhile, puree the preserves, horseradish, honey, remaining salt and pepper and, if desired, liquid smoke in a blender.

3. Drain ribs. Place 1 rib rack on a large piece of aluminum foil. Brush with the apricot-horseradish mixture; wrap tightly. Repeat with remaining ribs. Refrigerate up to 2 days.

4. Prepare campfire or grill for medium heat. Remove the ribs from foil; grill until they are browned, 10-15 minutes, turning them occasionally.

★ ★ ★ ★ ★ **READER REVIEW**

"Really good. Making ahead is a great way to have ribs when camping. Did save some glaze aside and basted with it over the campfire. Yum!"

MZGRINDER TASTEOFHOME.COM

CHILI SKILLET

We're a family of farmers, so down-home cooking goes over big in our house. Chili in particular is a family favorite. With all the vegetables, cheese and ground beef in this recipe, this quick dish is a hearty meal-in-one. I serve it frequently in fall and winter.
—**Katherine Brown** Fredericktown, OH

Prep: 10 min. • **Cook:** 35 min.
Makes: 4 servings

- 1 pound ground beef
- 1 cup chopped onion
- ½ cup chopped green pepper
- 1 garlic clove, minced
- 1 can (16 ounces) kidney beans, rinsed and drained
- 1 cup tomato juice
- ½ cup water
- 4 teaspoons chili powder
- 1 teaspoon dried oregano
- 1 teaspoon salt
- ½ cup uncooked long grain rice
- 1 cup canned or frozen corn
- ½ cup sliced ripe olives
- 1 cup shredded cheddar or Monterey Jack cheese
  Thinly sliced green onions, optional

1. In a large skillet over medium heat, cook beef, onion, pepper and garlic until meat is no longer pink; drain. Add the next seven ingredients; simmer, covered, until rice is tender, about 25 minutes.

2. Stir in corn and olives; cover and cook 5 minutes more. Sprinkle with the cheese; cook, covered, until the cheese is melted, about 5 minutes. If desired, top the chili with green onions.

SWEET-AND-SOUR PORK

I used to visit my sister at her university on weekends. She often made this wonderful and tangy pork dish. Now, every time I make it for my family, it reminds me of those special visits. Everyone who tries it loves it.

—Cherry Williams St. Albert, AB

Start to Finish: 25 min.
Makes: 4 servings

- 1 can (14 ounces) pineapple tidbits
- 2 tablespoons cornstarch
- 2 tablespoons brown sugar
- ¾ teaspoon salt
- ¼ teaspoon ground ginger
- ¼ teaspoon pepper
- ⅓ cup water
- ⅓ cup ketchup
- 2 tablespoons white vinegar
- 2 tablespoons reduced-sodium soy sauce
- 1 pound pork tenderloin, cut into 1½-inch x ¼-inch strips
- 1 medium onion, chopped
- 2 tablespoons canola oil
- 1 green pepper, cut into thin strips
  Hot cooked rice

1. Drain the pineapple, reserving juice; set aside. In a small bowl, combine the cornstarch, brown sugar, salt, ginger and pepper. Stir in the water, ketchup, vinegar, soy sauce and reserved juice until smooth.
2. In a large skillet or wok, stir-fry pork and onion in oil for 4-8 minutes or until tender. Stir pineapple juice mixture; add to the skillet. Bring to a boil; cook and stir for 1-2 minutes or until thickened.
3. Add the green pepper and reserved pineapple. Reduce heat; cover and cook for 5 minutes. Serve with rice.

CHICKEN CURRY LASAGNA

My family digs Indian food, and I thought the creamy tomato-based sauce in our favorite curry would be very tasty as part of a lasagna. I was right! We can't get enough of this comforting twist on the classic.

—Elisabeth Larsen Pleasant Grove, UT

Prep: 30 min. • **Bake:** 40 min. + standing
Makes: 12

- 1 tablespoon canola oil
- 1 medium onion, chopped
- 4 teaspoons curry powder
- 3 garlic cloves, minced
- 1 can (6 ounces) tomato paste
- 2 cans (13.66 ounces each) coconut milk
- 1 pound (about 4 cups) shredded rotisserie chicken, skin removed
- 12 lasagna noodles, uncooked
- 2 cups part-skim ricotta cheese
- 2 large eggs
- ½ cup chopped fresh cilantro, divided
- 1 package (10 ounces) frozen chopped spinach, thawed and squeezed dry
- ½ teaspoon salt
- ¼ teaspoon pepper
- 2 cups shredded part-skim mozzarella cheese
  Lime wedges

1. Preheat oven to 350°. In a large skillet, heat oil over medium-high heat. Add the onion; cook and stir until softened, about 5 minutes. Add curry powder and garlic; cook 1 minute more. Stir in tomato paste; pour coconut milk into skillet. Bring to a boil. Reduce heat and simmer 5 minutes. Stir in cooked chicken.
2. Meanwhile, cook lasagna noodles according to package directions. Drain. Combine ricotta, eggs, ¼ cup cilantro, spinach and seasonings.
3. Spread one-fourth of chicken mixture into a 13x9-in. baking dish coated with cooking spray. Layer with four noodles, half of ricotta mixture, one-fourth of chicken mixture and ½ cup mozzarella. Repeat layers. Top with the remaining noodles, remaining chicken mixture and remaining mozzarella.
4. Bake, uncovered, until bubbly, 40-45 minutes. Cool 10 minutes before cutting. Top with remaining cilantro; serve with lime wedges.

BEST SPAGHETTI & MEATBALLS

We had unexpected company one evening. Since I had some of these meatballs left over in the freezer, I warmed them up as appetizers. Everyone raved! This classic recipe makes a big batch and is perfect for entertaining.

—**Mary Lou Koskella** Prescott, AZ

Prep: 30 min. • **Cook:** 2 hours
Makes: 16 servings

- 2 tablespoons olive oil
- 1½ cups chopped onions
- 3 garlic cloves, minced
- 2 cans (12 ounces each) tomato paste
- 3 cups water
- 1 can (29 ounces) tomato sauce
- ⅓ cup minced fresh parsley
- 1 tablespoon dried basil
- 2 teaspoons salt
- ½ teaspoon pepper

MEATBALLS

- 4 large eggs, lightly beaten
- 2 cups soft bread cubes (cut into ¼-inch pieces)
- 1½ cups whole milk
- 1 cup grated Parmesan cheese
- 3 garlic cloves, minced
- 2 teaspoons salt
- ½ teaspoon pepper
- 3 pounds ground beef
- 2 tablespoons canola oil
- 2 pounds spaghetti, cooked

1. In a Dutch oven, heat the olive oil over medium heat. Add the onions; saute until softened. Add the garlic; cook 1 minute longer. Stir in the tomato paste; cook 3-5 minutes. Add next six ingredients. Bring to a boil. Reduce the heat; simmer, covered, for 50 minutes.

2. Combine the first seven meatball ingredients. Add beef; mix lightly but thoroughly. Shape into 1½-in. balls.

3. In a large skillet, heat canola oil over medium heat. Add meatballs; brown in batches until no longer pink. Drain. Add to sauce; bring to a boil. Reduce the heat; simmer, covered, until flavors are blended, about 1 hour, stirring occasionally. Serve with hot cooked spaghetti.

TEST KITCHEN TIP
Instead of frying the meatballs, you can bake them at 400° on a rack placed over a rimmed baking sheet. Bake about 20 minutes or until golden brown.

OLD-FASHIONED CABBAGE ROLLS

It was an abundance of dill in my garden that led me to try this. My family liked the taste so much that from then on, the dill became a permanent addition to my cabbage rolls.

—**Florence Krantz** Bismarck, ND

Prep: 25 min. • **Bake:** 1½ hours
Makes: 6 servings

- 1 medium head cabbage (3 pounds)
- ½ pound uncooked ground beef
- ½ pound uncooked ground pork
- 1 can (15 ounces) tomato sauce, divided
- 1 small onion, chopped
- ½ cup uncooked long grain rice
- 1 tablespoon dried parsley flakes
- ½ teaspoon salt
- ½ teaspoon snipped fresh dill or dill weed
- ⅛ teaspoon cayenne pepper
- 1 can (14½ ounces) diced tomatoes, undrained
- ½ teaspoon sugar

1. Cook cabbage in boiling water just until the outer leaves pull away easily from the head. Set aside 12 large leaves for the rolls. In a small bowl, combine the beef, pork, ½ cup tomato sauce, onion, rice, parsley, salt, dill and cayenne; mix well.

2. Cut out the thick vein from the bottom of each leaf, making a V-shaped cut. Place about ¼ cup of meat mixture on a cabbage leaf; overlap the cut ends of leaf. Fold in the sides. Beginning from the cut end, roll up. Repeat.

3. Slice the remaining cabbage; place in an ovenproof Dutch oven. Arrange the cabbage rolls seam side down over sliced cabbage. Combine the tomatoes, sugar and remaining tomato sauce; pour over the rolls. Cover and bake at 350° for 1½ hours or until cabbage rolls are tender.

CASSEROLE ENTREES

Some of the best memories are made while gathered around the table with loved ones, waiting in sweet anticipation for that family favorite casserole. Versatile, easy to clean up after and warm-you-up hearty, it's no wonder these one-pan meals remain dinnertime staples.

CHICKEN PENNE CASSEROLE

I make this family favorite casserole every week or two and we never tire of it. I like that I can put it together and then relax while it bakes.
—**Carmen Vanosch** Vernon, BC

Prep: 35 min. • **Bake:** 45 min.
Makes: 4 servings

1½ cups uncooked penne pasta
 1 tablespoon canola oil
 1 pound boneless skinless chicken thighs, cut into 1-inch pieces
 ½ cup chopped onion
 ½ cup chopped green pepper
 ½ cup chopped sweet red pepper
 1 teaspoon dried basil
 1 teaspoon dried oregano
 1 teaspoon dried parsley flakes
 ½ teaspoon salt
 ½ teaspoon crushed red pepper flakes
 3 garlic cloves, minced
 1 can (14½ ounces) diced tomatoes, undrained
 3 tablespoons tomato paste
 ¾ cup chicken broth
 2 cups shredded part-skim mozzarella cheese
 ½ cup grated Romano cheese

1. Preheat the oven to 350°. Cook pasta according to package directions. Meanwhile, in a large saucepan, heat oil over medium heat. Add chicken, onion, peppers and seasonings; saute until chicken is no longer pink. Add garlic; cook 1 minute longer.
2. In a blender, pulse tomatoes and tomato paste, covered, until blended. Add to chicken mixture. Stir in broth; bring to a boil over medium-high heat. Reduce heat; cover and simmer until slightly thickened, 10-15 minutes.
3. Drain pasta; toss with chicken mixture. Spoon half of the mixture into a greased 2-qt. baking dish. Sprinkle with half of the cheeses. Repeat layers.
4. Cover and bake 30 minutes. Uncover; bake until casserole is heated through, 15-20 minutes longer.

CHEDDAR CHICKEN POTPIE

I love cheese soup, but it's too rich for my husband's tastes. I slightly tweaked the ingredients and came up with a cheesy variation of potpie we both enjoy. If I'm in a hurry and don't have the time this takes to bake, I'll leave off the crust, add extra milk and serve it as a chowder.
—**Sandra Cothran** Ridgeland, SC

Prep: 30 min. • **Bake:** 40 min.
Makes: 6 servings

CRUST
- 1   cup all-purpose flour
- ½   teaspoon salt
- 5   tablespoons cold butter, cubed
- 3   tablespoons cold water

FILLING
- 1½ cups chicken broth
- 2   cups peeled cubed potatoes
- 1   cup sliced carrots
- ½   cup sliced celery
- ½   cup chopped onion
- ¼   cup all-purpose flour
- 1½ cups whole milk
- 2   cups shredded sharp cheddar cheese
- 4   cups cubed cooked chicken
- ¼   teaspoon poultry seasoning
     Salt and pepper to taste

1. For crust, in a small bowl, combine the flour and salt. Cut the butter into the flour until the mixture resembles coarse crumbs. Gradually add the water, mixing gently with a fork. Gather into a ball. Cover with plastic wrap and chill at least 30 minutes.

2. For filling, place the chicken broth in a Dutch oven; bring to a boil over high heat. Add vegetables. Reduce heat; simmer for 10-15 minutes or until the vegetables are tender.

3. In a small bowl, combine flour and milk; stir into broth mixture. Cook and stir over medium heat until slightly thickened and bubbly. Stir in cheese, chicken, poultry seasoning, salt and pepper. Heat until the cheese melts. Spoon mixture into a 10-in. (2½ to 3-qt.) casserole. Set aside.

4. On a lightly floured surface, roll crust to fit top of casserole, trimming edges as necessary. Place on casserole over filling; seal edges. Make several slits in center of crust for steam to escape.

5. Bake at 425° for 40 minutes or until golden brown.

HAM & SWISS POTATO CASSEROLE

One night I wanted to use up ingredients I had on hand, so I started experimenting—and hit a home run! The classic trio of potatoes, ham and Swiss comes together in this comforting bake, which is now one of my go-to recipes to feed a crowd.
—**Sarah Wilham** Elkhart, IL

Prep: 25 min. • **Bake:** 20 min.
Makes: 8 servings

- 5   large potatoes (about 4 pounds), peeled and cut into ¾-inch pieces
- ¼   cup butter, cubed
- 1   medium onion, chopped
- 1   garlic clove, minced
- ⅓   cup all-purpose flour
- 2   cups 2% milk
- 1⅓ cups roasted red pepper Alfredo sauce
- 1   teaspoon dried basil
- ¼   teaspoon salt
- ¼   teaspoon dill weed
- ¼   teaspoon pepper
- 2   cups cubed fully cooked ham
- 2   cups shredded Swiss cheese
- ¼   cup seasoned bread crumbs
- 1   tablespoon butter, melted

1. Preheat oven to 375°. Place potatoes in a large saucepan; add water to cover. Bring to a boil. Reduce heat; simmer, covered, 8-10 minutes or until crisp-tender. Meanwhile, in a large skillet, heat butter over medium-high heat. Add onion; cook and stir 6-8 minutes or until tender. Add garlic; cook and stir 1 minute. Stir in flour until blended; gradually whisk in milk. Bring to a boil, stirring constantly; cook and stir 1-2 minutes or until thickened. Stir in Alfredo sauce and seasonings; heat through.

2. Drain potatoes; transfer to a greased 13x9-in. baking dish. Layer potatoes with ham, cheese and sauce. In a small bowl, combine the bread crumbs and butter. Sprinkle over the top. Bake, uncovered, 18-22 minutes or until topping is golden brown and cheese is melted. Let stand 5 minutes before serving.

To make ahead: This can be made a day in advance. Prepare recipe as directed, layering ham, cheese and sauce in baking dish. Cover and refrigerate overnight. Remove from the refrigerator 30 minutes before baking. Prepare crumb topping; sprinkle over top. Bake as directed.

FIRECRACKER CASSEROLE

My husband and I love this Southwestern-style casserole. The flavor reminds us of enchiladas, but this handy recipe doesn't require the extra time to roll them up.

—Teressa Eastman El Dorado, KS

Prep: 15 min. • **Bake:** 25 min.
Makes: 8 servings

- 2 **pounds ground beef**
- 1 **medium onion, chopped**
- 1 **can (15 ounces) black beans, rinsed and drained**
- 1 **to 2 tablespoons chili powder**
- 2 **to 3 teaspoons ground cumin**
- ½ **teaspoon salt**
- 4 **flour tortillas (6 inches)**
- 1 **can (10¾ ounces) condensed cream of mushroom soup, undiluted**
- 1 **can (10 ounces) diced tomatoes and green chilies, undrained**
- 1 **cup shredded cheddar cheese**

1. In a large skillet, cook ground beef and onion until the meat is no longer pink; drain. Add the black beans, chili powder, cumin and salt.

2. Transfer to a greased 13x9-in. baking dish. Arrange tortillas over top. Combine soup and tomatoes; pour over tortillas. Sprinkle with cheese.

3. Bake casserole, uncovered, at 350° for 25-30 minutes or until heated through.

UPSIDE-DOWN PIZZA BAKE

I've been serving this easy and exceptionally delicious bake to my kids and grandkids for over 30 years. You can't go wrong with the flavor of pizza in a casserole.

—Sandy Bastian Tinley Park, IL

Prep: 20 min. • **Bake:** 25 min.
Makes: 4 servings

- ½ **pound Italian sausage links, cut into ¼-inch slices**
- 1 **cup spaghetti sauce**
- ½ **cup sliced fresh mushrooms**
- ½ **cup julienned green pepper**
- 1 **cup shredded part-skim mozzarella cheese, divided**
- 1 **cup biscuit/baking mix**
- 1 **large egg**
- ½ **cup 2% milk**

1. In a large skillet, cook sausage over medium heat until no longer pink; drain.

2. Pour spaghetti sauce into a greased 8-in. square baking dish. Layer with mushrooms, green pepper, sausage and ½ cup cheese.

3. In a small bowl, combine the biscuit mix, egg and milk until blended. Pour over top. Sprinkle with remaining cheese.

4. Bake casserole, uncovered, at 400° for 25-30 minutes or until golden brown.

BROCCOLI TURKEY CASSEROLE

Whenever I serve this hearty, cheesy hot dish, everyone asks for the recipe!

—Muriel Shand Isanti, MN

Prep: 20 min. • **Bake:** 25 min.
Makes: 8 servings

- ¼ **cup chopped onion**
- ¼ **cup chopped celery**
- ¼ **cup butter, cubed**
- 4 **cups cubed cooked turkey breast**
- 1 **package (16 ounces) frozen broccoli florets, thawed**
- 1 **can (10¾ ounces) condensed cream of mushroom soup, undiluted**
- 1 **can (10¾ ounces) condensed cream of chicken soup, undiluted**
- 1 **cup cooked rice**
- ½ **cup shredded part-skim mozzarella cheese**
- 1 **can (2.8 ounces) French-fried onions**

1. In a large skillet, saute onion and celery in butter until tender. Stir in the turkey, broccoli, soups and rice; transfer to a greased shallow 2½ qt. baking dish.

2. Bake casserole, uncovered, at 350° for 25-30 minutes or until bubbly. Sprinkle with cheese and French-fried onions; bake 5 minutes longer or until cheese is melted.

Freeze option: Sprinkle mozzarella cheese and French-fried onions over unbaked casserole. Cover and freeze. To use, partially thaw in refrigerator overnight. Remove from refrigerator 30 minutes before baking. Preheat oven to 350°. Bake as directed, increasing time as necessary to heat through and for a thermometer inserted in center to read 165°.

FAST FIX

CONTEST-WINNING REUBEN CASSEROLE

Here sauerkraut, kielbasa and Swiss cheese combine for a creamy, Reuben-style entree. I've had this recipe for a long time, and from the smudges on it, you can tell it's been well used.

—**Sally Mangel** Bradford, PA

Start to Finish: 30 min.
Makes: 2 servings

- 1½ cups uncooked egg noodles
- ⅔ cup condensed cream of mushroom soup, undiluted
- ⅓ cup 2% milk
- 2 tablespoons chopped onion
- ¾ teaspoon prepared mustard
- 1 can (8 ounces) sauerkraut, rinsed and well drained
- ⅓ pound smoked kielbasa or Polish sausage, cut into ½-inch slices
- ½ cup shredded Swiss cheese
- 3 tablespoons soft whole wheat bread crumbs
- 1½ teaspoons butter, melted

1. Cook noodles according to package directions. Meanwhile, in a small bowl, combine the soup, milk, onion and mustard; set aside.
2. Spread sauerkraut into a 1-qt. baking dish coated with cooking spray. Drain noodles; place over sauerkraut. Layer with soup mixture and kielbasa; sprinkle with Swiss cheese.
3. In a small bowl, combine bread crumbs and butter; sprinkle over casserole. Bake, uncovered, at 350° for 15-20 minutes or until bubbly.

★ ★ ★ ★ ★ **READER REVIEW**

"I don't usually give five stars, but this dish was that good! I did add a touch of Thousand Island dressing to give it more of a Reuben taste, and it was perfect."

LPHJKITCHEN TASTEOFHOME.COM

TEXAS-STYLE LASAGNA

With its spicy flavor, this dish is a real crowd-pleaser. It goes great with picante sauce, guacamole and tortilla chips.
—**Effie Gish** Fort Worth, TX

Prep: 40 min. • **Bake:** 30 min. + standing
Makes: 12 servings

- 1½ pounds ground beef
- 1 teaspoon seasoned salt
- 1 package (1¼ ounces) taco seasoning
- 1 can (14½ ounces) diced tomatoes, undrained
- 1 can (15 ounces) tomato sauce
- 1 can (4 ounces) chopped green chilies
- 2 cups 4% cottage cheese
- 2 large eggs, lightly beaten
- 12 corn tortillas (6 inches), torn
- 3½ to 4 cups shredded Monterey Jack cheese
    Optional toppings: crushed tortilla chips, salsa and cubed avocado

1. In a large skillet, cook beef over medium heat until no longer pink; drain. Add the seasoned salt, taco seasoning, tomatoes, tomato sauce and chilies. Reduce heat; simmer, uncovered, for 15-20 minutes. In a small bowl, combine cottage cheese and eggs.
2. In a greased 13x9-in. baking dish, layer half of each of the following: meat sauce, corn tortillas, cottage cheese mixture and Monterey Jack cheese. Repeat layers.
3. Bake lasagna, uncovered, at 350° for 30 minutes or until bubbly. Let stand 10 minutes before serving. Garnish with toppings if desired.
Freeze option: Cover and freeze unbaked lasagna for up to 3 months. Thaw in the refrigerator overnight. Remove from the refrigerator 30 minutes before baking. Bake as directed, increasing time as necessary for a thermometer to read 160°.

TUNA MUSHROOM CASSEROLE

The first time I made this dish, my uncle asked for seconds, even though tuna casseroles are not usually his favorite. The green beans add texture, color and flavor.
—Jone Furlong Santa Rosa, CA

Prep: 30 min. • **Bake:** 25 min.
Makes: 4-6 servings

- ½ cup water
- 1 teaspoon chicken bouillon granules
- 1 package (9 ounces) frozen cut green beans
- 1 cup chopped onion
- 1 cup sliced fresh mushrooms
- ¼ cup chopped celery
- 1 garlic clove, minced
- ½ teaspoon dill weed
- ½ teaspoon salt
- ⅛ teaspoon pepper
- 4 teaspoons cornstarch
- 1½ cups cold whole milk
- ½ cup shredded Swiss cheese
- ¼ cup mayonnaise
- 2½ cups egg noodles, cooked and drained
- 1 can (12 ounces) light tuna in water, drained and flaked
- ⅓ cup dry bread crumbs
- 1 tablespoon butter

1. In a large saucepan, bring water and bouillon to a boil; stir until bouillon is dissolved. Add the next eight ingredients; bring to a boil. Reduce heat; cover and simmer for 5 minutes or until vegetables are tender.

2. In a small bowl, combine cornstarch and milk until smooth; gradually add to vegetable mixture. Bring to a boil; cook and stir for 2 minutes or until thickened. Remove from the heat; stir in cheese and mayonnaise until cheese is melted. Fold in noodles and tuna.

3. Pour into a greased 2½-qt. baking dish. In a small skillet, brown bread crumbs in butter; sprinkle over casserole. Bake, uncovered, at 350° for 25-30 minutes or until heated through.

PORTOBELLO PASTA BAKE

I turn to this recipe the day after Thanksgiving. Leftover turkey never tasted so good.
—Preci D'Silva
Dubai, United Arab Emirates

Prep: 20 min. • **Bake:** 20 min.
Makes: 4 servings

- 2½ cups uncooked multigrain spiral pasta
- 3 large portobello mushrooms
- 1 tablespoon olive oil
- 1 tablespoon butter
- 3 garlic cloves, minced
- 3 tablespoons all-purpose flour
- 1½ cups 2% milk
- ⅓ cup heavy whipping cream
- 2 cups cubed cooked turkey
- ¾ teaspoon salt
- ¼ teaspoon pepper
- 1 cup shredded part-skim mozzarella cheese, divided
- 2 tablespoons grated Parmesan cheese

1. Preheat oven to 350°. Cook pasta according to package directions. With a spoon, scrape and remove gills of mushrooms; slice caps.
2. In a large skillet, heat oil and butter over medium-high heat. Add sliced mushrooms; cook and stir until tender. Add garlic; cook 1 minute longer. Stir in flour until blended; gradually add milk and cream. Bring to a boil; cook and stir 2 minutes or until thickened. Stir in turkey, salt and pepper; heat through.
3. Drain pasta; add to turkey mixture and toss to coat. Stir in ¾ cup of mozzarella.
4. Transfer mixture to a greased 8-in. square baking dish. Sprinkle with Parmesan cheese and remaining mozzarella cheese. Bake, uncovered, 20-25 minutes or until cheese is melted.

SPAGHETTI MEATBALL BAKE

Some nights we're in the mood for pasta— and it seems nothing else will do! I came up with this saucy dish to satisfy our cravings.
—Kimberly Forni Laconia, NH

Prep: 45 min. • **Bake:** 30 min.
Makes: 10 servings

- 1½ cups dry bread crumbs, divided
- 3 large eggs, lightly beaten
- 1½ cups cooked spaghetti (3 ounces uncooked), coarsely chopped
- 2 garlic cloves, minced
- 2 teaspoons dried basil
- ¾ teaspoon salt
- 1 teaspoon dried oregano
- 1 teaspoon pepper
- 2 pounds ground beef

SAUCE
- 2 jars (24 ounces each) meatless pasta sauce
- 1 small onion, finely chopped
- 2 garlic cloves, minced
- 2 teaspoons dried basil
- 1 teaspoon dried oregano
- 2 cups shredded part-skim mozzarella cheese

1. Preheat oven to 375°. Place 1 cup of bread crumbs in a shallow bowl. In a large bowl, combine eggs, chopped spaghetti, garlic, seasonings and remaining bread crumbs. Add ground beef; mix lightly but thoroughly. Shape into 1½-in. balls.
2. Roll meatballs in bread crumbs; place in a greased 13x9-in. baking dish. Bake 15-20 minutes or until cooked through.
3. In a large saucepan, combine the pasta sauce, onion, garlic and seasonings; bring to a boil over medium heat, stirring occasionally. Pour over meatballs; sprinkle with cheese. Bake 15-20 minutes longer or until cheese is lightly browned.

TURKEY MUSHROOM CASSEROLE

My mother developed this recipe. The Parmesan cheese and splash of sherry make it elegant enough to serve at a dinner party.

—Peggy Kroupa Leawood, KS

Prep: 50 min. • **Cook:** 30 min.
Makes: 2 casseroles (4 servings each)

- 1 pound uncooked spaghetti
- ½ pound sliced fresh mushrooms
- 1 cup chopped onion
- 2 tablespoons olive oil
- ½ teaspoon minced garlic
- 3 cans (10¾ ounces each) condensed cream of mushroom soup, undiluted
- 3 cups cubed cooked turkey
- 1 cup chicken broth
- ⅓ cup sherry or additional chicken broth
- 1 teaspoon Italian seasoning
- ¾ teaspoon pepper
- 2 cups grated Parmesan cheese, divided

1. Cook spaghetti according to directions on package.

2. Meanwhile, in a Dutch oven, saute mushrooms and onion in oil until tender. Add the garlic; cook 1 minute longer. Stir in the soup, turkey, broth, sherry, Italian seasoning, pepper and 1 cup cheese. Drain spaghetti; stir into turkey mixture.

3. Transfer mixture to two greased 8-in. square baking dishes. Sprinkle with remaining cheese. Cover and freeze one casserole for up to 3 months. Cover and bake the remaining casserole at 350° for 30-40 minutes or until heated through.

To use frozen casserole: Thaw in the refrigerator overnight. Remove from the refrigerator 30 minutes before baking. Cover and bake at 350° for 45 minutes. Uncover and bake 5-10 minutes longer or until bubbly.

PUFF PASTRY CHICKEN POTPIE

When my wife is craving comfort food, I whip up my chicken potpie. It's easy to make, sticks to your ribs and delivers soul-satisfying flavor.

—Nick Iverson Denver, CO

Prep: 45 min. • **Bake:** 45 min. + standing
Makes: 8 servings

- 1 package (17.3 ounces) frozen puff pastry, thawed
- 2 pounds boneless skinless chicken breasts, cut into 1-inch pieces
- 1 teaspoon salt, divided
- 1 teaspoon pepper, divided
- 4 tablespoons butter, divided
- 1 large onion, chopped
- 2 garlic cloves, minced
- 1 teaspoon minced fresh thyme or ¼ teaspoon dried thyme
- 1 teaspoon minced fresh sage or ¼ teaspoon rubbed sage
- ½ cup all-purpose flour
- 2 cups chicken broth
- 1 cup plus 1 tablespoon half-and-half cream, divided
- 2 cups frozen mixed vegetables (about 10 ounces)
- 1 tablespoon lemon juice
- 1 large egg yolk

1. Preheat oven to 400°. On a lightly floured surface, roll each pastry sheet into a 12x10-in. rectangle. Cut one sheet crosswise into six 2-in. strips; cut the remaining sheet lengthwise into five 2-in. strips. On a baking sheet, closely weave strips to make a 12x10-in. lattice. Freeze while making filling.

2. Toss chicken with ½ teaspoon each salt and pepper. In a large skillet, heat 1 tablespoon butter over medium-high heat; saute the chicken until browned, 5-7 minutes. Remove from pan.

3. In same skillet, heat remaining butter over medium-high heat; saute onion until tender, 5-7 minutes. Stir in the garlic and herbs; cook 1 minute. Stir in flour until blended; cook and stir 1 minute. Gradually stir in broth and 1 cup cream. Bring to a boil, stirring constantly; cook and stir until thickened, about 2 minutes.

4. Stir in vegetables, lemon juice, chicken and the remaining salt and pepper; return to a boil. Transfer to a greased 2-qt. oblong baking dish. Top with lattice; trim to fit.

5. Whisk together egg yolk and remaining cream; brush over pastry. Bake potpie, uncovered, until bubbly and golden brown, 45-55 minutes. Let stand for 15 minutes before serving.

CHILI MAC CASSEROLE

This nicely spiced entree uses several of my family's favorite ingredients, including macaroni, kidney beans, tomatoes and cheese. Just add a green salad to make it a complete meal.

—**Marlene Wilson** Rolla, ND

Prep: 15 min. • **Bake:** 30 min.
Makes: 10 servings

- 1 cup uncooked elbow macaroni
- 2 pounds lean ground beef (90% lean)
- 1 medium onion, chopped
- 2 garlic cloves, minced
- 1 can (28 ounces) diced tomatoes, undrained
- 1 can (16 ounces) kidney beans, rinsed and drained
- 1 can (6 ounces) tomato paste
- 1 can (4 ounces) chopped green chilies
- 1¼ teaspoons salt
- 1 teaspoon chili powder
- ½ teaspoon ground cumin
- ½ teaspoon pepper
- 2 cups shredded reduced-fat Mexican cheese blend
  Thinly sliced green onions, optional

1. Cook macaroni according to package directions. Meanwhile, in a large nonstick skillet, cook the beef, onion and garlic over medium heat until meat is no longer pink; drain. Stir in the tomatoes, beans, tomato paste, chilies and seasonings. Drain the macaroni; add to beef mixture.

2. Transfer to a 13x9-in. baking dish coated with cooking spray. Cover and bake at 375° for 25-30 minutes or until bubbly. Uncover; sprinkle with cheese. Bake 5-8 minutes longer or until cheese is melted. If desired, top with sliced green onions.

✳

TEST KITCHEN TIP

To transport a casserole to an event, wrap it in an insulated carrying case that keeps foods warm for short periods of time. Be sure to follow manufacturer's directions for recommended maximum holding times for these carriers to ensure your food stays safe. If there's an oven available at your destination, cook, chill and transport food in a cooler for safe traveling, then reheat upon arrival.

POTLUCK CORDON BLEU CASSEROLE

Whenever I'm invited to attend a potluck, I am usually asked to bring this tempting casserole. The turkey, ham and cheese are delectable combined with the crunchy topping. When I bake a turkey, I prepare the leftovers for this dish, knowing I'll be making it again soon.

—**Joyce Paul** Moose Jaw, SK

Prep: 25 min. • **Bake:** 30 min.
Makes: 10 servings

- 4 cups cubed cooked turkey
- 3 cups cubed fully cooked ham
- 1 cup shredded cheddar cheese
- 1 cup chopped onion
- ¼ cup butter, cubed
- ⅓ cup all-purpose flour
- 2 cups half-and-half cream
- 1 teaspoon dill weed
- ⅛ teaspoon ground mustard
- ⅛ teaspoon ground nutmeg

TOPPING
- 1 cup dry bread crumbs
- 2 tablespoons butter, melted
- ¼ teaspoon dill weed
- ¼ cup shredded cheddar cheese
- ¼ cup chopped walnuts

1. In a large bowl, combine the turkey, ham and cheese; set aside. In a large saucepan, saute onion in butter until tender. Add flour; stir until blended. Gradually add cream, stirring constantly. Bring mixture to a boil; cook and stir for 1-2 minutes or until thickened. Stir in the dill, mustard and nutmeg. Remove from the heat and pour over meat mixture.

2. Spoon into a greased 13x9-in. baking dish. In a small bowl, combine the bread crumbs, butter and dill. Stir in cheese and walnuts. Sprinkle over the top.

3. Bake casserole, uncovered, at 350° for 30 minutes or until heated through.

BEEF ENCHILADA LASAGNA CASSEROLE

Whenever I make this cheesy layered casserole, guests rave about it and ask for the recipe. I serve it with French bread or toasted garlic bread.
—**Charlene Griffin** Minocqua, WI

Prep: 45 min. • **Bake:** 30 min. + standing
Makes: 12 servings

- 1½ pounds ground beef
- 1 medium onion, chopped
- 1 garlic clove, minced
- 1 can (14½ ounces) stewed tomatoes, undrained
- 1 can (10 ounces) enchilada sauce
- 1 to 2 teaspoons ground cumin
- 1 large egg, beaten
- 1½ cups 4% cottage cheese
- 3 cups shredded Mexican cheese blend
- 8 flour tortillas (8 inches), cut in half
- 1 cup shredded cheddar cheese

1. In a large skillet, cook the beef, onion and garlic over medium heat until meat is no longer pink; drain. Stir in the tomatoes, enchilada sauce and cumin. Bring to a boil. Reduce heat; simmer, uncovered, for 20 minutes.
2. In a small bowl, combine egg and cottage cheese; set aside. Spread a third of the meat sauce into a greased 13x9-in. baking dish. Layer with half each of the cheese blend, tortillas, cottage cheese mixture and remaining meat sauce. Repeat layers. Sprinkle with cheddar cheese.
3. Cover and bake at 350° for 20 minutes. Uncover; bake 10 minutes longer or until casserole is bubbly. Let stand 15 minutes before cutting.

CHICKEN & SWISS CASSEROLE

What's Sunday dinner without a casserole? This comforting pasta bake is a classic crowd-pleaser.
—**Christina Petri** Alexandria, MN

Prep: 30 min. • **Bake:** 10 min.
Makes: 8 servings

- 5½ cups uncooked egg noodles (about ½ pound)
- 3 tablespoons olive oil
- 3 shallots, chopped
- 3 small garlic cloves, minced
- ⅓ cup all-purpose flour
- 2 cups chicken broth
- ¾ cup 2% milk
- 1½ teaspoons dried thyme
- ¾ teaspoon grated lemon peel
- ½ teaspoon salt
- ¼ teaspoon ground nutmeg
- ¼ teaspoon pepper
- 5 cups cubed rotisserie chicken
- 1½ cups frozen peas
- 2 cups shredded Swiss cheese
- ¾ cup dry bread crumbs
- 2 tablespoons butter, melted

1. Preheat oven to 350°. Cook noodles according to package directions; drain. In a large skillet, heat oil over medium heat. Add shallots and garlic; cook and stir for 45 seconds. Stir in flour; cook and stir 1 minute. Add broth, milk, thyme, lemon peel, salt, nutmeg and pepper. Stir in cubed chicken and peas; heat mixture through. Stir in noodles and cheese.
2. Transfer to a greased 13x9-in. baking dish. In a small bowl, mix bread crumbs and butter; sprinkle over top. Bake for 8-10 minutes or until top is browned.

STUFFING & TURKEY CASSEROLE

Gathering around the table with loved ones is all about quality time spent together. But good food makes those special times even more memorable. This is a plate full of love, comfort and happiness.

—**Debbie Fabre** Fort Myers, FL

Prep: 15 min. • **Bake:** 45 min. + standing
Makes: 12 servings

- 4 cups leftover stuffing
- 1 cup dried cranberries
- 1 cup chopped pecans
- ¾ cup chicken broth
- 1 large egg, lightly beaten
- 2 cups shredded part-skim mozzarella cheese
- 1 cup whole-milk ricotta cheese
- 4 cups cubed cooked turkey, divided
- 1 cup shredded cheddar cheese

1. Preheat oven to 350°. Place stuffing, cranberries and pecans in a large bowl; stir in broth. In a small bowl, mix egg with mozzarella and ricotta cheeses.
2. In a greased 13x9-in. baking dish, layer 2 cups turkey, 3 cups stuffing mixture and ricotta cheese mixture. Top with remaining turkey and stuffing mixture. Sprinkle with cheddar cheese.
3. Bake, covered, for 40-45 minutes or until heated through. Bake, uncovered, 5 minutes longer. Let stand 10 minutes before serving.

★ ★ ★ ★ ★ **READER REVIEW**

"This was the perfect recipe to pull all of my Thanksgiving leftovers together into one tasty casserole! After a long week of holiday prep, there's nothing better than the ease of putting together this quick dish."

GINA.KAPFHAMER TASTEOFHOME.COM

WHITE SEAFOOD LASAGNA

We make lasagna with shrimp and scallops as part of the traditional Italian Feast of the Seven Fishes. Every bite delivers a tasty jewel from the sea.

—**Joe Colamonico** North Charleston, SC

Prep: 1 hour
Bake: 40 min. + standing
Makes: 12 servings

- 9 uncooked lasagna noodles
- 1 tablespoon butter
- 1 pound uncooked shrimp (31 to 40 per pound), peeled and deveined
- 1 pound bay scallops
- 5 garlic cloves, minced
- ¼ cup white wine
- 1 tablespoon lemon juice
- 1 pound fresh crabmeat

CHEESE SAUCE
- ¼ cup butter, cubed
- ¼ cup all-purpose flour
- 3 cups 2% milk
- 1 cup shredded part-skim mozzarella cheese
- ½ cup grated Parmesan cheese
- ½ teaspoon salt
- ¼ teaspoon pepper
  Dash ground nutmeg

RICOTTA MIXTURE
- 1 carton (15 ounces) part-skim ricotta cheese
- 1 package (10 ounces) frozen chopped spinach, thawed and squeezed dry
- 1 cup shredded part-skim mozzarella cheese
- ½ cup grated Parmesan cheese
- ½ cup seasoned bread crumbs
- 1 large egg, lightly beaten

TOPPING
- 1 cup shredded part-skim mozzarella cheese
- ¼ cup grated Parmesan cheese
  Minced fresh parsley

1. Preheat oven to 350°. Cook lasagna noodles according to directions on the package; drain.

2. Meanwhile, in a large skillet, heat butter over medium heat. Add the shrimp and scallops in batches; cook 2-4 minutes or until shrimp turn pink and scallops are firm and opaque. Remove from pan.

3. Add garlic to same pan; cook 1 minute. Add white wine and lemon juice, stirring to loosen browned bits from pan. Bring to a boil; cook 1-2 minutes or until liquid is reduced by half. Add crab; heat through. Stir in shrimp and scallops.

4. For cheese sauce, melt butter over medium heat in a large saucepan. Stir in flour until smooth; gradually whisk in milk. Bring to a boil, stirring constantly; cook and stir for 1-2 minutes or until thickened. Remove from heat; stir in remaining cheese sauce ingredients. In a large bowl, combine ricotta mixture ingredients; stir in 1 cup cheese sauce.

5. Spread ½ cup cheese sauce into a greased 13x9-in. baking dish. Layer with three noodles, half of the ricotta mixture, half of the seafood mixture and ⅔ cup cheese sauce. Repeat layers. Top with the remaining noodles and cheese sauce. Sprinkle with remaining mozzarella and Parmesan cheese.

6. Bake, uncovered, for 40-50 minutes or until bubbly and top is golden brown. Let stand 10 minutes before serving. Sprinkle with parsley.

CHICKEN TATER BAKE

You'll please everyone with this inviting dish. It tastes like chicken potpie with a crispy Tater Tot crust.

—Fran Allen St. Louis, MO

Prep: 20 min. • **Bake:** 30 min.
Makes: 2 casseroles (6 servings each)

- 2 cans (10¾ ounces each) condensed cream of chicken soup, undiluted
- ½ cup 2% milk
- ¼ cup butter, cubed
- 3 cups cubed cooked chicken
- 1 package (16 ounces) frozen peas and carrots, thawed
- 1½ cups shredded cheddar cheese, divided
- 1 package (32 ounces) frozen Tater Tots

1. In a large saucepan, combine the soup, milk and butter. Cook and stir mixture over medium heat until heated through. Remove from the heat; stir in the chicken, peas and carrots and 1 cup cheese.
2. Transfer to two greased 8-in. square baking dishes. Top with Tater Tots.
3. Cover and freeze one casserole for up to 3 months. Bake the remaining casserole at 400° for 25-30 minutes or until bubbling. Sprinkle with ¼ cup cheddar cheese; bake 5 minutes longer or until cheese is melted.
To use frozen casserole: Remove from the freezer 30 minutes before baking (do not thaw). Sprinkle with ¼ cup cheese. Cover and bake at 350° for 1½-1¾ hours or until heated through.

ZUCCHINI ENCHILADAS

Every summer my garden overflows with zucchini, and this is my go-to recipe to make the most of it. My family loves the freshness of this classic dish.

—Angela Leinenbach Mechanicsvlle, VA

Prep: 1½ hours • **Bake:** 30 min.
Makes: 12 servings

- 1 medium sweet yellow pepper, chopped
- 1 medium green pepper, chopped
- 1 large sweet onion, chopped
- 2 tablespoons olive oil
- 2 garlic cloves, minced
- 2 cans (15 ounces each) tomato sauce
- 2 cans (14½ ounces each) no-salt-added diced tomatoes, undrained
- 2 tablespoons chili powder
- 2 teaspoons sugar
- 2 teaspoons dried marjoram
- 1 teaspoon dried basil
- 1 teaspoon ground cumin
- ¼ teaspoon salt
- ¼ teaspoon cayenne pepper
- 1 bay leaf
- 3 pounds zucchini, shredded (about 8 cups)
- 24 corn tortillas (6 inches), warmed
- 4 cups shredded reduced-fat cheddar cheese
- 2 cans (2¼ ounces each) sliced ripe olives, drained
- ½ cup minced fresh cilantro
  Reduced-fat sour cream, optional

1. In a large saucepan, saute peppers and onion in oil until tender. Add garlic; cook 1 minute longer. Stir in the tomato sauce, tomatoes, chili powder, sugar, marjoram, basil, cumin, salt, cayenne and bay leaf. Bring to a boil. Reduce heat; simmer, uncovered, 30-35 minutes or until slightly thickened. Discard bay leaf.
2. Preheat oven to 350°. Place ⅓ cup zucchini down the center of each tortilla; top each with 2 tablespoons cheese and 2 teaspoons olives. Roll up and place seam side down in two 13x9-in. baking dishes coated with cooking spray. Pour sauce over top of enchiladas; sprinkle with the remaining cheese.
3. Bake, uncovered, for 30-35 minutes or until heated through. Sprinkle with fresh cilantro. Serve with sour cream if desired.

NEW ENGLAND BEAN & BOG CASSOULET

When I moved to New England, I embraced the regional cuisine. My cassoulet with baked beans pays tribute to both my new locale and a French classic.
—**Devon Delaney** Westport, CT

Prep: 15 min. • **Cook:** 35 min.
Makes: 8 servings (3½ quarts)

- 5 tablespoons olive oil, divided
- 8 boneless skinless chicken thighs (about 2 pounds)
- 1 package (12 ounces) fully cooked Italian chicken sausage links, cut into ½-in. slices
- 4 shallots, finely chopped
- 2 teaspoons minced fresh rosemary or ½ teaspoon dried rosemary, crushed
- 2 teaspoons minced fresh thyme or ½ teaspoon dried thyme
- 1 can (28 ounces) fire-roasted diced tomatoes, undrained
- 1 can (16 ounces) baked beans
- 1 cup chicken broth
- ½ cup fresh or frozen cranberries
- 3 day-old croissants, cubed (about 6 cups)
- ½ teaspoon lemon-pepper seasoning
- 2 tablespoons minced fresh parsley

1. Preheat oven to 400°. In a Dutch oven, heat 2 tablespoons oil over medium heat. In batches, brown chicken thighs on both sides; remove from pan, reserving the drippings. Add sausage; cook and stir until lightly browned. Remove from pan.
2. In the same pan, heat 1 tablespoon oil over medium heat. Add shallots, rosemary and thyme; cook and stir until shallots are tender, 1-2 minutes. Stir in tomatoes, beans, chicken broth and cranberries. Return chicken and sausage to pan; bring to a boil. Bake, covered, until chicken is tender, 20-25 minutes.
3. Toss croissant pieces with remaining oil; sprinkle with lemon pepper. Arrange over chicken mixture. Bake, uncovered, until the croissants are golden brown, 12-15 minutes. Sprinkle with parsley.

FIESTA CHICKEN

Chili powder and picante sauce add just the right dash of spice to this hearty main dish. The recipe calls for convenient pantry staples, so it's a snap to assemble.
—**Teresa Peterson** Kasson, MN

Prep: 15 min. • **Bake:** 40 min.
Makes: 8 servings

- 1 can (10¾ ounces) condensed cream of chicken soup, undiluted
- 1 can (10¾ ounces) condensed cream of mushroom soup, undiluted
- 2 small tomatoes, chopped
- ⅓ cup picante sauce
- 1 medium green pepper, chopped
- 1 small onion, chopped
- 2 to 3 teaspoons chili powder
- 12 corn tortillas (6 inches), cut into 1-inch strips
- 3 cups cubed cooked chicken
- 1 cup shredded Colby cheese

1. In a large bowl, combine the soups, tomatoes, picante sauce, green pepper, onion and chili powder. In a greased 13x9-in. baking dish, layer half each of the tortilla strips, chicken, soup mixture and cheese. Repeat layers.
2. Cover and bake in a 350° oven for 40-50 minutes or until bubbly.
Freeze option: Cover and freeze unbaked casserole. To use, partially thaw in the refrigerator overnight. Remove from refrigerator 30 minutes before baking. Preheat oven to 350°. Bake casserole as directed, increasing time as necessary to heat through and for a thermometer inserted in center to read 165°.

CHICKEN ALFREDO LASAGNA

My crew was growing tired of traditional red sauce lasagna, so I created this fun twist using a creamy homemade Alfredo sauce. Store-bought rotisserie chicken keeps prep simple and fast.

—**Caitlin MacNeilly** Uncasville, CT

Prep: 35 min. • **Bake:** 45 min. + standing
Makes: 12 servings

- 4 ounces thinly sliced pancetta, cut into strips
- 3 ounces thinly sliced prosciutto or deli ham, cut into strips
- 3 cups shredded rotisserie chicken
- 5 tablespoons unsalted butter, cubed
- ¼ cup all-purpose flour
- 4 cups whole milk
- 2 cups shredded Asiago cheese, divided
- 2 tablespoons minced fresh parsley, divided
- ¼ teaspoon coarsely ground pepper
  Pinch ground nutmeg
- 9 no-cook lasagna noodles
- 1½ cups shredded part-skim mozzarella cheese
- 1½ cups shredded Parmesan cheese

1. In a large skillet, cook the pancetta and prosciutto over medium heat until browned. Drain on paper towels. Transfer to a large bowl; add shredded chicken and toss to combine.

2. For sauce, in a large saucepan, melt butter over medium heat. Stir in flour until smooth; gradually whisk in milk. Bring to a boil, stirring constantly; cook and stir for 1-2 minutes or until thickened. Remove from the heat; stir in ½ cup Asiago cheese, 1 tablespoon parsley, pepper and nutmeg.

3. Preheat oven to 375°. Spread ½ cup sauce into a greased 13x9-in. baking dish. Layer with a third of each of the following: noodles, Alfredo sauce, meat mixture, Asiago, mozzarella and Parmesan cheeses. Repeat layers twice.

4. Bake, covered, 30 minutes. Uncover; bake 15 minutes longer or until bubbly. Sprinkle with remaining parsley. Let stand 10 minutes before serving.

PORK & GREEN CHILI CASSEROLE

I'm always on the lookout for tasty, quick recipes to fix for my family. I work at a local hospital and also part time for some area doctors, so my co-workers and I often exchange recipes. One of them brought this casserole when I hosted a picnic at my house. People raved about it.

—Dianne Esposite New Middletown, OH

Prep: 20 min. • **Bake:** 30 min.
Makes: 6 servings

- 1½ pounds boneless pork, cut into ½-inch cubes
- 1 tablespoon canola oil
- 1 can (15 ounces) black beans, rinsed and drained
- 1 can (10¾ ounces) condensed cream of chicken soup, undiluted
- 1 can (14½ ounces) diced tomatoes, undrained
- 2 cans (4 ounces each) chopped green chilies
- 1 cup quick-cooking brown rice
- ¼ cup water
- 2 to 3 tablespoons salsa
- 1 teaspoon ground cumin
- ½ cup shredded cheddar cheese

1. Preheat oven to 350°. In a large skillet, brown pork in oil; drain. Stir in the beans, soup, tomatoes, chilies, rice, water, salsa and cumin.

2. Pour into an ungreased 2-qt. baking dish. Bake, uncovered, 30 minutes or until bubbly. Sprinkle with the cheese; let stand 5 minutes before serving.

Freeze option: Sprinkle cheese over cooled unbaked casserole. Cover and freeze. To use, partially thaw in refrigerator overnight. Remove from the refrigerator 30 minutes before baking. Preheat oven to 350°. Bake casserole as directed, increasing the time as necessary to heat through and for a thermometer inserted in the center to read 165°.

PAN BURRITOS

We love Mexican food, so this zesty bake is a favorite. I like that I can enjoy the full flavor of burritos in the serving size of my choice.

—Joyce Kent Grand Rapids, MI

Prep: 35 min. • **Bake:** 35 min. + standing
Makes: 8-10 servings

- 2 packages (1½ ounces each) enchilada sauce mix
- 3 cups water
- 1 can (12 ounces) tomato paste
- 1 garlic clove, minced
- ¼ teaspoon pepper
  Salt to taste
- 2 pounds ground beef
- 9 large flour tortillas (9-inch)
- 4 cups shredded cheddar cheese or Mexican cheese blend
- 1 can (16 ounces) refried beans, warmed
  Taco sauce, sour cream, chili peppers, chopped onion and/or guacamole, optional

1. In a saucepan, combine the first six ingredients; simmer for 15-20 minutes.

2. In a skillet, brown the beef. Drain; stir in one third of the sauce. Spread another third on the bottom of a greased 13x9-in. baking pan.

3. Place three tortillas over sauce, tearing to fit bottom of pan. Spoon half of the meat mixture over tortillas; sprinkle with 1½ cups cheese. Add three more tortillas. Spread refried beans over tortillas; top with the remaining meat. Sprinkle with 1½ cups of cheese. Layer remaining tortillas; top with the remaining sauce. Sprinkle with remaining cheese.

4. Bake, uncovered, in a 350° oven for 35-40 minutes. Let stand for 10 minutes before cutting. Serve with taco sauce, sour cream, chili peppers, chopped onion and/or guacamole if desired.

SPAGHETTI SQUASH CASSEROLE

Spaghetti squash, like zucchini, can take over a garden. This is an excellent way to put that abundance to good use. I got the original recipe at a cooking class, and I've made it many times since.
—**Mina Dick** Boissevain, MB

Prep: 20 min. • **Bake:** 45 min.
Makes: 6-8 servings

- 1 small spaghetti squash (1½ to 2 pounds)
- ½ cup water
- 1 pound ground beef
- ½ cup chopped onion
- ½ cup chopped sweet red pepper
- 1 garlic clove, minced
- 1 cup canned diced tomatoes
- ½ teaspoon dried oregano
- ¼ teaspoon salt
- ⅛ teaspoon pepper
- 1 cup shredded mozzarella or cheddar cheese
- 1 tablespoon chopped fresh parsley

1. Cut squash in half lengthwise; scoop out seeds. Place with cut side down in a baking dish; add water. Cover and bake at 375° for 20-30 minutes or until squash is easily pierced with a fork. When cool enough to handle, scoop out the squash, separating the strands with a fork.
2. In a large skillet, cook beef, onion, red pepper and garlic until meat is browned and the vegetables are tender. Drain; add the tomatoes, oregano, salt, pepper and squash. Cook and stir for 1-2 minutes or until liquid is absorbed. Transfer to an ungreased 1½-qt. baking dish. Bake, uncovered, at 350° for 25 minutes. Sprinkle with the cheese and parsley; let stand a few minutes before serving.

TEST KITCHEN TIP

With its hard shell, spaghetti squash can be difficult to cut in half. Here's a method that doesn't rely on strength alone. You'll need a rubber mallet and a large knife, such as a French chef's knife. Cover mallet with a food storage bag and secure to the handle with a rubber band or twist tie. Insert the knife lengthwise into the middle of the squash. Hold the knife handle with one hand and hit the top of the blade near the handle with the mallet. Continue hitting the knife with the mallet until the squash splits in half.

OLÉ POLENTA CASSEROLE

This casserole has been a favorite of ours for several years. I like to dollop sour cream on each serving.
—**Angela Biggin** Lyons, IL

Prep: 1 hour + chilling
Bake: 45 min. + standing
Makes: 6 servings

- 1 cup yellow cornmeal
- 1 teaspoon salt
- 4 cups water, divided
- 1 pound ground beef
- 1 cup chopped onion
- ½ cup chopped green pepper
- 2 garlic cloves, minced
- 1 can (14½ ounces) diced tomatoes, undrained
- 1 can (8 ounces) tomato sauce
- ½ pound sliced fresh mushrooms
- 1 teaspoon each dried basil, oregano and dill weed
  Dash hot pepper sauce
- 1½ cups shredded part-skim mozzarella cheese
- ¼ cup grated Parmesan cheese

1. For polenta, in a small bowl, whisk cornmeal, salt and 1 cup water until smooth. In a large saucepan, bring remaining water to a boil. Add cornmeal mixture, stirring constantly. Bring to a boil; cook and stir 3 minutes or until thickened.
2. Reduce heat to low; cover and cook for 15 minutes. Divide mixture between two greased 8-in. square baking dishes. Cover and refrigerate until firm, about 1½ hours.
3. In a large skillet, cook the beef, onion, green pepper and garlic over medium heat until meat is no longer pink; drain. Stir in the tomatoes, tomato sauce, mushrooms, herbs and hot pepper sauce; bring to a boil. Reduce heat; simmer, uncovered, for 20 minutes or until thickened.
4. Loosen one polenta from sides and bottom of dish; invert onto a waxed paper-lined baking sheet and set aside. Spoon half of the meat mixture over the remaining polenta. Sprinkle with half each of the mozzarella and Parmesan cheeses. Top with reserved polenta and remaining meat mixture.
5. Cover and bake at 350° for 40 minutes or until heated through. Uncover; sprinkle with remaining cheese. Bake for 5 minutes longer or until cheese is melted. Let stand for 10 minutes before cutting.

FAVORITE COMPANY CASSEROLE

Even my friends who don't eat a lot of broccoli or mushrooms admit that this casserole is a winner. It's so easy to throw together, and the leftovers are delicious.
—**Suzann Verdun** Lisle, IL

....

Prep: 15 min. • **Bake:** 45 min.
Makes: 8 servings

- 1 package (6 ounces) wild rice, cooked
- 3 cups frozen chopped broccoli, thawed
- 1½ cups cubed cooked chicken
- 1 cup cubed cooked ham
- 1 cup shredded cheddar cheese
- 1 jar (4½ ounces) sliced mushrooms, drained
- 1 cup mayonnaise
- 1 teaspoon prepared mustard
- ½ to 1 teaspoon curry powder
- 1 can (10¾ ounces) condensed cream of mushroom soup, undiluted
- ¼ cup grated Parmesan cheese

1. Preheat oven to 350°. In a greased 2-qt. baking dish, layer the first six ingredients in the order listed. Combine the mayonnaise, mustard, curry powder and soup. Spread over top. Sprinkle with Parmesan cheese.
2. Bake, uncovered, 45-60 minutes or until top is light golden brown.

PASTITSIO

Guests gobble up this authentic Greek beef and pasta casserole. The creamy white sauce is to die for. Try it—I bet you'll agree!
—**Amanda Briggs** Greenfield, WI

....

Prep: 35 min. • **Bake:** 30 min. + standing
Makes: 4 servings

- 1 package (7 ounces) uncooked elbow macaroni
- 1 pound ground beef or lamb
- 1 medium onion, chopped
- 1 garlic clove, minced
- 1 can (8 ounces) tomato sauce
- 1 teaspoon salt, divided
- ¼ teaspoon dried oregano
- ⅛ teaspoon pepper
- ¼ teaspoon ground cinnamon, optional
- ½ cup grated Parmesan cheese, divided
- 3 tablespoons butter
- 3 tablespoons all-purpose flour
- 1½ cups 2% milk
- 1 large egg, lightly beaten

1. Cook macaroni according to package directions. Meanwhile, in a large skillet, cook beef and onion over medium heat until meat is no longer pink. Add garlic; cook 1 minute longer. Drain. Stir in the tomato sauce, ½ teaspoon salt, oregano, pepper and, if desired, cinnamon; heat mixture through.
2. Drain macaroni; place half in a greased 9-in. square baking pan. Sprinkle with ¼ cup cheese. Layer with meat mixture and remaining macaroni. Set aside.
3. Preheat the oven to 350°. In a small saucepan, melt butter; stir in flour and remaining salt until smooth. Gradually add milk. Bring to a boil; cook and stir for 2 minutes or until thickened.
4. Remove from heat. Stir a small amount of the hot mixture into the egg; return all to pan, stirring constantly. Bring to a gentle boil; cook and stir for 2 minutes. Remove from heat; stir in the remaining cheese. Pour sauce over macaroni.
5. Bake, uncovered, 30-35 minutes or until golden brown. Let stand 10 minutes before serving.

SLOW COOKER DINNERS

Looking for comfort food without all the fuss? Low and slow is the way to go! Pull out your old faithful kitchen companion for a perfect all-in-one meal. From classic pot roast to hearty jambalaya, these recipes make it easy to put a home-cooked meal on the table at the end of the day, even when you've been away.

SAUCY CHICKEN THIGHS

Everyone raves about the delectable sauce on these tender slow-cooked chicken thighs. Add your favorite side dish for a terrific meal.
—**Kim Puckett** Reagan, TN

Prep: 20 min. • **Cook:** 4 hours
Makes: 9 servings

- 9 bone-in chicken thighs (about 3¼ pounds)
- ½ teaspoon salt
- ¼ teaspoon pepper
- 1½ cups barbecue sauce
- ½ cup honey
- 2 teaspoons prepared mustard
- 2 teaspoons Worcestershire sauce
- ⅛ to ½ teaspoon hot pepper sauce

1. Sprinkle chicken with salt and pepper. Place on a broiler pan. Broil 4-5 in. from the heat for 3-4 minutes on each side or until lightly browned. Transfer to a 5-qt. slow cooker.
2. In a small bowl, combine the barbecue sauce, honey, mustard, Worcestershire sauce and pepper sauce. Pour over the chicken; stir to coat. Cover and cook on low 4-5 hours or until chicken is tender.

★ ★ ★ ★ ★ **READER REVIEW**
"This is a wonderful weeknight dish. It's great to come home from work and have this all ready to go. I like serving it with rice pilaf. The sauce is so good!"
LVARNER TASTEOFHOME.COM

PORK BURRITOS

As a working mom, I depend on my slow cooker to help feed my family good food. We all love the spicy, slightly sweet flavor of these tender burritos.

—Kelly Gengler Theresa, WI

Prep: 25 min. • **Cook:** 8 hours
Makes: 10 burritos

- 1 boneless pork shoulder butt roast (3 to 4 pounds)
- 1 can (14½ ounces) diced tomatoes with mild green chilies, undrained
- ¼ cup chili powder
- 3 tablespoons minced garlic
- 2 tablespoons lime juice
- 2 tablespoons honey
- 1 tablespoon chopped seeded jalapeno pepper
- 1 teaspoon salt
- 10 flour tortillas (8 inches), warmed
   Sliced avocado, sour cream and minced fresh cilantro, optional

1. Cut pork roast in half; place in a 5-qt. slow cooker. In a blender, combine the tomatoes, chili powder, garlic, lime juice, honey, jalapeno and salt; cover and process until smooth. Pour over pork. Cover and cook on low for 8-10 hours or until meat is tender.

2. Remove roast; cool slightly. Shred pork with two forks and return to slow cooker. Using a slotted spoon, place about ½ cup pork mixture down the center of each tortilla; top with avocado, sour cream and cilantro if desired. Fold sides and ends over filling and roll up.

Freeze option: Omit the avocado, sour cream and cilantro. Individually wrap cooled burritos in paper towels and foil; freeze in a resealable plastic freezer bag. To use, remove the foil; microwave paper towel-wrapped burrito on high for 3-4 minutes or until heated through, turning once. Let stand 20 seconds. If desired, serve with sliced avocado, sour cream and cilantro.

Note: Wear disposable gloves when cutting hot peppers; the oils can burn skin. Avoid touching your face.

SLOW COOKER SAUSAGE LASAGNA

This deep-dish lasagna is especially good on a cold winter day. My family loves mild Italian sausage, but I prefer the spicy version, which gives it a bit more zing.

—Cindi DeClue Anchorage, AK

Prep: 40 min. • **Cook:** 3½ hours + standing
Makes: 8 servings

- 1 pound ground beef
- 1 pound ground mild Italian sausage
- 1 medium onion, finely chopped
- 1 garlic clove, minced
- 1 jar (24 ounces) spaghetti sauce
- 1 can (14½ ounces) diced tomatoes in sauce, undrained
- ½ cup water
- 1 teaspoon dried basil
- 1 teaspoon dried oregano
- 1 carton (15 ounces) whole-milk ricotta cheese
- 2 large eggs, lightly beaten
- ½ cup grated Parmesan cheese
- 9 uncooked lasagna noodles
- 4 cups shredded part-skim mozzarella cheese
   Minced fresh basil, optional

1. Line sides of an oval 6-qt. slow cooker with heavy-duty foil; coat foil with cooking spray. In a Dutch oven, cook beef, sausage, onion and garlic over medium heat for 8-10 minutes or until meat is no longer pink, breaking up beef and sausage into crumbles; drain. Stir in spaghetti sauce, tomatoes, water and herbs; heat through.

2. In a small bowl, mix ricotta, eggs and Parmesan. Spread 1½ cups meat sauce onto bottom of prepared slow cooker. Layer with three noodles (breaking to fit), ¾ cup ricotta mixture, 1 cup mozzarella cheese and 2 cups meat sauce. Repeat layers twice. Sprinkle with remaining mozzarella cheese.

3. Cook, covered, on low for 3½-4 hours or until the noodles are tender. Turn off slow cooker; remove insert. Let stand for 15 minutes. If desired, sprinkle lasagna with fresh basil.

PORK CHILI VERDE

Pork slowly stews with jalapenos, onion, green enchilada sauce and spices in this flavor-packed Mexican dish. It's great on its own or stuffed in a warm tortilla with sour cream, grated cheese or olives on the side.
—**Kimberly Burke** Chico, CA

Prep: 25 min. • **Cook:** 6½ hours
Makes: 8 servings

- 1 boneless pork sirloin roast (3 pounds), cut into 1-inch cubes
- 4 medium carrots, sliced
- 1 medium onion, thinly sliced
- 4 garlic cloves, minced
- 3 tablespoons canola oil
- 1 can (28 ounces) green enchilada sauce
- ¼ cup cold water
- 2 jalapeno peppers, seeded and chopped
- 1 cup minced fresh cilantro
  Hot cooked rice
  Flour tortillas, warmed

In a large skillet, saute the pork, carrots, onion and garlic in oil in batches until pork is browned. Transfer mixture to a 5-qt. slow cooker. Add the enchilada sauce, water, jalapenos and cilantro. Cover and cook on low for 6 hours or until meat is tender. Serve with rice and tortillas.
Note: Wear disposable gloves when cutting hot peppers; the oils can burn skin. Avoid touching your face.

BUSY MOM'S CHICKEN FAJITAS

Staying at home with a 9-month-old makes preparing dinner a challenge, but the slow cooker provides an easy way to make a healthy meal.
—**Sarah Newman** Mahtomedi, MN

Prep: 15 min. • **Cook:** 5 hours
Makes: 6 servings

- 1 pound boneless skinless chicken breast halves
- 1 can (16 ounces) kidney beans, rinsed and drained
- 1 can (14½ ounces) diced tomatoes with mild green chilies, drained
- 1 medium green pepper, julienned
- 1 medium sweet red pepper, julienned
- 1 medium sweet yellow pepper, julienned
- 1 medium onion, halved and sliced
- 2 teaspoons ground cumin
- 2 teaspoons chili powder
- 1 garlic clove, minced
- ¼ teaspoon salt
- 6 flour tortillas (8 inches), warmed
  Shredded lettuce and chopped tomatoes, optional

1. In a 3-qt. slow cooker, combine the first 11 ingredients. Cook, covered, on low until the chicken is tender, 5-6 hours. Remove chicken; cool slightly. Shred and return to slow cooker; heat through.
2. Spoon about ¾ cup chicken mixture down the center of each tortilla. If desired, top with lettuce and tomatoes.

MEAT SAUCE FOR SPAGHETTI

Here's a hearty meat sauce that turns ordinary spaghetti with marinara into a feast. Don't have spaghetti noodles? I've successfully swirled up this sauce with every pasta shape in my pantry.
—**Mary Tallman** Arbor Vitae, WI

Prep: 30 min. • **Cook:** 8 hours
Makes: 9 servings

- 1 pound ground beef
- 1 pound bulk Italian sausage
- 1 can (28 ounces) crushed tomatoes, undrained
- 1 medium green pepper, chopped
- 1 medium onion, chopped
- 2 medium carrots, finely chopped
- 1 cup water
- 1 can (8 ounces) tomato sauce
- 1 can (6 ounces) tomato paste
- 1 tablespoon brown sugar
- 1 tablespoon Italian seasoning
- 2 garlic cloves, minced
- ½ teaspoon salt
- ¼ teaspoon pepper
  Hot cooked spaghetti

1. In a large skillet, cook ground beef and sausage over medium heat until no longer pink; drain.

2. Transfer to a 5-qt. slow cooker. Stir in the tomatoes, green pepper, onion, carrots, water, tomato sauce, tomato paste, brown sugar, Italian seasoning, garlic, salt and pepper. Cover; cook on low for 8-10 hours or until bubbly. Serve with spaghetti.

Freeze option: Do not cook spaghetti. Freeze meat sauce in freezer containers. To use, partially thaw in the refrigerator overnight. Cook spaghetti according to package directions. Place sauce in a large skillet; heat through, stirring occasionally and adding a little water if necessary. Serve over spaghetti.

SLOW-COOKED HEARTY JAMBALAYA

I love anything with Cajun spices, so I came up with this slow-cooker jambalaya that's just as good as restaurant versions. If you can't find andouille sausage, try hot links, smoked sausage or chorizo. I garnish the stew with sliced green onions and serve it with warm cornbread.
—**Jennifer Fulk** Moreno Valley, CA

Prep: 20 min. • **Cook:** 6¼ hours
Makes: 8 servings

- 1 can (28 ounces) diced tomatoes, undrained
- 1 pound fully cooked andouille sausage links, cubed
- ½ pound boneless skinless chicken breasts, cut into 1-inch cubes
- 1 can (8 ounces) tomato sauce
- 1 cup diced onion
- 1 small sweet red pepper, diced
- 1 small green pepper, diced
- 1 cup chicken broth
- 1 celery rib with leaves, chopped
- 2 tablespoons tomato paste
- 2 teaspoons dried oregano
- 2 teaspoons Cajun seasoning
- 1½ teaspoons minced garlic
- 2 bay leaves
- 1 teaspoon Louisiana-style hot sauce
- ½ teaspoon dried thyme
- 1 pound cooked medium shrimp, peeled and deveined
  Hot cooked rice

In a 5-qt. slow cooker, combine the first 16 ingredients. Cover and cook on low for 6-7 hours or until chicken is no longer pink. Stir in shrimp. Cover and cook 15 minutes longer or until heated through. Discard bay leaves. Serve with rice.

SLOW-COOKED VEGETABLE CURRY

Slow cooker recipes get a bad rap for having no flavor. This cozy, spiced-up dish proves that theory wrong.
—**Susan Smith** Mead, WA

Prep: 35 min. • **Cook:** 5 hours
Makes: 6 servings

 1 tablespoon canola oil
 1 medium onion, finely chopped
 4 garlic cloves, minced
 3 teaspoons ground coriander
 1½ teaspoons ground cinnamon
 1 teaspoon ground ginger
 1 teaspoon ground turmeric
 ½ teaspoon cayenne pepper
 2 tablespoons tomato paste
 2 cans (15 ounces each) garbanzo beans or chickpeas, rinsed and drained
 3 cups cubed peeled sweet potatoes (about 1 pound)
 3 cups fresh cauliflower florets (about 8 ounces)
 4 medium carrots, cut into ¾-inch pieces (about 2 cups)
 2 medium tomatoes, seeded and chopped
 2 cups chicken broth
 1 cup light coconut milk
 ½ teaspoon pepper
 ¼ teaspoon salt
   Minced fresh cilantro
   Hot cooked brown rice
   Lime wedges
   Plain yogurt, optional

1. In a large skillet, heat oil over medium heat; saute onion until soft and lightly browned, 5-7 minutes. Add garlic and spices; cook and stir 1 minute. Stir in the tomato paste; cook 1 minute. Transfer to a 5- or 6-qt. slow cooker.
2. Mash 1 can of beans until smooth; add to slow cooker. Stir in remaining beans, vegetables, broth, coconut milk, pepper and salt.
3. Cook, covered, on low until vegetables are tender, 5-6 hours. Sprinkle with the cilantro. Serve with rice, lime wedges and, if desired, yogurt.

POT ROAST WITH GRAVY

It doesn't get much more down-home than pot roast. My family loves this tangy slow-cooked take with its rich onion and mushroom gravy. We even look forward to leftovers.

—Deborah Dailey Vancouver, WA

Prep: 30 min. • **Cook:** 6½ hours
Makes: 10 servings

- 1 beef rump roast or bottom round roast (5 pounds)
- 6 tablespoons balsamic vinegar, divided
- 1 teaspoon salt
- ½ teaspoon garlic powder
- ¼ teaspoon pepper
- 2 tablespoons canola oil
- 3 garlic cloves, minced
- 4 bay leaves
- 1 large onion, thinly sliced
- 3 teaspoons beef bouillon granules
- ½ cup boiling water
- 1 can (10¾ ounces) condensed cream of mushroom soup, undiluted
- 4 to 5 tablespoons cornstarch
- ¼ cup cold water

1. Cut roast in half; rub with 2 tablespoons vinegar. Combine the salt, garlic powder and pepper; rub over the meat. In a large skillet, brown the roast in oil on all sides. Transfer to a 5-qt. slow cooker.

2. Place the garlic, bay leaves and onion on roast. In a small bowl, dissolve bouillon in boiling water; stir in soup and remaining vinegar. Slowly pour over roast. Cover and cook on low for 6-8 hours or until the meat is tender.

3. Remove roast; keep warm. Discard bay leaves. Whisk cornstarch and cold water until smooth; stir into the cooking juices. Cover and cook on high for 30 minutes or until gravy is thickened. Slice roast; return to slow cooker and heat through.

MEATBALLS IN HONEY BUFFALO SAUCE

We declared this recipe an instant favorite for the amazing flavor. The meatballs start sweet but finish with a little heat!

—Anne Ormond Dover, NH

Prep: 45 min. • **Cook:** 2 hours
Makes: about 2½ dozen

- 2 large eggs, lightly beaten
- 15 Ritz crackers, crushed
- ½ medium onion, finely chopped
- ¼ cup 2% milk
- 4 teaspoons brown sugar
- ½ teaspoon garlic powder
- ½ teaspoon ground chipotle pepper
- ¼ teaspoon smoked paprika
- ¼ teaspoon salt
- ⅛ teaspoon pepper
- ½ pound ground beef
- ½ pound ground pork
- ½ pound ground veal

SAUCE
- ½ cup honey
- ¼ cup Buffalo wing sauce
- ¼ cup packed brown sugar
- 2 tablespoons orange marmalade
- 2 tablespoons apricot spreadable fruit
- 2 tablespoons reduced-sodium soy sauce
- ¼ teaspoon crushed red pepper flakes
  Hot cooked rice or pasta
  Sliced celery, optional

1. Preheat oven to 400°. Combine the first 10 ingredients. Add meat; mix lightly but thoroughly. Shape the meat mixture into 1½-in. balls; bake on a greased rack in a 15x10x1-in. baking pan lined with foil until lightly browned, 12-15 minutes. Meanwhile, in a saucepan over medium heat, whisk together sauce ingredients until brown sugar is dissolved.

2. Transfer the meatballs to a 3-qt. slow cooker; add sauce. Cook, covered, on low until meatballs are cooked through, about 2 hours. Serve with hot cooked rice and, if desired, sliced celery.

Freeze option: Freeze cooled meatballs and sauce in freezer containers. To use, partially thaw in refrigerator overnight. Heat through in a covered saucepan, stirring gently and adding a little water or broth if necessary. Serve as directed.

BEEF BRISKET IN BEER

One bite of this tender brisket and your family will be hooked! The rich gravy is perfect for spooning over a side of creamy mashed potatoes.
—**Eunice Stoen** Decorah, IA

Prep: 15 min. • **Cook:** 8 hours
Makes: 6 servings

- 1 fresh beef brisket (2½ to 3 pounds)
- 2 teaspoons liquid smoke, optional
- 1 teaspoon celery salt
- ½ teaspoon pepper
- ¼ teaspoon salt
- 1 large onion, sliced
- 1 can (12 ounces) beer or nonalcoholic beer
- 2 teaspoons Worcestershire sauce
- 2 tablespoons cornstarch
- ¼ cup cold water

1. Cut brisket in half; rub with liquid smoke, if desired, and celery salt, pepper and salt. Place in a 3-qt. slow cooker. Top with sliced onion. Combine the beer and Worcestershire sauce; pour over meat. Cover and cook on low for 8-9 hours or until tender.

2. Remove brisket and keep warm. Strain the cooking juices; transfer to a saucepan. In a small bowl, combine cornstarch and water until smooth; stir into juices. Bring to a boil; cook and stir for 2 minutes or until thickened. Serve beef with gravy.

TEST KITCHEN TIP
Liquid smoke is a great addition to this recipe, as it adds a nice depth of flavor. Be careful not to overdo it; a very small amount goes a long way. Look for liquid smoke in the grocery store near the spices and marinades.

SWEET & TANGY CHICKEN

If you need an easy dish for a casual dinner party, this is just the thing. Spicy barbecue sauce blends with sweet pineapple for a crowd-pleasing entree.
—**Mary Zawlocki** Gig Harbor, WA

Prep: 10 min. • **Cook:** 5 hours
Makes: 8 servings

- 8 boneless skinless chicken breast halves (4 ounces each)
- 1 bottle (18 ounces) barbecue sauce
- 1 can (20 ounces) pineapple chunks, undrained
- 1 medium green pepper, chopped
- 1 medium onion, chopped
- 2 garlic cloves, minced
     Hot cooked rice

1. Place four chicken breasts in a 5-qt. slow cooker. Combine the barbecue sauce, pineapple, green pepper, onion and garlic; pour half over the chicken. Top with the remaining chicken and sauce.

2. Cover and cook on low until chicken is 165°, about 5 hours. Thicken sauce if desired. Serve the chicken and sauce with hot cooked rice.

DID YOU KNOW?

The United States Department of Agriculture advises against washing or rinsing chicken before cooking, as it can cause bacteria to spread to kitchen surfaces and utensils and contaminate other foods.

(5) INGREDIENTS

SLOW COOKER KALUA PORK & CABBAGE

My slow cooker pork has four ingredients and takes less than 10 minutes to prep. The result tastes just like the kalua pork made in Hawaii that's slow roasted all day in an underground oven.
—**Rholinelle DeTorres** San Jose, CA

Prep: 10 min. • **Cook:** 9 hours
Makes: 12 servings

- 7 bacon strips, divided
- 1 boneless pork shoulder butt roast (3 to 4 pounds), well trimmed
- 1 tablespoon coarse sea salt
- 1 medium head cabbage (about 2 pounds), coarsely chopped

1. Line bottom of a 6-qt. slow cooker with four bacon strips. Sprinkle all sides of roast with salt; place in slow cooker. Arrange the remaining bacon over top of roast.
2. Cook, covered, on low for 8-10 hours or until the pork is tender. Add cabbage, spreading it around roast. Cook, covered, 1-1¼ hours or until cabbage is tender.
3. Remove pork to a serving bowl; shred with two forks. Using a slotted spoon, add cabbage to pork and toss to combine. If desired, skim fat from some of the cooking juices; stir juices into pork mixture or serve on the side.

APPLE & ONION BEEF POT ROAST

I thicken the cooking juices from this roast to make a pleasing apple gravy that's wonderful over the beef and onions.
—**Rachel Koistinen** Hayti, SD

Prep: 30 min. • **Cook:** 5 hours + standing
Makes: 8 servings

- 1 beef sirloin tip roast (3 pounds), cut in half
- 1 cup water
- 1 teaspoon seasoned salt
- ½ teaspoon reduced-sodium soy sauce
- ½ teaspoon Worcestershire sauce
- ¼ teaspoon garlic powder
- 1 large tart apple, quartered
- 1 large onion, sliced
- 2 tablespoons cornstarch
- 2 tablespoons cold water
- ⅛ teaspoon browning sauce

1. In a large nonstick skillet coated with cooking spray, brown roast on all sides. Transfer to a 5-qt. slow cooker. Add water to skillet, stirring to loosen any browned bits; pour over the roast. Sprinkle with seasoned salt, soy sauce, Worcestershire sauce and garlic powder. Top with apple and onion.
2. Cover and cook on low for 5-6 hours or until the meat is tender.
3. Remove roast and onion; let stand for 15 minutes before slicing. Strain cooking liquid into a saucepan, discarding apple. Bring liquid to a boil; cook until reduced to 2 cups, about 15 minutes. Combine cornstarch and cold water until smooth; stir in browning sauce. Stir into cooking liquid. Bring to a boil; cook and stir for 2 minutes or until thickened. Serve with beef and onion.

SECRET'S IN THE SAUCE BBQ RIBS

Slow cooking makes these ribs so tender the meat literally falls off the bones. And the sweet, rich sauce is simply wonderful.

—**Tanya Reid** Winston Salem, NC

Prep: 10 min. • **Cook:** 6 hours
Makes: 5 servings

4½ pounds pork baby back ribs
1½ teaspoons pepper
2½ cups barbecue sauce
¾ cup cherry preserves
1 tablespoon Dijon mustard
1 garlic clove, minced

Cut ribs into serving-size pieces; sprinkle with pepper. Place in a 5- or 6-qt. slow cooker. Combine remaining ingredients; pour over ribs. Cover and cook on low for 6-8 hours or until meat is tender. Serve with sauce.

FRENCH BEEF STEW

When it comes to making a thick and hearty beef stew, I let my slow cooker do the work for me. Once it's done simmering, I toss together a green salad and slice some bread, and dinner is ready!

—**Iola Egle** Bella Vista, AR

Prep: 20 min. • **Cook:** 9 hours
Makes: 8-10 servings

3 medium potatoes, peeled and cubed
2 pounds beef stew meat
4 medium carrots, sliced
2 medium onions, sliced
3 celery ribs, sliced
2 cups tomato juice
1 cup water
⅓ cup quick-cooking tapioca
1 tablespoon sugar
1 tablespoon salt
1 teaspoon dried basil
½ teaspoon pepper

1. Place the cubed potatoes in a greased 5-qt. slow cooker. Top with the stew meat, carrots, onions and celery. In a large bowl, combine the remaining ingredients. Pour over the vegetables.
2. Cover and cook on low for 9-10 hours or until meat and vegetables are tender.

BBQ CHICKEN & SMOKED SAUSAGE

My barbecue recipe works equally great for parties and weeknights dinners. With just a few minutes of prep time, you get that low-and-slow flavor folks crave. Throw in some minced jalapenos for extra oomph.

—**Kimberly Young** Mesquite, TX

Prep: 30 min. • **Cook:** 4 hours
Makes: 8 servings

1 medium onion, chopped
1 large sweet red pepper, cut into 1-inch pieces
4 bone-in chicken thighs, skin removed
4 chicken drumsticks, skin removed
1 package (12 ounces) smoked sausage links, cut into 1-inch pieces
1 cup barbecue sauce
 Sliced seeded jalapeno pepper, optional

1. Place first five ingredients in a 4 or 5-qt. slow cooker; top with barbecue sauce. Cook, covered, on low until chicken is tender and a thermometer inserted in chicken reads at least 170°, 4-5 hours.
2. Remove the chicken, sausage and vegetables from slow cooker; keep warm. Transfer cooking juices to a saucepan; bring to a boil. Reduce heat and simmer, uncovered, until thickened, 15-20 minutes, stirring occasionally.
3. Serve chicken, sausage and vegetables with sauce. If desired, top with jalapeno.
Health tip: Swap smoked turkey sausage for regular smoked sausage to lighten up this dish. Serve with hot cooked rice and steamed green beans for a complete meal.

SLOW COOKER TURKEY PESTO LASAGNA

My cheesy lasagna makes any slow cooker skeptic a believer. I'll usually bring more pesto and marinara to the table for our resident sauce lovers.

—Blair Lonergan Rochelle, VA

Prep: 25 min. • **Cook:** 3 hours + standing
Makes: 8 servings

- 1 **pound ground turkey**
- 1 **small onion, chopped**
- 2 **teaspoons Italian seasoning**
- ½ **teaspoon salt**
- 2 **cups shredded part-skim mozzarella cheese, divided**
- 1 **container (15 ounces) whole-milk ricotta cheese**
- ¼ **cup prepared pesto**
- 1 **jar (24 ounces) marinara sauce**
- 9 **no-cook lasagna noodles**
  Grated Parmesan cheese

1. Cut three 25x3-in. strips of heavy-duty foil; crisscross so they resemble spokes of a wheel. Place strips on bottom and up sides of a greased 5-qt. slow cooker. Coat strips with cooking spray.

2. In a large skillet, cook turkey and onion over medium heat 6-8 minutes or until the turkey is no longer pink, breaking up turkey into crumbles; drain. Stir in the Italian seasoning and salt.

3. In a small bowl, mix 1 cup mozzarella cheese, ricotta and pesto. In prepared slow cooker, layer a third of each of the following: marinara sauce, noodles (breaking noodles if necessary to fit), turkey mixture and cheese mixture. Repeat layers twice. Sprinkle with the remaining mozzarella cheese.

4. Cook, covered, on low until noodles are tender, 3-4 hours. Turn off the slow cooker; remove the insert. Let stand, uncovered, 30 minutes before serving. Using foil strips, remove the lasagna to a platter. Serve with Parmesan cheese.

FABULOUS FAJITAS

I've enjoyed cooking since I was a young girl growing up in the Southwest. When friends ask me for new recipes, I suggest these flavorful fajitas. It's great being able to put the beef in the slow cooker before church and come home to a hot, delicious meal.

—**Janie Reitz** Rochester, MN

Prep: 20 min. • **Cook:** 3 hours
Makes: 8 servings

- 1½ pounds beef top sirloin steak, cut into thin strips
- 2 tablespoons canola oil
- 2 tablespoons lemon juice
- 1 garlic clove, minced
- 1½ teaspoons ground cumin
- 1 teaspoon seasoned salt
- ½ teaspoon chili powder
- ¼ to ½ teaspoon crushed red pepper flakes
- 1 large sweet red pepper, julienned
- 1 large onion, julienned
- 8 mini flour tortillas (5 inches)
  Optional toppings: shredded cheddar cheese, fresh cilantro leaves, sliced jalapeno pepper and avocado

1. In a large skillet, brown steak in oil over medium heat. Place steak and drippings in a 3-qt. slow cooker. Stir in the lemon juice, garlic, cumin, salt, chili powder and red pepper flakes.

2. Cover and cook on high until meat is almost tender, 2 hours. Add red pepper and onion; cover and cook until meat and vegetables are tender, 1 hour.

3. Warm tortillas according to package directions; spoon beef and vegetables down the center. Top as desired.

HEARTY NEW ENGLAND DINNER

This favorite slow cooker recipe came from a friend. At first, my husband was a bit skeptical about a roast that wasn't made in the oven, but he loves the old-fashioned goodness of this version. The horseradish in the gravy is a nice touch.

—**Claire McCombs** San Diego, CA

Prep: 20 min. • **Cook:** 7½ hours
Makes: 6-8 servings

- 2 medium carrots, sliced
- 1 medium onion, sliced
- 1 celery rib, sliced
- 1 boneless beef chuck roast (about 3 pounds)
- 1 teaspoon salt, divided
- ¼ teaspoon pepper
- 1 envelope onion soup mix
- 2 cups water
- 1 tablespoon white vinegar
- 1 bay leaf
- ½ small head cabbage, cut into wedges
- 3 tablespoons butter
- 2 tablespoons all-purpose flour
- 1 tablespoon dried minced onion
- 2 tablespoons prepared horseradish

1. Place the carrots, onion and celery in a 5-qt. slow cooker. Cut the roast in half. Place roast over vegetables; sprinkle with ½ teaspoon salt and pepper. Add the soup mix, water, vinegar and bay leaf. Cover and cook on low for 7-9 hours or until the beef is tender.

2. Remove beef and keep warm; discard the bay leaf. Add cabbage. Cover and cook on high for 30-40 minutes or until cabbage is tender.

3. Meanwhile, melt the butter in a small saucepan; stir in flour and onion. Skim fat from cooking liquid in slow cooker. Add 1½ cups cooking liquid to the saucepan. Stir in the horseradish and remaining salt; bring to a boil. Cook and stir for 2 minutes or until thickened and bubbly. Serve with roast and vegetables.

MEAT LOAF FROM THE SLOW COOKER

This simple, easy-to-make meat loaf is one of my personal favorites. I'm often asked for the recipe.

—Laura Burgess Mount Vernon, SD

Prep: 25 min. • **Cook:** 3 hours
Makes: 8 servings

- ½ cup tomato sauce
- 2 large eggs, lightly beaten
- ¼ cup ketchup
- 1 teaspoon Worcestershire sauce
- 1 small onion, chopped
- ⅓ cup crushed saltines
  (about 10 crackers)
- ¾ teaspoon minced garlic
- ¼ teaspoon seasoned salt
- ⅛ teaspoon seasoned pepper
- 1½ pounds lean ground beef (90% lean)
- ½ pound reduced-fat bulk pork sausage

SAUCE
- ½ cup ketchup
- 3 tablespoons brown sugar
- ¾ teaspoon ground mustard
- ¼ teaspoon ground nutmeg

1. Cut three 25x3-in. strips of heavy-duty foil; crisscross so they resemble spokes of a wheel. Place strips on the bottom and up the sides of a 4- or 5-qt. slow cooker. Coat strips with cooking spray.
2. In a large bowl, combine the first nine ingredients. Crumble beef and sausage over mixture and mix well (mixture will be moist). Shape into a loaf. Place meat loaf in the center of the strips.
3. In a small bowl, combine the sauce ingredients. Spoon over meat loaf. Cover and cook on low 3-4 hours or until no pink remains and a thermometer reads 160°. Using foil strips as handles, remove the meat loaf to a platter.

TEST KITCHEN TIP
When making meat loaf, start by combining all of the ingredients except the ground meat. This will allow you to distribute the seasonings more evenly without much effort.

SLOW COOKER ROAST CHICKEN

Tender roasted chicken is easy to make in a slow cooker. I shred some and save it in the freezer to use on busy nights.

—**Courtney Stultz** Weir, KS

Prep: 20 min. • **Cook:** 4 hours + standing
Makes: 6 servings

- 2 medium carrots, cut into 1-inch pieces
- 1 medium onion, cut into 1-inch pieces
- 2 garlic cloves, minced
- 2 teaspoons olive oil
- 1 teaspoon dried parsley flakes
- 1 teaspoon pepper
- ¾ teaspoon salt
- ½ teaspoon dried oregano
- ½ teaspoon rubbed sage
- ½ teaspoon chili powder
- 1 broiler/fryer chicken (4 to 5 pounds)

1. Place carrots and onion in a 6-qt. slow cooker. In a small bowl, mix garlic and oil. In another bowl, mix dry seasonings.
2. Tuck the wings under the chicken; tie drumsticks together. Carefully loosen skin from chicken breast with fingers; rub garlic mixture under the skin. Secure skin to the underside of breast with toothpicks.
3. Place chicken in slow cooker over the carrots and onions, breast side up; sprinkle with seasoning mixture. Cook, covered, on low 4-5 hours (a thermometer inserted in thigh should read at least 170°).
4. Remove chicken from slow cooker; tent with foil. Discard vegetables. Let chicken stand 15 minutes before carving.

SLOW COOKER TAMALE PIE

Canned beans and cornbread/muffin mix speed up the prep on this popular main dish. It's perfect for busy evenings and carry-in dinners.
—**Jill Pokrivka** York, PA

Prep: 25 min. • **Cook:** 7 hours
Makes: 8 servings

- 1 pound ground beef
- 1 teaspoon ground cumin
- ½ teaspoon salt
- ½ teaspoon chili powder
- ¼ teaspoon pepper
- 1 can (15 ounces) black beans, rinsed and drained
- 1 can (14½ ounces) diced tomatoes with mild green chilies, undrained
- 1 can (11 ounces) whole kernel corn, drained
- 1 can (10 ounces) enchilada sauce
- 2 green onions, chopped
- ¼ cup minced fresh cilantro
- 1 package (8½ ounces) cornbread/muffin mix
- 2 large eggs
- 1 cup shredded Mexican cheese blend
  Sour cream and additional minced fresh cilantro, optional

1. In a large skillet, cook beef over medium heat until no longer pink; drain. Stir in cumin, salt, chili powder and pepper.
2. Transfer to a 4-qt. slow cooker; stir in the beans, tomatoes, corn, enchilada sauce, onions and cilantro. Cover and cook on low for 6-8 hours or until mixture is heated through.
3. In a small bowl, combine cornbread mix and eggs; spoon over meat mixture. Cover and cook 1 hour longer or until a toothpick inserted in the center comes out clean.
4. Sprinkle with cheese; cover and let stand 5 minutes. Serve with sour cream and additional cilantro if desired.

SLOW COOKER PIZZA

Always a hit at our church dinners, this hearty casserole keeps folks coming back for more. You can't lose with pizza fixings.
—**Julie Sterchi** Jackson, Missouri

Prep: 20 min. • **Cook:** 2 hours
Makes: 6 servings

- 1 package (16 ounces) wide egg noodles
- 1½ pounds ground beef or turkey
- ¼ cup chopped onion
- 1 jar (26 ounces) spaghetti sauce
- 1 jar (4½ ounces) sliced mushrooms, drained
- 1½ teaspoon Italian seasoning
- 1 package (3½ ounces) sliced pepperoni, halved
- 3 cups shredded part-skim mozzarella cheese
- 3 cups shredded cheddar cheese

1. Cook noodles according to package directions. Meanwhile, in a large skillet, cook beef and onion over medium heat until meat is no longer pink; drain. Stir in the spaghetti sauce, mushrooms and Italian seasoning. Drain noodles.
2. In a 5-qt. slow cooker coated with cooking spray, spread a third of the meat sauce. Cover with a third each of the noodles and pepperoni. Sprinkle with a third of the cheese. Repeat layers twice. Press down to compact.
3. Cover; cook on low 2-3 hours or until heated through and cheese is melted.

STUFFED CHICKEN ROLLS

Just thinking about this dish sparks my appetite. The ham and cheese rolled inside make a tasty surprise, and it's especially nice served over rice or pasta.

—**Jean Sherwood** Kenneth City, FL

Prep: 25 min. + chilling • **Cook:** 4 hours
Makes: 6 servings

- 6 boneless skinless chicken breast halves (8 ounces each)
- 6 slices fully cooked ham
- 6 slices Swiss cheese
- ¼ cup all-purpose flour
- ¼ cup grated Parmesan cheese
- ½ teaspoon rubbed sage
- ¼ teaspoon paprika
- ¼ teaspoon pepper
- ¼ cup canola oil
- 1 can (10¾ ounces) condensed cream of chicken soup, undiluted
- ½ cup chicken broth
  Chopped fresh parsley, optional

1. Flatten chicken to ¼-in. thickness; top with ham and cheese. Roll up and tuck in ends; secure with toothpicks.
2. In a shallow bowl, combine the flour, cheese, sage, paprika and pepper; coat chicken on all sides. In a large skillet, brown chicken in oil over medium-high heat.
3. Transfer to a 5-qt. slow cooker. Combine soup and broth; pour over top. Cover and cook on low for 4-5 hours or until chicken is tender. Remove toothpicks. Garnish with parsley if desired.
Freeze option: Cool chicken. Freeze in freezer containers. To use, partially thaw in refrigerator overnight. Heat through slowly in a covered skillet, stirring occasionally, until a thermometer inserted in chicken reads 165°.

BBQ CHICKEN BAKED POTATOES

These baked potatoes boast a smoky barbecue flavor that will make your mouth water. Top them with your favorite cheese and garnishes. With so much heartiness, they're practically meals in themselves!

—**Amber Massey** Argyle, TX

Prep: 15 min. • **Cook:** 6 hours
Makes: 10 servings

- 4½ pounds bone-in chicken breast halves, skin removed
- 2 tablespoons garlic powder
- 1 large red onion, sliced into thick rings
- 1 bottle (18 ounces) honey barbecue sauce
- 1 cup Italian salad dressing
- ½ cup packed brown sugar
- ½ cup cider vinegar
- ¼ cup Worcestershire sauce
- 2 tablespoons liquid smoke, optional
- 10 medium potatoes, baked
  Crumbled blue cheese and chopped green onions, optional

1. Place chicken in a greased 5- or 6-qt. slow cooker; sprinkle with garlic powder and top with onion. Combine the barbecue sauce, salad dressing, brown sugar, cider vinegar, Worcestershire sauce and liquid smoke if desired; pour over chicken.
2. Cover and cook on low for 6-8 hours or until chicken is tender. When cool enough to handle, remove chicken from bones; discard bones and onion. Skim fat from cooking juices.
3. Shred meat with two forks and return to slow cooker; heat through. Serve with potatoes and, if desired, blue cheese and green onions.

✱

TEST KITCHEN TIP

To prepare potatoes for baking, scrub with a vegetable brush under cold water. Remove eyes or sprouts. When working with lots of potatoes, peel and place in cold water to prevent discoloration. Before baking a whole potato, pierce with a fork.

SLOW-COOKED MESQUITE RIBS

When we're missing the grill during winter, these tangy ribs give us that same smoky barbecue taste we love. They're simple to make and fall-off-the-bone delicious.
—**Sue Evans** Marquette, MI

Prep: 10 min. • **Cook:** 6½ hours
Makes: 8 servings

- 1 cup water
- 2 tablespoons cider vinegar
- 1 tablespoon soy sauce
- 2 tablespoons mesquite seasoning
- 4 pounds pork baby back ribs, cut into serving-size portions
- ½ cup barbecue sauce

1. In a 6-qt. slow cooker, mix the water, cider vinegar and soy sauce. Rub ribs with mesquite seasoning; place in slow cooker.
2. Cook, covered, on low until tender, 6-8 hours. Remove ribs to a platter. Brush with barbecue sauce; return to the slow cooker. Cook, covered, on low until ribs are glazed, about 30 minutes.

BEEF IN ONION GRAVY

We have a family of four, but I double this recipe so I have leftovers to send with my husband to work. His coworkers tell him he's lucky to have someone who fixes him such special meals. It's our secret that it's an easy slow cooker dinner!
—**Denise Albers** Freeburg, IL

Prep: 5 min. + standing • **Cook:** 6 hours
Makes: 3 servings

- 1 can (10¾ ounces) condensed cream of mushroom soup, undiluted
- 2 tablespoons onion soup mix
- 2 tablespoons beef broth
- 1 tablespoon quick-cooking tapioca
- 1 pound beef stew meat, cut into 1-inch cubes
  Hot cooked noodles or mashed potatoes

In a 1½-qt. slow cooker, combine the soup, soup mix, broth and tapioca; let stand for 15 minutes. Stir in the stew meat. Cover and cook on low for 6-8 hours or until meat is tender. Serve over noodles or mashed potatoes.

BEER-BRAISED PULLED HAM

To jazz up leftover ham, I slow cook it with a beer sauce. Buns loaded with ham, pickles and mustard are irresistible.
—**Ann Sheehy** Lawrence, MA

Prep: 10 min.
Cook: 7 hours
Makes: 16 servings

- 2 bottles (12 ounces each) beer or nonalcoholic beer
- ¾ cup German or Dijon mustard, divided
- ½ teaspoon coarsely ground pepper
- 1 fully cooked bone-in ham (about 4 pounds)
- 4 fresh rosemary sprigs
- 16 pretzel hamburger buns, split
  Dill pickle slices, optional

1. In a 5-qt. slow cooker, whisk together beer and ½ cup mustard. Stir in pepper. Add ham and rosemary. Cook, covered, on low until tender, 7-9 hours.
2. Remove ham; cool slightly. Discard rosemary sprigs. Skim fat. When ham is cool enough to handle, shred meat with two forks. Discard bone. Return to slow cooker; heat through.
3. Using tongs, place shredded ham on pretzel buns; top with remaining mustard and, if desired, dill pickle slices.
Freeze option: Freeze cooled ham mixture in freezer containers. To use, partially thaw in refrigerator overnight. Heat through in a covered saucepan, stirring gently and adding a little water if necessary.

PENNSYLVANIA POT ROAST

This heartwarming one-dish meal is adapted from a Pennsylvania Dutch recipe. I get the pot roast cooking before I leave for church, toss in the vegetables when I get home, and then just sit back and relax until it's done.
—**Donna Wilkinson** Monrovia, MD

Prep: 10 min. • **Cook:** 5 hours
Makes: 6 servings

- 1 boneless pork shoulder butt roast (2½ to 3 pounds), halved
- 1½ cups beef broth
- ½ cup sliced green onions
- 1 teaspoon dried basil
- 1 teaspoon dried marjoram
- ½ teaspoon salt
- ½ teaspoon pepper
- 1 bay leaf
- 6 medium red potatoes, cut into 2-inch chunks
- 4 medium carrots, cut into 2-inch chunks
- 7 to 8 fresh mushrooms, quartered
- ¼ cup all-purpose flour
- ½ cup cold water
   Browning sauce, optional

1. Place roast in a 5-qt. slow cooker; add the broth, onions and seasonings. Cook, covered, on high for 4 hours. Add the potatoes, carrots and mushrooms. Cook, covered, on high 1 hour longer or until vegetables are tender. Remove meat and vegetables; keep warm. Discard bay leaf.
2. In a medium saucepan, combine the flour and cold water until smooth; stir in 1½ cups cooking juices. Bring to a boil. Cook and stir for 2 minutes or until thickened. Add the browning sauce if desired. Serve with roast and vegetables.

CINCINNATI CHILI DOGS

My in-laws are from Ohio, so we have Cincinnati chili at many of our family gatherings. I spiced up this family classic with cinnamon and cocoa powder and ladled it over hot dogs. It's perfect for game day, tailgates and potlucks.
—**Jennifer Gilbert** Brighton, MI

Prep: 20 min. • **Cook:** 4 hours
Makes: 10 servings

- 1½ pounds ground beef
- 2 small yellow onions, chopped and divided
- 2 cans (15 ounces each) tomato sauce
- 1½ teaspoons baking cocoa
- ½ teaspoon ground cinnamon
- ¼ teaspoon chili powder
- ¼ teaspoon paprika
- ¼ teaspoon garlic powder
- 2 tablespoons Worcestershire sauce
- 1 tablespoon cider vinegar
- 10 hot dogs
- 10 hot dog buns, split
   Shredded cheddar cheese

1. In a large skillet over medium heat, cook and stir ground beef, crumbling meat, until no longer pink; drain.
2. In a 3-qt. slow cooker, combine beef with one chopped onion; add next eight ingredients. Cook, covered, on low for about 2 hours; add hot dogs. Continue cooking, covered, on low until heated through, about 2 hours longer.
3. Serve on buns; top with shredded cheese and remaining chopped onion.

SLOW COOKER BARBACOA

My husband adores this roast. I serve it over rice flavored with cilantro and lime.
—**Aundrea McCormick** Denver, CO

Prep: 45 min. • **Cook:** 7 hours
Makes: 8 servings

- ¼ cup lime juice
- ¼ cup cider vinegar
- 3 chipotle peppers in adobo sauce
- 4 garlic cloves, thinly sliced
- 4 teaspoons ground cumin
- 3 teaspoons dried oregano
- 1½ teaspoons pepper
- ¾ teaspoon salt
- ½ teaspoon ground cloves
- 1 cup reduced-sodium chicken broth
- 1 boneless beef chuck roast (3 to 4 pounds)
- 3 bay leaves

RICE

- 3 cups water
- 2 cups uncooked jasmine rice, rinsed and drained
- 3 tablespoons butter
- 1½ teaspoons salt
- ½ cup minced fresh cilantro
- 2 tablespoons lime juice

1. Place first nine ingredients in a blender; cover and process until smooth. Add the broth; pulse to combine.
2. Place roast and bay leaves in a 4- or 5-qt. slow cooker; pour sauce over top. Cook, covered, on low 7-9 hours or until meat is tender.
3. Prepare rice about 30 minutes before serving. In a large saucepan, combine water, rice, butter and salt; bring to a boil. Reduce heat and simmer, covered, for 12-15 minutes or until liquid is absorbed and rice is tender. Remove from heat; gently stir in cilantro and lime juice.
4. Remove roast from slow cooker; cool slightly. Discard bay leaves and skim fat from cooking juices. Shred beef with two forks; return to slow cooker. Serve roast with rice.

SLOW COOKER SWEET-AND-SOUR PORK

We love Chinese takeout, and it's tempting to place an order whenever the craving calls. So I decided to lighten up one of our favorite dishes. As the pork cooks, the aroma is beyond mouthwatering.
—**Elyse Ellis** Layton, UT

Prep: 15 min. • **Cook:** 6¼ hours
Makes: 4 servings

- ½ cup sugar
- ½ cup packed brown sugar
- ½ cup chicken broth
- ⅓ cup white vinegar
- 3 tablespoons lemon juice
- 3 tablespoons reduced-sodium soy sauce
- 3 tablespoons tomato paste
- ½ teaspoon garlic powder
- ¼ teaspoon ground ginger
- ¼ teaspoon pepper
- 1½ pounds boneless pork loin chops, cut into 1-inch cubes
- 1 large onion, cut into 1-inch pieces
- 1 large green pepper, cut into 1-inch pieces
- 1 can (8 ounces) pineapple chunks, drained
- 3 tablespoons cornstarch
- ⅓ cup chicken broth
  Hot cooked rice

1. In a 3- or 4-qt. slow cooker, mix first 10 ingredients. Stir in pork, onion, green pepper and pineapple. Cook, covered, on low 6-8 hours or until pork is tender.
2. In a small bowl, mix the cornstarch and chicken broth until smooth; gradually stir into cooking juices. Cook, covered, on low 15-20 minutes longer or until the sauce is thickened. Serve with rice.

To make ahead: In a large resealable plastic freezer bag, combine first 10 ingredients. Add cubed pork, onion, green pepper and pineapple; seal bag, turn to coat, then freeze. To use, place filled freezer bag in refrigerator for 48 hours or until contents are completely thawed. Cook as directed.

BREADS
& ROLLS

Quick breads, yeast breads, muffins, rolls, biscuits and even pizza dough—nothing says home cooking like homemade breads. Whether you're making breakfast, lunch or dinner, treat your family to the mouthwatering aromas of fresh-baked bread!

HONEY CORNBREAD

It's a pleasure to serve this cornbread to family and guests. Honey gives it a slightly sweet taste. Most people find it's difficult to eat just one piece.
—Adeline Piscitelli Sayreville, NJ

....

Start to Finish: 30 min.
Makes: 9 servings

1	cup all-purpose flour
1	cup yellow cornmeal
¼	cup sugar
3	teaspoons baking powder
½	teaspoon salt
2	large eggs
1	cup heavy whipping cream
¼	cup canola oil
¼	cup honey

1. Preheat oven to 400°. Combine flour, cornmeal, sugar, baking powder and salt. In a small bowl, beat the eggs. Add cream, oil and honey; beat well. stir into the dry ingredients just until moistened. Pour into a greased 9-in. square baking pan.
2. Bake for 20-25 minutes or until a toothpick inserted in the center comes out clean. Serve warm.

★ ★ ★ ★ ★ **READER REVIEW**

"Excellent. My family loved this cornbread. I baked it as muffins, and they took about 12 minutes."

MRPINTER TASTEOFHOME.COM

PUMPKIN KNOT ROLLS

These rolls are the lightest, most delicious ones I've ever tasted...and everyone else seems to agree. The pumpkin gives them mild flavor, moist texture and a pretty golden color.

—**Dianna Shimizu** Issaquah, WA

Prep: 30 min. + rising • **Bake:** 15 min.
Makes: 2 dozen

- 2 packages (¼ ounce each) active dry yeast
- 1 cup warm whole milk (110° to 115°)
- ⅓ cup butter, softened
- ½ cup sugar
- 1 cup canned pumpkin
- 3 large eggs
- 1½ teaspoons salt
- 5½ to 6 cups all-purpose flour
- 1 tablespoon cold water
  Sesame or poppy seeds, optional

1. In a bowl, dissolve yeast in warm milk. Add the butter, sugar, pumpkin, 2 eggs, salt and 3 cups flour. Beat until smooth. Stir in enough remaining flour to form a soft dough. Turn onto a lightly floured surface; knead until smooth and elastic, 6-8 minutes. Place in a greased bowl, turning once to grease top. Cover and let rise in a warm place until doubled, about 1 hour.

2. Punch dough down. Turn onto a lightly floured surface; divide in half. Shape each portion into 12 balls. Roll each ball into a 10-in. rope; tie into a knot and tuck ends under. Place 2 in. apart on greased baking sheets. Cover and let rise until doubled, about 30 minutes.

3. In a small bowl, beat water and the remaining egg. Brush over rolls. Sprinkle with sesame or poppy seeds if desired. Bake at 350° for 15-17 minutes or until golden brown. Remove from pans to wire racks to cool.

SALLY LUNN BATTER BREAD

The tantalizing aroma when this golden loaf is baking always draws people into my mother's kitchen. With its circular shape, it's a pretty bread, too. I've never seen it last more than a day or two once it's out of the oven!

—**Jeanne Voss** Anaheim Hills, CA

Prep: 15 min. + rising • **Bake:** 25 min.
Makes: 12-16 servings

- 1 package (¼ ounce) active dry yeast
- ½ cup warm water (110° to 115°)
- 1 cup warm whole milk (110° to 115°)
- ½ cup butter, softened
- ¼ cup sugar
- 2 teaspoon salt
- 3 large eggs
- 5½ to 6 cups all-purpose flour

HONEY BUTTER
- ½ cup butter, softened
- ½ cup honey

1. In a large bowl, dissolve yeast in warm water. Add the milk, butter, sugar, salt, eggs and 3 cups flour; beat until smooth. Stir in enough remaining flour to form a soft dough.

2. Do not knead. Place in a greased bowl, turning once to grease the top. Cover and let rise in a warm place until doubled, about 1 hour.

3. Stir the dough down. Spoon into a greased and floured 10-in. tube pan. Cover and let rise until doubled, about 1 hour.

4. Bake at 400° for 25-30 minutes or until golden brown. Remove from pan to a wire rack to cool.

5. Combine the honey butter ingredients until smooth. Serve with bread.

PINA COLADA ZUCCHINI BREAD

At my husband's urging, I entered this recipe at the Pennsylvania Farm Show. It won first place! I think you'll love the cake-like texture and tropical flavors.
—**Sharon Rydbom** Tipton, PA

Prep: 25 min. • **Bake:** 45 min. + cooling
Makes: 3 loaves (12 slices each)

- 4 cups all-purpose flour
- 3 cups sugar
- 2 teaspoons baking powder
- 1½ teaspoons salt
- 1 teaspoon baking soda
- 4 large eggs
- 1½ cups canola oil
- 1 teaspoon each coconut, rum and vanilla extracts
- 3 cups shredded zucchini
- 1 cup canned crushed pineapple, drained
- ½ cup chopped walnuts or chopped pecans

1. Preheat oven to 350°. Line the bottoms of three greased and floured 8x4-in. loaf pans with waxed paper and grease the paper; set aside.
2. In a large bowl, combine the flour, sugar, baking powder, salt and baking soda. In another bowl, whisk the eggs, oil and extracts. Stir into the dry ingredients just until moistened. Fold in the zucchini, pineapple and walnuts.
3. Transfer to prepared pans. Bake for 45-55 minutes or until a toothpick inserted in the center comes out clean. Cool for 10 minutes before removing from pans to wire racks. Gently remove waxed paper.

CREAM-FILLED CHOCOLATE SUPREME MUFFINS

My mom earned quite the reputation as a baker. She used to sell muffins at my dad's workplace. Among my favorites were these cupcake-like treats.
—**Susanne Spicker** North Ogden, UT

Prep: 30 min. • **Bake:** 25 min. + cooling
Makes: 1 dozen

- 3 cups all-purpose flour
- 2 cups sugar
- ½ cup baking cocoa
- 2 teaspoons baking soda
- 1 teaspoon salt
- 2 cups cold water
- ¾ cup canola oil
- 1 large egg
- 2 tablespoons white vinegar
- 2 teaspoons vanilla extract

FILLING
- 4 ounces cream cheese, softened
- ¼ cup sugar
- ⅛ teaspoon salt
- 2 tablespoons beaten egg
- ½ teaspoon vanilla extract
- ¾ cup milk chocolate chips
  Confectioners' sugar, optional

1. Preheat oven to 350°. In a large bowl, combine flour, sugar, cocoa, baking soda and salt. In another bowl, combine water, oil, egg, vinegar and vanilla. Stir into the dry ingredients just until moistened.
2. For filling, beat cream cheese, sugar and salt until smooth. Beat in egg and vanilla. Fold in chips.
3. Fill 12 paper-lined jumbo muffin cups half full with batter. Drop a rounded tablespoonful of the cream cheese mixture into the center of each; cover with the remaining batter.
4. Bake 25-30 minutes or until a toothpick inserted in muffin comes out clean. Cool for 5 minutes before removing from pans to wire racks to cool completely. Sprinkle with confectioners' sugar if desired.

FAVORITE IRISH SODA BREAD

My best friend Rita shared this irresistible Irish soda bread recipe with me. It bakes up high, with a golden brown top and a combination of sweet and savory flavors.
—**Jan Alfano** Prescott, AZ

Prep: 20 min. • **Bake:** 45 min. + cooling
Makes: 1 loaf (12 wedges)

- 3 cups all-purpose flour
- ⅔ cup sugar
- 3 teaspoons baking powder
- 1 teaspoon salt
- 1 teaspoon baking soda
- 1 cup raisins
- 2 large eggs, beaten
- 1½ cups buttermilk
- 1 tablespoon canola oil

1. Preheat oven to 350°. In a large bowl, combine the first five ingredients. Stir in raisins. Set aside 1 tablespoon beaten egg. In a bowl, combine buttermilk, oil and the remaining eggs; stir into the flour mixture just until moistened (dough will be sticky). Transfer to a greased 9-in. round baking pan; brush top with the reserved egg.
2. Bake 45-50 minutes or until a toothpick inserted in the center comes out clean. Cool for 10 minutes before removing from pan to a wire rack to cool. Cut loaf into wedges.

★ ★ ★ ★ ★ **READER REVIEW**

"Moist and delicious... I made more than a dozen of these for my church's two-day St. Patrick's Day bake sale and they sold out in a flash."

KRISTINECHAYES TASTEOFHOME.COM

ICEBOX BUTTERHORNS

If you like a roll that melts in your mouth, try my Mom's recipe. She had a way with the dough, giving it just the right touch to turn out beautiful buttery rolls every time.
—**Judy Clark** Elkhart, IN

Prep: 15 min. + chilling • **Bake:** 15 min.
Makes: 2 dozen

- 2 packages (¼ ounce each) active dry yeast
- ¼ cup warm water (110° to 115°)
- 2 cups warm whole milk (110° to 115°)
- ¾ cup butter, melted
- ½ cup sugar
- 1 large egg
- 1 teaspoon salt
- 6½ cups all-purpose flour
  Additional melted butter

1. In a small bowl, dissolve yeast in warm water. In a large bowl, combine the milk, butter, sugar, egg, salt, yeast mixture and 3 cups flour; beat on medium speed until smooth. Stir in enough of the remaining flour to form a soft, sticky dough.
2. Do not knead. Place in a greased bowl, turning once to grease the top. Cover with plastic wrap and refrigerate overnight.
3. Punch down dough. Turn onto a lightly floured surface; divide in half. Roll each half into a 12-in. circle; cut each circle into 12 wedges. Roll up each wedge from the wide ends. Place rolls 2 in. apart on greased baking sheets, point side down. Cover with kitchen towels; let rise in a warm place until doubled, about 1 hour.
4. Bake at 350° for 15-20 minutes or until golden brown. Immediately brush with additional melted butter. Remove from pans to wire racks to cool.

APPLE STREUSEL MUFFINS

These muffins remind us of coffee cake, and my husband and kids love them as a quick breakfast or snack on the run. The drizzle of glaze makes them pretty enough for company.

—**Dulcy Grace** Roaring Spring, PA

Prep: 20 min. • **Bake:** 15 min. + cooling
Makes: 1 dozen

- 2 cups all-purpose flour
- 1 cup sugar
- 1 teaspoon baking powder
- ½ teaspoon baking soda
- ½ teaspoon salt
- 2 large eggs
- ½ cup butter, melted
- 1¼ teaspoons vanilla extract
- 1½ cups peeled chopped tart apples

STREUSEL TOPPING
- ⅓ cup packed brown sugar
- 1 tablespoon all-purpose flour
- ⅛ teaspoon ground cinnamon
- 1 tablespoon cold butter

GLAZE
- ¾ cup confectioners' sugar
- 2 to 3 teaspoons 2% milk
- 1 teaspoon butter, melted
- ⅛ teaspoon vanilla extract
  Dash salt

1. Preheat oven to 375°. Whisk together the first five ingredients. In another bowl, whisk together eggs, melted butter and vanilla; add to the flour mixture, stirring just until moistened (batter will be stiff). Fold in apples.

2. Fill greased or paper-lined muffin cups three-fourths full. For topping, mix brown sugar, flour and cinnamon; cut in butter until crumbly. Sprinkle over batter.

3. Bake until a toothpick inserted in the center comes out clean, 15-20 minutes. Cool for 5 minutes before removing from pan to a wire rack to cool completely. Mix the glaze ingredients; drizzle over tops.

SUNFLOWER SEED & HONEY WHEAT BREAD

I've tried other bread recipes, but this one is a staple in our home. I won $50 in a baking contest with a loaf that I had been storing in the freezer.

—**Mickey Turner** Grants Pass, OR

Prep: 40 min. + rising
Bake: 35 min. + cooling
Makes: 3 loaves (12 slices each)

- 2 packages (¼ ounce each) active dry yeast
- 3¼ cups warm water (110° to 115°)
- ¼ cup bread flour
- ⅓ cup canola oil
- ⅓ cup honey
- 3 teaspoons salt
- 6½ to 7½ cups whole wheat flour
- ½ cup sunflower kernels
- 3 tablespoons butter, melted

1. In a large bowl, dissolve yeast in warm water. Add the bread flour, oil, honey, salt and 4 cups of the whole wheat flour. Beat until smooth. Stir in sunflower kernels and enough of the remaining flour to form a firm dough.

2. Turn onto a floured surface; knead until smooth and elastic, 6-8 minutes. Place in a greased bowl, turning once to grease the top. Cover and let rise in a warm place until doubled, about 1 hour.

3. Punch dough down; divide into three portions. Shape into loaves; place in three greased 8x4-in. loaf pans. Cover and let rise until doubled, about 30 minutes.

4. Bake at 350° for 35-40 minutes or until golden brown. Brush with melted butter. Remove from pans to wire racks to cool.

Freeze option: Securely wrap and freeze cooled loaves in foil, and place in resealable plastic freezer bags. To use, thaw at room temperature.

TEST KITCHEN TIP

Whole wheat flour can be substituted for for all-purpose flour, and vice versa. For best results, it is recommended that equal proportions of whole wheat flour and all-purpose flour be used. Keep in mind that baked goods made with whole wheat flour tend to be denser and have a coarser texture.

ANGEL BISCUITS

These light, airy biscuits are a delicious treat—whether on their own, with butter and honey or used for sandwiches!

—**Faye Hintz** Springfield, MO

Prep: 20 min. + rising • **Bake:** 10 min.
Makes: 2½ dozen

- 2 packages (¼ ounce each) active dry yeast
- ¼ cup warm water (110° to 115°)
- 2 cups warm buttermilk (110° to 115°)
- 5 to 5½ cups all-purpose flour
- ⅓ cup sugar
- 2 teaspoons salt
- 2 teaspoons baking powder
- 1 teaspoon baking soda
- 1 cup shortening
  Melted butter

1. In a small bowl, dissolve yeast in warm water. Let stand 5 minutes. Stir in warm buttermilk; set aside.

2. In a large bowl, combine flour, sugar, salt, baking powder and baking soda. Cut in shortening with a pastry blender until the mixture resembles coarse crumbs. Stir in the yeast mixture.

3. Turn onto a lightly floured surface; knead lightly 3-4 times. Roll out to ½-in. thickness; cut with a 2½-in. round biscuit cutter. Place 2 in. apart on lightly greased baking sheets. Cover with kitchen towels, and let rise in a warm place until almost doubled, about 1 hour.

4. Bake at 450° for 8-10 minutes or until golden brown. Lightly brush tops with melted butter. Serve warm.

HERBED BUBBLE BREAD

It takes just four additional ingredients to turn a package of frozen rolls into this buttery, crusty loaf.

—**Anita Whorton** Powder Springs, GA

Prep: 10 min. + rising • **Bake:** 15 min.
Makes: 12 servings

- ¼ cup butter, melted
- 1 teaspoon garlic powder
- 1 teaspoon dried oregano
- ½ teaspoon dried thyme
- 1 package (16 ounces) frozen dinner roll dough, thawed

1. In a small bowl, combine butter, garlic powder, oregano and thyme. Cut each roll in half; dip into the butter mixture.
2. Arrange in a greased 12-cup fluted tube pan. Pour the remaining herb mixture over top. Cover and let rise in a warm place for 1 hour or until doubled.
3. Bake at 350° for 15-20 minutes or until golden brown.

CHOCOLATE CHIP OATMEAL MUFFINS

I saw this recipe in a newspaper years ago and have changed it quite a bit over time. I make these muffins at least once a month and get many requests for the recipe.

—**Cheryl Bohn** Dominion City, MB

Prep: 10 min. • **Bake:** 25 min.
Makes: 12 muffins

- ½ cup butter, softened
- ¾ cup packed brown sugar
- 1 large egg
- 1 cup all-purpose flour
- 1 teaspoon baking powder
- ¼ teaspoon baking soda
- ¼ teaspoon salt
- ¾ cup applesauce
- 1 cup rolled oats
- 1 cup (6 ounces) semisweet chocolate chips

In a large bowl, cream butter and sugar. Beat in egg. Combine dry ingredients; add alternately with applesauce to the creamed mixture. Stir in oats and chips. Fill 12 paper-lined muffin cups three-fourths full. Bake at 350° for 25 minutes.

FRESH PEAR BREAD

When our trees are loaded with ripe, juicy pears, I treat my family and friends to this cinnamon-spiced bread studded with walnuts and pears. I always receive rave reviews.

—**Linda Patrick** Houston, TX

Prep: 15 min. • **Bake:** 55 min. + cooling
Makes: 2 loaves

- 3 large eggs
- 1½ cups sugar
- ¾ cup vegetable oil
- 1 teaspoon vanilla extract
- 3 cups all-purpose flour
- 2 teaspoons baking powder
- 2 teaspoons ground cinnamon
- 1 teaspoon baking soda
- 1 teaspoon salt
- 4 cups finely chopped peeled ripe pears (about 4 medium)
- 1 teaspoon lemon juice
- 1 cup chopped walnuts

1. Preheat oven to 350°. In a bowl, combine the eggs, sugar, oil and vanilla; mix well. Combine flour, baking powder, cinnamon, baking soda and salt; stir into the egg mixture just until moistened. Toss pears with lemon juice. Stir pears and walnuts into batter (batter will be thick).
2. Spoon into two greased 9x5-in. loaf pans. Bake for 55-60 minutes or until a toothpick inserted in the center comes out clean. Cool for 10 minutes before removing from pans to wire racks.

DOUBLE CHOCOLATE BANANA MUFFINS

Combining two favorite flavors—rich chocolate and sweet banana—makes these muffins doubly good.
—Donna Brockett Kingfisher, OK

....

Prep: 15 min. • **Bake:** 20 min.
Makes: about 1 dozen

- 1½ cups all-purpose flour
- 1 cup sugar
- ¼ cup baking cocoa
- 1 teaspoon baking soda
- ½ teaspoon salt
- ¼ teaspoon baking powder
- 1⅓ cups mashed ripe bananas (about 3 medium)
- ⅓ cup canola oil
- 1 large egg
- 1 cup (6 ounces) miniature semisweet chocolate chips

1. Preheat oven to 350°. Whisk together the first six ingredients. In a separate bowl, whisk bananas, oil and egg until blended.

Add to the flour mixture; stir just until moistened. Fold in chocolate chips.

2. Fill greased or paper-lined muffin cups three-fourths full. Bake until a toothpick inserted in the center comes out clean, 20-25 minutes. Cool for 5 minutes before removing from the pan to a wire rack. Serve warm.

Optional streusel topping (pictured): Combine ½ cup sugar, ⅓ cup all-purpose flour and ½ teaspoon ground cinnamon; cut in ¼ cup cold butter until crumbly. Before baking, sprinkle over filled muffin cups; bake as directed.

CINNAMON CHIP SCONES

These scones will melt in your mouth. They're delicious hot, warm or even cold!
—Barbara Humiston Tampa, FL

....

Prep: 25 min. • **Bake:** 10 min.
Makes: 1 dozen

- 3¼ cups all-purpose flour
- ⅓ cup plus 2 tablespoons sugar, divided
- 2½ teaspoons baking powder
- ½ teaspoon baking soda
- ½ teaspoon salt
- ¾ cup cold butter, cubed
- 1 cup buttermilk
- 1 package (10 ounces) cinnamon baking chips
- 2 tablespoons butter, melted

1. Preheat oven to 425°. In a large bowl, combine flour, ⅓ cup of sugar, baking powder, baking soda and salt. Cut in the butter until the mixture resembles coarse crumbs. Stir in the buttermilk just until moistened. Fold in chips.

2. Turn onto a lightly floured surface; knead gently 10-12 times or until the dough is no longer sticky. Divide in half; gently pat or roll each portion into a 7-in. circle. Brush with butter and sprinkle with remaining sugar.

3. Cut each circle into six wedges. Separate the wedges and place on an ungreased baking sheet. Bake scones for 10-13 minutes or until lightly browned. Serve warm.

RUSTIC RYE BREAD

This gorgeous rye bread has just a touch of sweetness and the perfect amount of caraway seeds. With a crusty top and firm texture, it holds up well in sandwiches... but a pat of butter will do the job, too.

—**Holly Wade** Harrisonburg, VA

Prep: 25 min. + rising
Bake: 30 min. + cooling
Makes: 2 loaves (12 slices each)

 1 package (¼ ounce) active dry yeast
1¾ cups warm water (110° to 115°), divided
 ¼ cup packed brown sugar
 ¼ cup light molasses
 3 tablespoons caraway seeds
 2 tablespoons canola oil
 1 tablespoon salt
1¾ cups rye flour
 ¾ cup whole wheat flour
2½ to 3 cups all-purpose flour

 1 large egg white, optional
   Additional caraway seeds, optional

1. Dissolve yeast in ¼ cup warm water. Stir in brown sugar, molasses, caraway seeds, oil, salt and remaining water. Add rye and whole wheat flours and 1 cup of the all-purpose flour; beat on medium speed until smooth. Stir in enough of the remaining all-purpose flour to form a firm dough.
2. Turn onto a floured surface; knead until smooth and elastic, 6-8 minutes. Place in a greased bowl, turning once to grease the top. Cover; let rise in a warm place until doubled, about 1½ hours.
3. Punch down dough. Turn onto a lightly floured surface; divide in half. Shape each into a round loaf; place on a baking sheet coated with cooking spray. Cover with kitchen towels; let rise in a warm place until almost doubled, about 1½ hours.

4. Bake at 350° until golden brown, 30-35 minutes. Remove from pan to wire racks to cool.
Note: For caraway topping, brush loaves with an egg white beaten lightly with water before baking; sprinkle with caraway seeds.

CRUSTY FRENCH LOAF

A delicate texture makes this bread absolutely wonderful. I sometimes use the dough to make breadsticks, which I brush with melted butter and sprinkle with garlic powder.

—**Deanna Naivar** Temple, TX

Prep: 20 min. + rising
Bake: 25 min. + cooling
Makes: 1 loaf (16 slices)

 1 package (¼ ounce) active dry yeast
 1 cup warm water (110° to 115°)
 2 tablespoons sugar
 2 tablespoons canola oil
1½ teaspoons salt
 3 to 3¼ cups all-purpose flour
   Cornmeal
 1 large egg white
 1 teaspoon cold water

1. In a large bowl, dissolve yeast in warm water. Add the sugar, oil, salt and 2 cups flour. Beat until blended. Stir in enough remaining flour to form a stiff dough.
2. Turn onto a floured surface; knead until smooth and elastic, 6-8 minutes. Place in a greased bowl, turning once to grease the top. Cover and let rise in a warm place until doubled, about 1 hour. Punch the dough down; return to bowl. Cover and let rise for 30 minutes.
3. Punch dough down. Turn onto a lightly floured surface. Shape into a 16x2½-in. loaf with tapered ends. Sprinkle a greased baking sheet with cornmeal; place loaf on baking sheet. Cover and let rise until doubled, about 25 minutes.
4. Beat egg white and cold water; brush over the dough. With a sharp knife, make diagonal slashes 2 in. apart across top of loaf. Bake at 375° for 25-30 minutes or until golden brown. Remove from pan to a wire rack to cool.

GARLIC-CHEESE CRESCENT ROLLS

Here's a recipe that just couldn't be much quicker or easier and is sure to add a nice extra touch to any dinner. The garlic and Parmesan flavors really come through.
—**Lori Abad** East Haven, CT

Start to Finish: 20 min.
Makes: 8 servings

- 1 tube (8 ounces) refrigerated crescent rolls
- 3 tablespoons butter, melted
- 1½ teaspoons garlic powder
- 1 teaspoon dried oregano
- 2 tablespoons grated Parmesan cheese

1. Preheat oven to 375°. Separate crescent dough into eight triangles. Roll up each triangle from the wide end; place rolls point side down 2 in. apart on an ungreased baking sheet. Curve ends to form a crescent.
2. Combine the butter, garlic powder and oregano; brush over the rolls. Sprinkle with cheese.
3. Bake for 10-12 minutes or until golden brown. Serve warm.

COUNTRY WHITE BREAD

Everyone loves a good slice of homemade bread, especially when it's spread with butter or jam. These loaves are especially nice because the crust stays tender. My husband makes most of the bread at our house, and this recipe is his favorite.
—**Joanne Shew Chuk** St. Benedict, SK

Prep: 20 min. + rising
Bake: 25 min. + cooling
Makes: 2 loaves (16 slices each)

- 2 packages (¼ ounce each) active dry yeast
- 2 cups warm water (110° to 115°)
- ½ cup sugar
- 2 teaspoons salt
- 2 large eggs
- ¼ cup canola oil
- 6½ to 7 cups all-purpose flour

1. In a large bowl, dissolve yeast in warm water. Add sugar, salt, eggs, oil and 3 cups flour; beat on medium speed until smooth. Stir in enough remaining flour to form a soft dough.
2. Turn dough onto a floured surface; knead until smooth and elastic, about 6-8 minutes. Place in a greased bowl, turning once to grease the top. Cover and let rise in a warm place until doubled, about 1 hour.
3. Punch down dough. Divide in half and shape into loaves. Place in two greased 9x5-in. loaf pans. Cover with kitchen towels; let rise in a warm place until doubled, about 1 hour.
4. Bake at 375° until golden brown, 25-30 minutes. Remove from pans to wire racks to cool.

JUDY'S CHOCOLATE CHIP BANANA BREAD

I got this recipe from a dear friend, Judy, more than 30 years ago. She said I'd never need another banana bread recipe. She was right, except I added chocolate chips.
—**Debra Keiser** St. Cloud, MN

Prep: 20 min.
Bake: 1 hour + cooling
Makes: 1 loaf (16 slices)

- ½ cup butter, softened
- 1¼ cups sugar
- 2 large eggs
- 1 cup mashed ripe bananas (about 2 medium)
- ¼ cup buttermilk
- 1 teaspoon vanilla extract
- 2 cups all-purpose flour
- 1 teaspoon baking powder
- ¾ teaspoon baking soda
- ½ teaspoon salt
- ¾ cup semisweet chocolate chips
- ¼ cup chopped walnuts, optional

1. Preheat oven to 350°. Line bottom of a greased 9x5-in. loaf pan with parchment paper; grease the paper.
2. In a large bowl, beat butter and sugar until crumbly. Add eggs, one at a time, beating well after each addition. Beat in bananas, buttermilk and vanilla. In another bowl, mix flour, baking powder, baking soda and salt; stir into creamed mixture. Fold in chocolate chips and, if desired, chopped walnuts.
3. Transfer to the prepared pan. Bake 60-65 minutes or until a toothpick inserted in the center comes out clean. Cool for 10 minutes before removing from pan to a wire rack; remove paper.

DID YOU KNOW?

If the chocolate chips or chopped nuts sink to the bottom of the bread, it's because the batter was too thin to support them. If you substituted a thinner milk for the buttermilk, switch back; or, try chopping the nuts smaller and using miniature chocolate chips.

---

⑤ INGREDIENTS
PERFECT PIZZA CRUST

I spent years trying different recipes and techniques looking for the perfect pizza crust recipe, and this is it! I'm amazed that I finally found a crust my family prefers over the pizza parlor's!
—**Lesli Dustin** Nibley, UT

Prep: 20 min. + rising • **Bake:** 20 min.
Makes: 8 servings

- 1 tablespoon active dry yeast
- 1½ cups warm water (110° to 115°)
- 2 tablespoons sugar
- ½ teaspoon salt
- 2 cups bread flour
- 1½ cups whole wheat flour
  Cornmeal
  Pizza toppings of your choice

1. In a large bowl, dissolve yeast in warm water. Add the sugar, salt, 1 cup of the bread flour and the whole wheat flour. Beat until smooth. Stir in enough of the remaining bread flour to form a soft dough (dough will be sticky).
2. Turn onto a floured surface; knead until smooth and elastic, 6-8 minutes. Place in a greased bowl, turning once to grease the top. Cover and let rise in a warm place until doubled, about 1 hour.
3. Punch dough down; roll into a 15-in. circle. Grease a 14-in. pizza pan and sprinkle with cornmeal. Transfer dough to prepared pan; build up edges slightly. Add pizza toppings of your choice.
4. Bake at 425° for 20-25 minutes or until crust is golden brown and toppings are lightly browned and heated through.

PRALINE-TOPPED APPLE BREAD

Apples and candied pecans make this bread so much better than the usual coffee cakes you see at brunches.
—**Sonja Blow** Nixa, MO

Prep: 30 min. • **Bake:** 50 min. + cooling
Makes: 1 loaf (16 slices)

- 2 cups all-purpose flour
- 2 teaspoons baking powder
- ½ teaspoon baking soda
- ½ teaspoon salt
- 1 cup sugar
- 1 cup (8 ounces) sour cream
- 2 large eggs
- 3 teaspoons vanilla extract
- 1½ cups peeled and chopped Granny Smith apples
- 1¼ cups chopped pecans, toasted, divided
- ½ cup butter, cubed
- ½ cup packed brown sugar

1. Preheat oven to 350°. In a large bowl, mix flour, baking powder, baking soda and salt. In another bowl, beat sugar, sour cream, eggs and vanilla until well blended. Stir into flour mixture just until moistened. Fold in apples and 1 cup pecans.
2. Transfer to a greased 9x5-in. loaf pan. Bake 50-55 minutes or until a toothpick inserted in the center comes out clean. Cool in pan 10 minutes. Remove to a wire rack to cool completely.
3. In a small saucepan, combine butter and brown sugar. Bring to a boil, stirring constantly to dissolve sugar; boil 1 minute. Spoon over bread. Sprinkle with remaining pecans; let stand until set.
Note: To toast nuts, bake in a shallow pan in a 350° oven for 5-10 minutes or cook in a skillet over low heat until lightly browned, stirring occasionally.

PUMPKIN-APPLE MUFFINS WITH STREUSEL TOPPING

My mother made these tasty muffins whenever our family got together at her house. Now they're a family favorite at my house, and my in-laws love them, too!
—**Carolyn Riley** Carlisle, PA

Prep: 20 min. • **Bake:** 30 min. + cooling
Makes: about 1½ dozen

- 2½ cups all-purpose flour
- 2 cups sugar
- 1 tablespoon pumpkin pie spice
- 1 teaspoon baking soda
- ½ teaspoon salt
- 2 large eggs, lightly beaten
- 1 cup canned pumpkin
- ½ cup vegetable oil
- 2 cups finely chopped peeled apples

TOPPING
- ¼ cup sugar
- 2 tablespoons all-purpose flour
- ½ teaspoon ground cinnamon
- 1 tablespoon butter or margarine

1. Preheat oven to 350°. In a large bowl, combine flour, sugar, pumpkin pie spice, baking soda and salt. Combine the eggs, pumpkin and vegetable oil; stir into the dry ingredients just until moistened. Fold in apples. Fill greased or paper-lined muffin cups three-fourths full.
2. For the topping, combine the sugar, flour and cinnamon. Cut in butter until the mixture resembles coarse crumbs; sprinkle 1 teaspoon over each muffin.
3. Bake until the muffins test done, 30-35 minutes. Cool in pan 10 minutes before removing to a wire rack.

SOUR CREAM CHIVE BREAD

This savory loaf, mildly flavored with chives, is delicious when served warm with a meal, soup, salad or stew. It also tastes wonderful toasted the next day for breakfast. Because it's made in a bread machine, it's extra-easy to have a loaf on hand.

—**Deborah Plank** West Salem, OH

....

Prep: 10 min. • **Bake:** 3 hours
Makes: 1 loaf (1½ pounds, 16 slices)

- ⅔ cup whole milk (70° to 80°)
- ¼ cup water (70° to 80°)
- ¼ cup sour cream
- 2 tablespoons butter
- 1½ teaspoons sugar
- 1½ teaspoons salt
- 3 cups bread flour
- ⅛ teaspoon baking soda
- ¼ cup minced chives
- 2¼ teaspoons active dry yeast

In bread machine pan, place all ingredients in the order suggested by manufacturer. Select basic bread setting. Choose crust color and loaf size if available. Bake according to bread machine directions (check dough after 5 minutes of mixing; add 1-2 tablespoons of water or flour if needed).

Note: We recommend you do not use a bread machine's time-delay feature for this recipe.

★ ★ ★ ★ ★ **READER REVIEW**

"I loved this recipe! Nice and moist and light. This is a keeper!"

COOKJAN TASTEOFHOME.COM

SWEET POTATO CINNAMON BREAD

My family loves quick breads. This one is moist and spicy, and it's become one of our favorites. If you don't have mini loaf pans, don't worry—it works just as well in regular-size pans.

—Nancy Foust Stoneboro, PA

Prep: 20 min. • **Bake:** 35 min. + cooling
Makes: 4 loaves (6 slices each)

- 3½ cups all-purpose flour
- 2⅔ cups sugar
- 2 teaspoons baking soda
- 1 teaspoon salt
- ½ teaspoon baking powder
- 1½ teaspoons ground cinnamon
- 1 teaspoon ground ginger
- ½ teaspoon ground cloves
- 4 large eggs
- 2 cups mashed sweet potatoes
- ⅔ cup canola oil
- ⅔ cup 2% milk
- 1½ cups raisins
- 1 cup chopped walnuts

1. Preheat oven to 350°. In a large bowl, whisk the first eight ingredients. In another bowl, whisk eggs, sweet potatoes, oil and milk until blended. Add to the flour mixture; stir just until moistened. Fold in raisins and walnuts.

2. Transfer to four greased 5¾x3x2-in. loaf pans. Bake for 35-40 minutes or until a toothpick inserted in center comes out clean. Cool in pans 10 minutes before removing to wire racks to cool.

For larger loaves: Prepare recipe as directed, using two greased 9x5-in. loaf pans. Bake in a preheated 350° oven for 55-60 minutes or until a toothpick comes out clean.

MAPLE BUTTER TWISTS

My stepmother passed on the recipe for this delicious yeast coffee cake that's shaped into pretty rings. When I make it for friends, they always ask for seconds.

—June Gilliland Hope, IN

Prep: 35 min. + rising
Bake: 25 min. + cooling
Makes: 2 coffee cakes

- 3¼ to 3½ cups all-purpose flour
- 3 tablespoons sugar
- 1½ teaspoons salt
- 1 package (¼ ounce) active dry yeast
- ¾ cup whole milk

- ¼ cup butter
- 2 large eggs

FILLING
- ⅓ cup packed brown sugar
- ¼ cup sugar
- 3 tablespoons butter, softened
- 3 tablespoons maple syrup
- 4½ teaspoons all-purpose flour
- ¾ teaspoon ground cinnamon
- ¾ teaspoon maple flavoring
- ⅓ cup chopped walnuts

GLAZE
- ½ cup confectioners' sugar
- ¼ teaspoon maple flavoring
- 2 to 3 teaspoons whole milk

1. In a large bowl, combine 1½ cups of flour, 3 tablespoons sugar, salt and yeast. In a saucepan, heat the milk and butter to 120°-130°. Add to the dry ingredients; beat just until moistened. Add eggs; beat on medium for 2 minutes. Stir in enough remaining flour to form a firm dough. Turn onto a floured surface; knead until smooth and elastic, 5-7 minutes.

Place in a greased bowl, turning once to grease the top. Cover and let rise in a warm place until doubled, about 70 minutes.

2. In a small bowl, combine first seven filling ingredients; beat for 2 minutes. Punch dough down; turn onto a lightly floured surface. Divide dough in half; roll each half into a 16x8-in. rectangle. Spread filling to within ½ in. of edges. Sprinkle with nuts. Roll up each rectangle jelly-roll style, starting with a long side.

3. With a sharp knife, cut each roll in half lengthwise. Open halves so cut side is up; gently twist the ropes together. Transfer to two greased 9-in. round baking pans. Coil into a circle. Tuck ends under; pinch to seal. Cover and let rise in a warm place until doubled, about 45 minutes.

4. Bake at 350° for 25-30 minutes or until golden brown. Cool for 10 minutes; remove from pans to wire racks. Combine the confectioners' sugar, maple flavoring and enough milk to achieve the desired consistency; drizzle over warm cakes.

APPLE-BACON MINI LOAVES

I came up with this recipe for a tailgate party at a University of Tennessee football game. The school colors are orange and white, so the cheddar cheese added a touch of team spirit.

—**Jay Davis** Knoxville, TN

Prep: 15 min. • **Bake:** 25 min. + cooling
Makes: 2 mini loaves (6 slices each)

- 1　cup all-purpose flour
- 2　tablespoons sugar
- 1　teaspoon baking powder
- ¼　teaspoon salt
- 1　large egg
- ½　cup 2% milk
- 2　tablespoons butter, melted
- 1　cup shredded sharp cheddar cheese
- ⅓　cup crumbled cooked bacon
- ¼　cup finely chopped apple

1. Preheat oven to 350°. In a large bowl, combine the flour, sugar, baking powder and salt. In another bowl, whisk egg, milk and butter. Stir into the dry ingredients just until moistened. Fold in the cheese, bacon and apple.

2. Transfer to two greased 5¾x3x2-in. loaf pans. Bake for 25-30 minutes or until a toothpick inserted in the center comes out clean. Cool for 10 minutes before removing from pans to wire racks.

CAN'T-EAT-JUST-ONE CINNAMON ROLLS

My cinnamon rolls have been known to vanish quickly. Once, I dropped off a dozen rolls for my brothers, and they emptied the pan in 10 minutes.

—**Regina Farmwald** West Farmington, OH

Prep: 1 hour + rising • **Bake:** 20 min.
Makes: 2 dozen

- 1　package (¼ ounce) active dry yeast
- 1　tablespoon sugar
- ¼　cup warm water (110° to 115°)
- 1　cup 2% milk
- ⅓　cup instant vanilla pudding mix (half of a 3.4-ounce package)
- 1　large egg
- ¼　cup butter, melted
- 1　teaspoon salt
- 3　to 3½ cups all-purpose flour

FILLING
- ¾　cup sugar
- 1　tablespoon ground cinnamon
- ¼　cup butter, melted

FROSTING
- ½　cup butter, softened
- 2　teaspoons vanilla extract
- 1　teaspoon water
- 1½　to 1¾ cups confectioners' sugar

1. In a small bowl, dissolve the yeast and 1 tablespoon sugar in warm water. In a large bowl, beat milk and pudding mix on low speed for 1 minute. Let stand 1 minute or until soft-set. Add egg, melted butter, salt, yeast mixture and 2 cups of flour; beat on medium until smooth. Stir in enough of the remaining flour to form a soft dough (dough will be sticky).

2. Turn onto a floured surface; knead until smooth and elastic, 6-8 minutes. Place in a greased bowl, turning once to grease the top. Cover and let rise in a warm place until doubled, about 1 hour.

3. For filling, in a small bowl, mix the sugar and cinnamon. Punch down dough; divide in half. Turn one portion of dough onto a lightly floured surface; roll into an 18x10-in. rectangle. Brush with half of the melted butter to within ¼ in. of edges; sprinkle with half the sugar mixture. Roll up jelly-roll style, starting with a long side; pinch seam to seal. Cut into 12 slices. Repeat with the remaining dough and filling ingredients.

4. Place all slices in a greased 13x9-in. baking pan, cut side down. Cover with a kitchen towel; let rise in a warm place until almost doubled, about 45 minutes.

5. Bake at 350° for 20-25 minutes or until golden brown. Cool in pan on a wire rack.

6. For frosting, in a small bowl, beat butter until creamy. Beat in vanilla, water and enough confectioners' sugar to reach desired consistency. Spread over warm rolls. Serve warm.

PUMPKIN SCONES WITH BERRY BUTTER

These delightful scones are perfect on a cold winter day with a steaming hot cup of coffee. They also make a wonderful hostess gift arranged in a basket.
—**Judy Wilson** Sun City West, AZ

Prep: 25 min. + chilling • **Bake:** 15 min.
Makes: 8 scones (about ½ cup berry butter)

- 2 tablespoons dried cranberries
- ½ cup boiling water
- ½ cup butter, softened
- 3 tablespoons confectioners' sugar

DOUGH

- 2¼ cups all-purpose flour
- ¼ cup packed brown sugar
- 2 teaspoons baking powder
- 1½ teaspoons pumpkin pie spice
- ¼ teaspoon salt
- ¼ teaspoon baking soda
- ½ cup cold butter, cubed
- 1 large egg
- ½ cup canned pumpkin
- ⅓ cup 2% milk
- 2 tablespoons chopped pecans, optional

1. Place cranberries in a small bowl; add boiling water. Let stand for 5 minutes; drain and chop. In a small bowl, beat butter until light and fluffy. Add confectioners' sugar and cranberries; mix well. Cover and refrigerate for at least 1 hour.

2. Preheat oven to 400°. In a large bowl, combine flour, brown sugar, baking powder, pie spice, salt and baking soda. Cut in cubed butter until the mixture resembles coarse crumbs. In a small bowl, whisk the egg, pumpkin and milk; add to crumb mixture just until moistened. Stir in pecans if desired.

3. Turn dough onto a floured surface; knead 10 times. Pat into an 8-in. circle. Cut into eight wedges; separate wedges and place on a greased baking sheet.

4. Bake 12-15 minutes or until golden brown. Serve warm with berry butter.

CRANBERRY ORANGE BAGELS

Dried cranberries and grated orange zest add bright flavor to these scrumptious morning treats. Doing the initial mixing in a bread machine takes a lot of the work out of it, too! Switch up the taste, if you'd like, by using raisins and cinnamon.
—**Kristy Reeves** LeRoy, KS

Prep: 30 min. + standing
Bake: 20 min. + cooling
Makes: 9 bagels

- 1 cup plus 4 tablespoons water (70° to 80°), divided
- ½ cup dried cranberries
- ⅓ cup packed brown sugar
- 4½ teaspoons grated orange zest
- 1 teaspoon salt
- ¼ teaspoon ground cloves
- 3 cups bread flour
- 1 package (¼ ounce) active dry yeast
- 1 tablespoon sugar
- 1 large egg white
- 1 tablespoon cornmeal

1. In bread machine pan, place 1 cup plus 2 tablespoons water, cranberries, brown sugar, orange zest, salt, cloves, flour and yeast in order suggested by manufacturer. Select the dough setting (check dough after 5 minutes of mixing; add 1-2 tablespoons of water or flour if needed).

2. When cycle is completed, turn dough onto a lightly floured surface. Shape into nine balls. Push thumb through centers to form a 1-in. hole. Stretch and shape dough to form an even ring. Cover and let rest for 10 minutes; flatten rings slightly.

3. Fill a Dutch oven two-thirds full with water; add sugar and bring to a boil. Drop bagels, two at a time, into boiling water. Cook for 45 seconds; turn bagels and cook 45 seconds longer. Remove with a slotted spoon; drain on paper towels.

4. Whisk egg white and remaining water; brush over bagels. Coat a baking sheet with cooking spray and sprinkle with cornmeal. Place the bagels 2 in. apart on prepared sheet. Bake at 400° for 18-22 minutes or until golden brown. Remove to wire racks to cool.

CAKES, PIES & DESSERTS

Whether you're hosting a party, going to a potluck or feeding your family, nothing makes eyes light up like dessert. Check out these cakes, pies and other sweet treats for the perfect way to end a meal!

SANDY'S CHOCOLATE CAKE

Years ago, I drove four-and-a-half hours to a cake contest, holding my entry on my lap the whole way. But it paid off. One bite and you'll see why this velvety beauty won first prize.
—Sandy Johnson Tioga, PA

Prep: 30 min. • **Bake:** 30 min. + cooling
Makes: 16 servings

- 1 cup butter, softened
- 3 cups packed brown sugar
- 4 large eggs
- 2 teaspoons vanilla extract
- 2⅔ cups all-purpose flour
- ¾ cup baking cocoa
- 3 teaspoons baking soda
- ½ teaspoon salt
- 1⅓ cups sour cream
- 1⅓ cups boiling water

FROSTING

- ½ cup butter, cubed
- 3 ounces unsweetened chocolate, chopped
- 3 ounces semisweet chocolate, chopped
- 5 cups confectioners' sugar
- 1 cup (8 ounces) sour cream
- 2 teaspoons vanilla extract

1. Preheat oven to 350°. Grease and flour three 9-in. round baking pans.
2. In a large bowl, cream butter and brown sugar until light and fluffy. Add eggs, one at a time, beating well after each addition. Beat in vanilla. In another bowl, whisk flour, cocoa, baking soda and salt; add to creamed mixture alternately with sour cream, beating well after each addition. Stir in water until blended.
3. Transfer batter to prepared pans. Bake until a toothpick comes out clean, 30-35 minutes. Cool in pans 10 minutes; remove to wire racks to cool completely.
4. For the frosting, in a metal bowl over simmering water, melt butter and both chocolates; stir until smooth. Cool mixture slightly.
5. In a bowl, combine confectioners' sugar, sour cream and vanilla. Add the chocolate mixture; beat until smooth. Spread frosting between layers and over top and sides of cake. Refrigerate any leftovers.

PUMPKIN SPICE CUPCAKES

I make these cupcakes each year for our Halloween party, but they're wonderful year-round. I sometimes bake them in decorative liners and top with sprinkles instead of nuts.

—**Amber Butzer** Gladstone, OR

Prep: 30 min. • **Bake:** 30 min. + cooling
Makes: 2 dozen

- 2 cups granulated sugar
- 1 can (15 ounces) solid-pack pumpkin
- 4 large eggs
- 1 cup canola oil
- 2 cups all-purpose flour
- 2 teaspoons baking powder
- 2 teaspoons ground cinnamon
- 1 teaspoon baking soda
- ½ teaspoon salt
- ½ teaspoon ground ginger
- ¼ teaspoon ground cloves
- 1 cup raisins

CREAM CHEESE FROSTING

- ⅓ cup butter, softened
- 3 ounces cream cheese, softened
- 1 teaspoon vanilla extract
- 2 cups confectioners' sugar
- ½ cup chopped walnuts, toasted

1. Preheat oven to 350°. Beat granulated sugar, pumpkin, eggs and oil until well blended. In another bowl, whisk the next seven ingredients; gradually beat into the pumpkin mixture. Stir in raisins.

2. Fill each of 24 paper-lined muffin cups with ¼ cup plus 1 teaspoon batter. Bake until a toothpick inserted in the center of a cupcake comes out clean, 28-32 minutes. Cool 10 minutes before removing from pans to wire racks to cool completely.

3. For frosting, beat butter and cream cheese until smooth. Beat in vanilla. Gradually add the confectioners' sugar. Frost cupcakes; sprinkle with walnuts. Refrigerate until serving.

Note: To toast nuts, bake in a shallow pan in a 350° oven for 5-10 minutes or cook in a skillet over low heat until lightly browned, stirring occasionally.

CARAMEL FUDGE CHEESECAKE

I combined several recipes to satisfy the chocolate lovers and cheesecake fans in my family. With a fudge brownie crust, crunchy pecans and a gooey layer of caramel, this gem is hard to resist!
—**Brenda Ruse** Truro, NS

Prep: 30 min. • **Bake:** 35 min. + chilling
Makes: 12 servings

- 1 package fudge brownie mix (8-inch square pan size)
- 1 package (14 ounces) caramels
- ¼ cup evaporated milk
- 1¼ cups coarsely chopped pecans
- 2 packages (8 ounces each) cream cheese, softened
- ½ cup sugar
- 2 large eggs, lightly beaten
- 2 ounces unsweetened chocolate, melted and cooled

1. Preheat oven to 350°. Prepare brownie batter according to package directions. Spread into a greased 9-in. springform pan. Place on a baking sheet. Bake for 20 minutes. Place pan on a wire rack for 10 minutes (leave oven on).
2. Meanwhile, in a microwave-safe bowl, melt caramels with milk. Pour over the brownie crust; sprinkle with pecans.
3. In a large bowl, beat cream cheese and sugar until light and fluffy. Add eggs; beat on low speed just until combined. Stir in melted chocolate. Pour over pecans. Return pan to baking sheet.
4. Bake 35-40 minutes or until center is almost set. Cool on a wire rack 10 minutes. Run a knife around edge of pan to loosen; cool 1 hour longer. Refrigerate overnight. Remove sides of pan.

DID YOU KNOW?

Cheesecakes don't set up completely until they've been thoroughly cooled or chilled. Our Test Kitchen determines a cheesecake's doneness by tapping the side of the pan with a wooden spoon. As a general rule, the "jiggle" in the center of the cake should be about the size of a walnut.

ORANGE GELATIN PRETZEL SALAD

Salty pretzels pair nicely with sweet oranges in this refreshing layered salad. It's a family favorite that's a slam-dunk at Thanksgiving and fall potlucks.
—**Peggy Boyd** Northport, AL

Prep: 20 min. + chilling
Bake: 10 min. + cooling
Makes: 12 servings

- ¾ cup butter, melted
- 1 tablespoon plus ¾ cup sugar, divided
- 2 cups finely crushed pretzels
- 2 cups boiling water
- 2 packages (3 ounces each) orange gelatin
- 2 cans (8 ounces each) crushed pineapple, drained
- 1 can (11 ounces) mandarin oranges, drained
- 1 package (8 ounces) cream cheese, softened
- 2 cups whipped topping
  Additional whipped topping and mandarin oranges, optional

1. Preheat oven to 350°. Mix melted butter and 1 tablespoon sugar; stir in pretzels. Press mixture onto the bottom of an ungreased 13x9-in. baking dish. Bake 10 minutes. Cool completely on a wire rack.
2. In a large bowl, add boiling water to gelatin; stir for 2 minutes to completely dissolve. Stir in fruit. Refrigerate until partially set, about 30 minutes.
3. Meanwhile, beat cream cheese and the remaining sugar until smooth. Fold in whipped topping. Spread over crust.
4. Gently spoon gelatin mixture over the top. Refrigerate, covered, until firm, 2-4 hours. To serve, cut into 12 squares. If desired, top with additional whipped topping and oranges.
Note: For single servings, prepare layers as directed. In each of twelve 9-ounce cups or ½-pint canning jars, layer 2 tablespoons of the pretzel mixture, 2 tablespoons cream cheese mixture and ⅓ cup gelatin mixture. Refrigerate and top as directed.

UPSIDE-DOWN APPLE PIE

This pie has won eight ribbons at area fairs. People say it looks and tastes like a giant apple-cinnamon bun! The recipe is many folks' favorite.

—Susan Frisch Germansville, PA

Prep: 30 min. + chilling
Bake: 50 min. + cooling
Makes: 8 servings

- 2 cups all-purpose flour
- ½ teaspoon salt
- 6 tablespoons shortening
- 2 tablespoons cold butter
- 5 to 7 tablespoons orange juice

FILLING
- 6 tablespoons butter, melted, divided
- ½ cup packed brown sugar
- ½ cup chopped pecans
- 8 cups thinly sliced peeled tart apples (about ⅛ inch thick)
- 1 cup sugar
- ⅓ cup all-purpose flour
- ¾ teaspoon ground cinnamon
- ¼ teaspoon ground nutmeg

GLAZE
- ½ cup confectioners' sugar
- 2 to 3 teaspoons orange juice

1. In a large bowl, combine flour and salt; cut in shortening and butter until crumbly. Gradually add orange juice, tossing with a fork until dough forms a ball. Divide dough into two balls. Wrap in plastic; refrigerate for at least 30 minutes.

2. Line a 9-in. deep-dish pie plate with heavy-duty foil, leaving 1½ in. of foil beyond the edge; coat foil with cooking spray. Combine 4 tablespoons butter, brown sugar and pecans; spoon into the prepared pie plate.

3. In a large bowl, combine the apples, sugar, flour, cinnamon, nutmeg and the remaining butter; toss gently.

4. On a sheet of waxed paper, roll out one ball of pastry to fit the pie plate. Place the pastry over the nut mixture, pressing firmly against mixture and sides of plate; trim to 1 in. beyond plate edge. Fill pastry with the apple mixture.

5. Roll out the remaining pastry to fit the top of pie; place over filling. Trim to ¼ in. beyond the plate edge. Fold the bottom pastry over the top pastry; seal and flute edges. Cut four 1-in. slits in top pastry.

6. Bake at 375° for 50-55 minutes or until the apples are tender and crust is golden brown (cover edges with foil during the last 20 minutes to prevent overbrowning if necessary).

7. Cool for 15 minutes on a wire rack. Invert onto a serving platter; carefully remove foil. Combine glaze ingredients; drizzle over pie.

BLUEBERRY LEMON TRIFLE

A refreshing lemon filling and fresh berries give this sunny dessert plenty of bright color. Don't worry about heating up the oven—this trifle doesn't require any baking at all.

—**Ellen Peden** Houston, TX

Prep: 15 min. + chilling
Makes: 12-14 servings

- 3 cups fresh blueberries, divided
- 2 cans (15¾ ounces each) lemon pie filling
- 2 cups (8 ounces) lemon yogurt
- 1 prepared angel food cake (8 to 10 ounces), cut into 1-inch cubes
- 1 carton (8 ounces) frozen whipped topping, thawed
  Lemon slices and fresh mint, optional

1. Set aside ¼ cup of the blueberries for garnish. In a large bowl, combine the pie filling and yogurt.

2. In a 3½-qt. trifle bowl, layer a third each of the cake cubes, lemon mixture and blueberries. Repeat layers twice. Top with whipped topping. Cover and refrigerate for at least 2 hours. Garnish with the reserved blueberries and, if desired, lemon and mint.

FAMILY-FAVORITE CHEESECAKE

This fluffy, delicate cheesecake has been a family favorite for almost 20 years. I've shared the recipe at many gatherings and have even started baking it for our friends instead of Christmas cookies.

—**Esther Wappner** Mansfield, OH

Prep: 20 min. + cooling
Bake: 1 hour + chilling
Makes: 12 servings

- 2½ cups graham cracker crumbs (about 40 squares)
- ⅓ cup sugar
- ½ teaspoon ground cinnamon
- ½ cup butter, melted

FILLING

- 3 packages (8 ounces each) cream cheese, softened
- 1½ cups sugar
- 1 teaspoon vanilla extract
- 4 large eggs, separated

TOPPING

- ½ cup sour cream
- 2 tablespoons sugar
- ½ teaspoon vanilla extract
- ½ cup heavy whipping cream, whipped

1. Preheat oven to 350°. In a small bowl, combine the cracker crumbs, sugar and cinnamon; stir in butter. Press onto the bottom and 2 in. up the sides of a greased 9-in. springform pan. Bake for 5 minutes. Cool on a wire rack. Reduce heat to 325°.

2. In a large bowl, beat the cream cheese, sugar and vanilla until smooth. Add egg yolks; beat on low just until combined.

3. In a small bowl, beat egg whites until soft peaks form; fold into cream cheese mixture. Pour over crust.

4. Bake for 1 hour or until the center is almost set. Cool on a wire rack for 10 minutes. Carefully run a knife around edge of pan to loosen; cool 1 hour longer. Refrigerate until completely cooled.

5. Combine the sour cream, sugar and vanilla; fold in whipped cream. Spread over cheesecake. Refrigerate overnight. Remove sides of pan.

PUMPKIN BARS

Nothing could be a more appropriate fall treat than a big pan of pumpkin-flavored bars—but my family loves these any time of year.
—Brenda Keller *Andalusia, AL*

Prep: 20 min. • **Bake:** 25 min. + cooling
Makes: 2 dozen

- 4 **large eggs**
- 1⅔ **cups sugar**
- 1 **cup canola oil**
- 1 **can (15 ounces) solid-pack pumpkin**
- 2 **cups all-purpose flour**
- 2 **teaspoons ground cinnamon**
- 2 **teaspoons baking powder**
- 1 **teaspoon baking soda**
- 1 **teaspoon salt**

ICING

- 6 **ounces cream cheese, softened**
- 2 **cups confectioners' sugar**
- ¼ **cup butter, softened**
- 1 **teaspoon vanilla extract**
- 1 **to 2 tablespoons whole milk**

1. Preheat oven to 350°. In a bowl, beat the eggs, sugar, oil and pumpkin until well blended. Combine flour, cinnamon, baking powder, baking soda and salt; gradually add to the pumpkin mixture and mix well. Pour into an ungreased 15x10x1-in. baking pan. Bake for 25-30 minutes or until set. Cool completely.

2. For icing, beat the cream cheese, confectioners' sugar, butter and vanilla in a small bowl. Add enough milk to achieve spreading consistency. Spread over bars. Store in the refrigerator.

FLOURLESS CHOCOLATE CAKE WITH ROSEMARY GANACHE

Moist, dense and chocolatey describes this rich cake. A silky chocolate ganache infused with rosemary really takes this dessert over the top.
—Kelly Gardner *Alton, IL*

Prep: 40 min. • **Bake:** 30 min.
Makes: 16 servings

- 1 **pound semisweet chocolate, chopped**
- 1 **cup butter, cubed**
- ¼ **cup dry red wine**
- 8 **large eggs**
- ½ **cup sugar**
- 1 **teaspoon vanilla extract**

GANACHE

- 9 **ounces bittersweet chocolate, chopped**
- 1 **cup heavy whipping cream**
- 2 **fresh rosemary sprigs**

1. Preheat oven to at 350°. Line the bottom of a greased 9-in. springform pan with parchment paper; grease the paper. Place on a double thickness of heavy-duty foil (about 18 in. square). Securely wrap foil around pan; set aside.

2. In a large heavy saucepan, melt the chocolate, butter and wine over low heat, stirring constantly. Remove from the heat. Cool to room temperature.

3. Meanwhile, in a large bowl, beat the eggs, sugar and vanilla until frothy and doubled in volume, about 5 minutes. Gradually fold the eggs into the chocolate mixture, one-third at a time, until well blended. Pour batter into prepared pan. Place springform pan in a large baking pan; add 1 in. of hot water to larger pan. Bake for 28-32 minutes or until outer edges are set (center will jiggle). Remove springform pan from water bath. Cool completely on a wire rack.

4. Carefully run a knife around the edge of the pan to loosen; remove sides of pan. Invert onto a serving platter; remove parchment paper.

5. Place chocolate in a small bowl. In a small saucepan, bring cream and rosemary just to a boil. Remove from heat; discard the rosemary. Pour cream over chocolate; whisk until smooth. Cool slightly, stirring occasionally. Pour over cake. Chill until set.

To make ahead: Cake can be made a day in advance. Cover and refrigerate. Remove from the refrigerator 1 hour before serving.

MOCHA TRUFFLE CHEESECAKE

I went through a phase when I couldn't get enough cheesecake or coffee, so I created this rich dessert. Its brownie-like crust and creamy mocha layer really hit the spot. It's excellent for get-togethers because it can be made in advance.

—Shannon Dormady Great Falls, MT

Prep: 20 min. • **Bake:** 50 min. + chilling
Makes: 16 servings

- 1 package devil's food cake mix (regular size)
- 6 tablespoons butter, melted
- 1 large egg
- 1 to 3 tablespoons instant coffee granules

FILLING/TOPPING

- 2 packages (8 ounces each) cream cheese, softened
- 1 can (14 ounces) sweetened condensed milk
- 2 cups (12 ounces) semisweet chocolate chips, melted and cooled
- 3 to 6 tablespoons instant coffee granules
- ¼ cup hot water
- 3 large eggs, lightly beaten
- 1 cup heavy whipping cream
- ¼ cup confectioners' sugar
- ½ teaspoon almond extract
- 1 tablespoon baking cocoa, optional

1. Preheat oven to 325°. In a large bowl, combine cake mix, butter, egg and coffee granules until well blended. Press onto the bottom and 2 in. up the sides of a greased 10-in. springform pan.

2. In another large bowl, beat the cream cheese until smooth. Beat in milk and melted chips. Dissolve coffee granules in water. Add coffee to the cream cheese mixture. Add eggs; beat on low speed just until combined. Pour into crust. Place pan on a baking sheet.

3. Bake for 50-55 minutes or until the center is almost set. Cool on a wire rack for 10 minutes. Carefully run a knife around the edge of the pan to loosen; cool 1 hour longer. Chill overnight.

4. Just before serving, in a large bowl, beat cream until soft peaks form. Beat in sugar and extract until stiff peaks form. Spread over top of the cheesecake. Sprinkle with cocoa powder if desired. Refrigerate leftovers.

GRANDMA'S STRAWBERRY SHORTCAKE

I can still taste the sweet, juicy berries piled over my grandmother's warm biscuits and topped with a huge dollop of fresh whipped cream. My father added more indulgence to this strawberry dessert by first buttering the biscuits.

—Shirley Joan Helfenbein Lapeer, MI

Prep: 30 min. • **Bake:** 20 min. + cooling
Makes: 6-8 servings

- 2 cups all-purpose flour
- 2 tablespoons sugar
- 3 teaspoons baking powder
- ½ teaspoon salt
- ½ cup cold butter, cubed
- 1 large egg, beaten
- ⅔ cup half-and-half cream
- 1 cup heavy whipping cream
- 2 tablespoons confectioners' sugar
- ⅛ teaspoon vanilla extract
   Additional butter
- 1½ cups fresh strawberries, sliced

1. Preheat oven to 450°. Combine the flour, sugar, baking powder and salt. Cut in butter until mixture resembles coarse crumbs. In another bowl, whisk egg and half-and-half. Add all at once to crumb mixture; stir just until moistened.

2. Spread the batter into a greased 8-in. round baking pan, slightly building up the edges. Bake cake until golden brown, 16-18 minutes. Remove from the pan; cool on a wire rack.

3. Beat heavy cream until it begins to thicken. Add confectioners' sugar and vanilla; beat until stiff peaks form. Split cake in half crosswise; butter the bottom layer. Spoon half the strawberries over the bottom layer. Spread with some whipped cream. Cover with the top cake layer. Top with the remaining berries and whipped cream. Cut into wedges.

CRANBERRY LAYER CAKE

I adapted a tube cake recipe to create this layer cake. Cranberries, walnuts and homemade frosting make it taste so delicious, you'd never guess it starts with a mix.

—**Sandy Burkett** Galena, OH

Prep: 20 min. • **Bake:** 30 min. + cooling
Makes: 12 servings

- 1 package white cake mix (regular size)
- 1⅓ cups water
- 3 large eggs
- ⅓ cup canola oil
- 1 tablespoon grated orange zest
- 1 cup fresh or frozen cranberries, thawed and coarsely chopped
- 1 cup finely chopped walnuts

CREAM CHEESE FROSTING
- 1 package (8 ounces) cream cheese, softened
- ½ cup butter, softened
- 1 teaspoon vanilla extract
- 3½ cups confectioners' sugar
- ½ teaspoon grated orange zest
- ¼ cup finely chopped walnuts

1. Preheat oven to 350°. Line bottoms of two greased 9-in. round baking pans with parchment paper; grease paper. In a large bowl, combine the first five ingredients; beat on low speed 30 seconds. Beat on medium 2 minutes. Stir in cranberries and walnuts. Transfer batter to prepared pans.
2. Bake 30-35 minutes or until a toothpick inserted in center comes out clean. Cool in pans 10 minutes before removing to wire racks; remove paper. Cool completely.
3. In a large bowl, beat cream cheese, butter and vanilla until blended. Gradually beat in confectioners' sugar and orange zest until smooth. Spread the frosting between layers and over the top and sides of the cake. Sprinkle with walnuts. Refrigerate leftovers.
Freeze option: Wrap cooled cake layers in plastic, then cover securely in foil; freeze. To use, thaw cakes before unwrapping. Assemble as directed.

APPLE DUMPLING BAKE

I received this recipe from a friend of mine, then tweaked it to suit my family's tastes. Mountain Dew is the secret ingredient in this rich dessert that's a snap to make.

—**Chris Shields** Monrovia, IN

Prep: 15 min. • **Bake:** 35 min.
Makes: 8 servings

- 2 medium Granny Smith apples
- 2 tubes (8 ounces each) refrigerated crescent rolls
- 1 cup sugar
- ⅓ cup butter, softened
- ½ teaspoon ground cinnamon
- ¾ cup Mountain Dew soda
  Vanilla ice cream

1. Preheat oven to 350°. Peel, core and cut each apple into eight wedges. Unroll both tubes of crescent dough; separate each into eight triangles. Wrap a triangle around each apple wedge. Place in a greased 13x9-in. baking dish.
2. In a bowl, mix the sugar, butter and cinnamon until blended; sprinkle over top of the dumplings. Slowly pour soda around the dumplings (do not stir).
3. Bake, uncovered, until golden brown and apples are tender, 35-40 minutes. Serve warm with ice cream.

CALIFORNIA LEMON POUND CAKE

Citrus trees grow abundantly in California, and I'm always looking for recipes to use the fruit from the orange and lemon trees in my yard. This is one of my favorites! My mother passed this recipe down to me.

—**Richard Killeaney** Spring Valley, CA

Prep: 15 min. • **Bake:** 70 min. + cooling
Makes: 12-16 servings

- 1 cup butter, softened
- ½ cup shortening
- 3 cups sugar
- 5 large eggs
- 1 tablespoon grated lemon zest
- 1 tablespoon lemon extract
- 3 cups all-purpose flour
- 1 teaspoon salt
- ½ teaspoon baking powder
- 1 cup whole milk

FROSTING

- ¼ cup butter, softened
- 1¾ cups confectioners' sugar
- 2 tablespoons lemon juice
- 1 teaspoon grated lemon zest

1. Preheat oven to 350°. In a large bowl, cream butter, shortening and sugar until light and fluffy, about 5 minutes. Add the eggs, one at a time, beating well after each addition. Stir in the lemon zest and extract. Combine flour, salt and baking powder; gradually add to the creamed mixture alternately with milk. Beat just until combined.

2. Pour batter into a greased 10-in. fluted tube pan. Bake for 70 minutes or until a toothpick inserted in the center comes out clean. Cool for 10 minutes before removing from pan to a wire rack to cool completely.

3. In a small bowl, combine the frosting ingredients; beat until smooth. Spread over the top of the cake.

TEST KITCHEN TIP

For extra nonstick insurance, grease your tube pan with shortening, then give the greased pan a spritz of cooking spray. Also, a flexible plastic knife works wonders to remove a cake from a fluted tube pan without damage. Slide the knife along the sides and center of the pan to loosen the cake before inverting it.

---

⑤ INGREDIENTS

SEMISWEET CHOCOLATE MOUSSE

A friend shared this rich, velvety mousse recipe with me. I love to cook and have tons of recipes, but this one is a favorite. Best of all, it's easy to make—and it's easy to double the recipe if you're feeding more than two people!

—**Judy Spencer** San Diego, CA

Prep: 20 min. + chilling
Makes: 2 servings

- ¼ cup semisweet chocolate chips
- 1 tablespoon water
- 1 large egg yolk, lightly beaten
- 1½ teaspoons vanilla extract
- ½ cup heavy whipping cream
- 1 tablespoon sugar
    Whipped cream and raspberries, optional

1. In a small saucepan, melt chocolate chips with water; stir until smooth. Stir a small amount of hot chocolate mixture into egg yolk; return all to the pan, stirring constantly. Cook and stir for 2 minutes or until slightly thickened. Remove from heat; stir in vanilla. Cool, stirring several times.

2. In a small bowl, beat whipping cream until it begins to thicken. Add sugar; beat until soft peaks form. Fold in the cooled chocolate mixture. Cover and refrigerate for at least 2 hours. Garnish with whipped cream and raspberries if desired.

PUMPKIN SHORTBREAD DESSERT

My family prefers this to traditional pumpkin pie, which is just fine with me. It feeds a crowd, so I only need to make one dessert instead of several pies.

—Edie DeSpain Logan, UT

Prep: 15 min. • **Bake:** 65 min. + chilling
Makes: 15 servings

- 1¾ cups sugar, divided
- 1½ cups all-purpose flour
- ½ cup cold butter
- 4 large eggs, lightly beaten
- 1 can (29 ounces) solid-pack pumpkin
- 1 teaspoon salt
- 1 teaspoon ground cinnamon
- 1 teaspoon ground ginger
- ½ teaspoon ground cloves
- 2 cans (12 ounces each) evaporated milk
- Whipped cream and additional ground cinnamon, optional

1. Preheat oven to 425°. In a bowl, combine ¼ cup sugar and the flour; cut in butter until the mixture resembles coarse crumbs. Press into an ungreased 13x9-in. baking pan.

2. Combine the eggs, pumpkin, salt, spices and remaining sugar. Stir in milk. Pour over the crust.

3. Bake for 15 minutes. Reduce heat to 350°; bake 50-55 minutes longer or until the filling is set. Cool on a wire rack. Cover and refrigerate overnight.

4. Cut into squares. If desired, top with whipped cream and sprinkle with additional cinnamon.

★★★★★ **READER REVIEW**

"Excellent, easy, delicious and feeds a crowd. I call it 'pumpkin cookie pie' because you get the best of both worlds. I like to garnish it with chopped pecans"

JCLYN TASTEOFHOME.COM

FAVORITE ITALIAN CAKE

Here's a scrumptious cake that melts in your mouth and makes you say, "grazie!"
—**Marilyn Morel** Keene, NH

Prep: 40 min. • **Bake:** 20 min. + cooling
Makes: 12 servings

- ½ cup butter, softened
- ½ cup shortening
- 2 cups granulated sugar
- 5 large eggs
- 1 teaspoon vanilla extract
- 2 cups all-purpose flour
- 1 teaspoon baking soda
- ¼ teaspoon salt
- 1 cup buttermilk
- 1 cup chopped pecans
- ½ cup sweetened shredded coconut

CREAM CHEESE FROSTING

- 11 ounces cream cheese, softened
- ½ cup butter, softened
- 3¾ cups confectioners' sugar
- 1 teaspoon vanilla extract
- 1 cup coarsely chopped pecans

1. Preheat oven to 350°. Cream butter, shortening and granulated sugar until light and fluffy. Add eggs, one at a time, beating well after each addition. Beat in vanilla. Combine flour, baking soda and salt; add to the creamed mixture alternately with the buttermilk, beating well after each addition. Fold in pecans and coconut.
2. Pour batter into three greased and floured 9-in. round pans. Bake until a toothpick inserted in center comes out clean, 20-25 minutes. Cool 10 minutes before removing from pans to wire racks to cool completely.
3. For frosting, beat cream cheese and butter until fluffy. Add confectioners' sugar and vanilla; beat until smooth. Spread frosting between layers and over top and sides of cake. Press pecans onto the sides of the cake. Refrigerate.

DID YOU KNOW?

If you don't have buttermilk, you can make your own soured milk as a substitute. For each cup of buttermilk, use 1 tablespoon of white vinegar or lemon juice plus enough milk to measure 1 cup. Stir, then let stand for 5 minutes. You can also use 1 cup of plain yogurt or 1¾ teaspoons cream of tartar plus 1 cup milk.

RUSTIC CARAMEL APPLE TART

Like an apple pie without the pan, this scrumptious tart has a crispy crust that cuts nicely and a yummy caramel topping.
—**Betty Fulks** Onia, AR

Prep: 20 min. + chilling • **Bake:** 25 min.
Makes: 4 servings

- ⅔ cup all-purpose flour
- 1 tablespoon sugar
- ⅛ teaspoon salt
- ¼ cup cold butter, cubed
- 6½ teaspoons cold water
- ⅛ teaspoon vanilla extract

FILLING

- 1½ cups chopped peeled tart apples
- 3 tablespoons sugar
- 1 tablespoon all-purpose flour

TOPPING

- 1 teaspoon sugar
- ¼ teaspoon ground cinnamon
- 1 large egg
- 1 tablespoon water
- 2 tablespoons caramel ice cream topping, warmed

1. In a large bowl, combine flour, sugar and salt; cut in the butter until crumbly. Gradually add water and vanilla, tossing with a fork until dough forms a ball. Cover and refrigerate for 30 minutes or until easy to handle.
2. Preheat oven to 400°. On a lightly floured surface, roll dough into a 10-in. circle. Transfer to a parchment paper-lined baking sheet. Combine filling ingredients; spoon over pastry to within 2 in. of edges. Fold up edges of pastry over filling, leaving the center uncovered. Combine sugar and cinnamon; sprinkle over the filling. Whisk egg and water; brush over the crust.
3. Bake 25-30 minutes or until the crust is golden and the filling is bubbly. Using the parchment paper, slide the tart onto a wire rack. Drizzle with caramel topping. Serve warm.

ZUCCHINI DESSERT SQUARES

We planted one too many zucchini plants a few summers ago and harvested a lot of zucchini that year. I was looking for ways to use them, and this delicious dessert is the result.

—**Nancy Morelli** Livonia, MI

Prep: 30 min. • **Bake:** 40 min.
Makes: 16-20 servings

- 4 cups all-purpose flour
- 2 cups sugar
- ½ teaspoon ground cinnamon
- ½ teaspoon salt
- 1½ cups cold butter

FILLING

- 8 to 10 cups cubed seeded peeled zucchini (4 to 5 pounds)
- ⅔ cup lemon juice
- 1 cup sugar
- 1 teaspoon ground cinnamon
- ½ teaspoon ground nutmeg

1. Preheat oven to 375°. In a large bowl, combine the flour, sugar, cinnamon and salt. Cut in butter until crumbly. Reserve 3 cups of the crumb mixture; pat the remaining mixture into a greased 13x9-in. baking pan. Bake for 12 minutes.
2. Meanwhile, for filling, place zucchini and lemon juice in a large saucepan; bring to a boil. Reduce heat; cover and cook for 6-8 minutes or until the zucchini is crisp-tender. Stir in the sugar, cinnamon and nutmeg; cover and simmer for 5 minutes (mixture will be thin).
3. Spoon over crust; sprinkle with the reserved crumb mixture. Bake at 375° until golden, 40-45 minutes.

PEANUT BUTTER-FILLED BROWNIE CUPCAKES

Folks love both brownies and cupcakes, so why not combine them? You'll watch these snacks disappear before your very eyes!

—**Carol Gillespie** Chambersburg, PA

Prep: 15 min. • **Bake:** 15 min. + cooling
Makes: 1 dozen

- 1 package fudge brownie mix (8-inch square pan size)
- ½ cup miniature semisweet chocolate chips
- ⅓ cup creamy peanut butter
- 3 tablespoons cream cheese, softened
- 1 large egg
- ¼ cup sugar
- Confectioners' sugar, optional

1. Preheat oven to 350°. Prepare brownie batter according to package directions; stir in chocolate chips. For filling, in a small bowl, beat peanut butter, cream cheese, egg and sugar until smooth.
2. Fill paper-lined muffin cups one-third full with batter. Drop filling by teaspoonfuls into the center of each cupcake. Cover with the remaining batter.
3. Bake 15-20 minutes or until a toothpick inserted in the brownie portion comes out clean. Cool 10 minutes before removing from pan to a wire rack to cool completely. If desired, dust tops with confectioners' sugar. Store in the refrigerator.

FIVE-STAR BROWNIES

When I entered these treats in the 1990 state fair, Kansas was celebrating the 100th birthday of Five-Star U.S. General and 34th President Dwight D. Eisenhower, who grew up in the central Kansas town of Abilene. So I renamed my brownies in honor of the rank he had achieved as a general, and cut them out with a star-shaped cookie cutter. They won a blue ribbon!

—Pam Buerki Rogers Victoria, KS

Prep: 15 min. • **Bake:** 30 min. + cooling
Makes: 1 dozen

- 3 large eggs
- 2 cups sugar
- 1½ teaspoons vanilla extract
- ½ cup butter, melted
- ¼ cup shortening, melted
- 1½ cups all-purpose flour
- ¾ cup baking cocoa
- ¾ teaspoon salt
- 1 cup chopped nuts, optional

1. Preheat oven to 350°. In a large bowl, beat the eggs, sugar and vanilla until blended. Beat in butter and shortening until smooth. Combine flour, cocoa and salt; gradually add to the egg mixture. Stir in nuts if desired.
2. Line a 13x9-in. baking pan with foil and grease the foil; pour the batter into the prepared pan. Bake for 30 minutes or until a toothpick inserted in the center comes out clean. Cool in pan on a wire rack.
3. Using foil, lift brownies out of pan. Discard foil. Cut brownies with a 3-in. star-shaped cookie cutter or into bars.

★ ★ ★ ★ ★ **READER REVIEW**

"I have been making this exact recipe since I was in the third grade. I've tried others over the years, but I always come back to this one. Perfect little crust on top and nice and moist in the center."

LAUREN TASTEOFHOME.COM

CRANBERRY-CHERRY NUT PIE

This delightful, stress-free pie using basic premade pie pastry combines cranberries with convenient cherry pie filling for a fresh, fun flavor.

—Taste of Home Test Kitchen

Prep: 20 min. • **Bake:** 40 min. + cooling
Makes: 8 servings

- 1 can (21 ounces) cherry pie filling
- 2 cups fresh or frozen cranberries, thawed
- ¾ cup sugar
- ½ cup chopped walnuts
- 2 tablespoons cornstarch
- 1 teaspoon vanilla extract
- ½ teaspoon ground cinnamon
- ⅛ teaspoon ground allspice
- 1 package (14.1 ounces) refrigerated pie pastry
- 2 tablespoons butter
- 1 teaspoon 2% milk
- 1 tablespoon coarse sugar

1. Preheat oven to 375°. For the filling, mix first eight ingredients. Unroll one pastry sheet into a 9-in. pie plate. Add filling; dot with butter.
2. Unroll the remaining pastry sheet onto a work surface; make cutout vents using small cookie cutters. Place top pastry over filling; seal and flute edge. Decorate top with cutouts. Brush with milk; sprinkle with coarse sugar.
3. Bake on a lower oven rack until the crust is golden brown and the filling is bubbly, 40-45 minutes. Cover the edge with foil during the last 30 minutes if needed to prevent overbrowning. Cool on a wire rack.

COFFEE-CHOCOLATE CAKE

This dark, moist cake is perfect for birthday parties or any special occasion. The buttery frosting has an unrivaled homemade flavor. If you want, mix it up by adding food coloring or using a different flavor extract.
—*Taste of Home* Test Kitchen

Prep: 25 min.
Bake: 25 min. + cooling
Makes: 12 servings

2 cups sugar
1 cup canola oil
1 cup whole milk
1 cup brewed coffee, room temperature
2 large eggs
1 teaspoon vanilla extract
2 cups all-purpose flour
¾ cup baking cocoa
2 teaspoons baking soda
1 teaspoon baking powder
1 teaspoon salt

BUTTERCREAM FROSTING

1 cup butter, softened
8 cups confectioners' sugar
2 teaspoons vanilla extract
½ to ¾ cup whole milk

1. Preheat oven to 325°. In a large bowl, beat the sugar, oil, milk, coffee, eggs and vanilla until well blended. Combine the flour, cocoa, baking soda, baking powder and salt; gradually beat into the sugar mixture until blended.
2. Pour batter into two greased and floured 9-in. round baking pans. Bake for 25-30 minutes or until a toothpick inserted in the center comes out clean. Cool in pans for 10 minutes before removing to wire racks to cool completely.
3. In a large bowl, beat butter until fluffy. Beat in confectioners' sugar and vanilla. Add milk until frosting reaches desired consistency. Spread frosting between layers and over top and sides of cake.

BUTTERSCOTCH BLISS LAYERED DESSERT

Every time I take this layered treat to a gathering, I bring home an empty dish.
—Janice Vernon Las Cruces, NM

Prep: 20 min. + chilling
Makes: 24 servings

1½ cups graham cracker crumbs
    Sugar substitute equivalent to ½ cup sugar, divided
6 tablespoons butter, melted
2 packages (8 ounces each) reduced-fat cream cheese
3 cups cold fat-free milk, divided
2 packages (1 ounce each) sugar-free instant butterscotch pudding mix
1 carton (8 ounces) frozen reduced-fat whipped topping, thawed
½ teaspoon rum extract

1. In a small bowl, combine the cracker crumbs, half of the sugar substitute and melted butter. Press into a 13x9-in. dish coated with cooking spray.
2. In a small bowl, beat the cream cheese, ¼ cup milk and remaining sugar substitute until smooth. Spread over crust.
3. In another bowl, whisk the remaining milk with the pudding mix for 2 minutes. Let stand for 2 minutes or until soft-set. Gently spread over the cream cheese layer. Combine whipped topping and extract; spread over the top. Refrigerate for at least 4 hours.
Note: This recipe was tested with Splenda no-calorie sweetener.

CHEESECAKE STRAWBERRY TRIFLE

The only drawback to this lovely dessert is that there's never any left over! For a patriotic look, replace one of the layers of strawberry pie filling with blueberry... or use whatever filling you prefer.
—**Lori Thorp** Frazee, MN

Start to Finish: 20 min.
Makes: 12-16 servings

- 1 package (8 ounces) cream cheese, softened
- 1 cup (8 ounces) sour cream
- ½ cup cold whole milk
- 1 package (3.4 ounces) instant vanilla pudding mix
- 1 carton (12 ounces) frozen whipped topping, thawed
- 1½ cups crushed butter-flavored crackers (about 38 crackers)
- ¼ cup butter, melted
- 2 cans (21 ounces each) strawberry pie filling

1. In a large bowl, beat cream cheese until smooth. Beat in the sour cream; mix well.
2. In a small bowl, beat milk and pudding mix on low speed for 2 minutes. Stir into the cream cheese mixture. Fold in the whipped topping.
3. In a small bowl, combine the crackers and butter.
4. In a 2½-qt. trifle bowl, layer half each of the cream cheese mixture, crumbs and pie filling. Repeat layers. Refrigerate trifle until serving.

WHITE CHOCOLATE CRANBERRY BLONDIES

The family often requests these bars. For a fancier presentation, cut them into triangles and drizzle white chocolate over each one individually.
—**Erika Busz** Kent, WA

Prep: 35 min. • **Bake:** 20 min. + cooling
Makes: 3 dozen

- ¾ cup butter, cubed
- 1½ cups packed light brown sugar
- 2 large eggs
- ¾ teaspoon vanilla extract
- 2¼ cups all-purpose flour
- 1½ teaspoons baking powder
- ¼ teaspoon salt
- ⅛ teaspoon ground cinnamon
- ½ cup dried cranberries
- 6 ounces white baking chocolate, coarsely chopped

FROSTING
- 1 package (8 ounces) cream cheese, softened
- 1 cup confectioners' sugar
- 1 tablespoon grated orange zest, optional
- 6 ounces white baking chocolate, melted
- ½ cup dried cranberries, chopped

1. Preheat the oven to 350°. In a large microwave-safe bowl, melt the butter; stir in the brown sugar. Cool slightly.
2. Beat in the eggs, one at a time, and the vanilla. In another bowl, whisk together flour, baking powder, salt and cinnamon; stir into butter mixture. Stir in cranberries and chopped chocolate (the batter will be thick). Spread into a greased 13x9-in. pan.
3. Bake until bars are golden brown and a toothpick inserted in center comes out clean, 18-21 minutes. (Do not overbake.) Cool completely on a wire rack.
4. For frosting, beat the cream cheese, confectioners' sugar and, if desired, orange zest until smooth. Gradually beat in half the melted white chocolate; spread over blondies. Sprinkle with cranberries; drizzle with the remaining melted white chocolate.
5. Cut into bars. Store in an airtight container in the refrigerator.

OLD-FASHIONED STRAWBERRY PIE

I've been cooking since I was a girl, and I especially enjoy making fresh, fruity desserts like this. It's a wonderful and light treat to follow dinner and a must when fresh berries are in season.
—**Erica Cooper** Elk River, MN

Prep: 30 min. • **Cook:** 10 min. + chilling
Makes: 8 servings

- 1 sheet refrigerated pie pastry
- 1 package (3 ounces) cook-and-serve vanilla pudding mix
- 1½ cups water
- 1 teaspoon lemon juice
- 1 package (.3 ounce) sugar-free strawberry gelatin
- ½ cup boiling water
- 4 cups sliced fresh strawberries
- 3 ounces reduced-fat cream cheese
- 2 cups reduced-fat whipped topping, divided
- 1 teaspoon vanilla extract
- 8 fresh strawberries

1. Preheat oven to 450°. On a lightly floured surface, unroll pie pastry. Transfer to a 9-in. pie plate. Trim pastry to ½ in. beyond edge of plate; flute edges. Line unpricked pastry with a double thickness of heavy-duty foil. Bake for 8 minutes. Remove foil; bake 5-7 minutes longer or until lightly browned. Cool on a wire rack.
2. In a small saucepan, combine pudding mix, water and lemon juice. Cook and stir over medium heat until the mixture comes to a boil. Cook and stir 1-2 minutes longer or until thickened. Remove from the heat; set aside.
3. In a large bowl, dissolve gelatin in boiling water. Gradually stir in pudding. Cover and refrigerate for 30 minutes or until thickened. Fold in sliced strawberries. Transfer to crust.
4. For topping, in another bowl, beat the cream cheese, ½ cup whipped topping and vanilla until smooth. Fold in the remaining whipped topping. Cut a small hole in the corner of a pastry or plastic bag; insert a medium star tip. Fill bag with topping. Pipe topping around the edges of pie; garnish with whole strawberries. Refrigerate for at least 1 hour before serving.

PINEAPPLE SHEET CAKE

This sheet cake is perfect for serving to a crowd. It keeps so well, you can easily prepare it a day ahead and it will stay moist. I often take it to church potlucks, and I have yet to take much of it home.
—**Kim Miller Spiek** Sarasota, FL

Prep: 15 min. • **Bake:** 35 min. + cooling
Makes: 24 servings

CAKE
- 2 cups all-purpose flour
- 2 cups sugar
- 2 large eggs
- 1 cup chopped nuts
- 2 teaspoons baking soda
- ½ teaspoon salt
- 1 teaspoon vanilla extract
- 1 can (20 ounces) crushed pineapple, undrained

CREAM CHEESE ICING
- 1 package (8 ounces) cream cheese, softened
- ½ cup butter, softened
- 3¾ cups confectioners' sugar
- 1 teaspoon vanilla extract
- ½ cup chopped nuts

1. Preheat oven to 350°. In a large bowl, combine the cake ingredients; beat until smooth. Pour into a greased 15x10x1-in. baking pan. Bake for 35 minutes. Cool.
2. For icing, in a small bowl, combine the cream cheese, butter, confectioners' sugar and vanilla until smooth. Spread over cake and sprinkle with nuts.

TEST KITCHEN TIP

Beat the batter just until smooth—overbeating can cause tunnels to form in the cake. For an even cake, rotate the pan halfway through the baking time. Don't worry if the top of this cake looks dark; cakes with large amounts of baking soda tend to darken because soda is a browning agent.

PEANUT BUTTER CHEESECAKE

The first time I served this cheesecake, my friends all went wild over it. They were surprised when I told them the crust is made of pretzels. It's sweet, salty, creamy, crunchy, peanut buttery and chocolatey.
—**Lois Brooks** Newark, DE

Prep: 20 min. + cooling
Bake: 55 min. + chilling
Makes: 12-14 servings

  1½ cups crushed pretzels
  ⅓ cup butter, melted
FILLING
  5 packages (8 ounces each) cream cheese, softened
  1½ cups sugar
  ¾ cup creamy peanut butter
  2 teaspoons vanilla extract
  3 large eggs, lightly beaten
  1 cup peanut butter chips
  1 cup (6 ounces) semisweet chocolate chips
TOPPING
  1 cup (8 ounces) sour cream
  3 tablespoons creamy peanut butter
  ½ cup sugar
  ½ cup finely chopped unsalted peanuts

1. Preheat oven to 350°. In a small bowl, combine pretzels and butter. Press onto the bottom and 1 in. up the sides of a greased 10-in. springform pan. Place pan on a baking sheet. Bake for 5 minutes. Cool on a wire rack.
2. In a large bowl, beat cream cheese and sugar until smooth. Add peanut butter and vanilla; mix well. Add eggs; beat on low just until combined. Stir in chips. Pour over the crust. Return pan to baking sheet.
3. Bake 50-55 minutes or until center is almost set. Remove from the oven; let stand for 15 minutes (leave oven on).
4. For topping, in a small bowl, combine the sour cream, peanut butter and sugar; spread over filling. Sprinkle with nuts. Bake for 5 minutes longer.
5. Cool on a wire rack for 10 minutes. Carefully run a knife around the edge of the pan to loosen; cool 1 hour longer. Refrigerate overnight. Remove the sides of the pan. Refrigerate leftovers.

MOIST PUMPKIN TUBE CAKE

This cake is perfect for fall. As it bakes, it fills the house with a spicy aroma.
—**Virginia Loew** Leesburg, FL

Prep: 10 min. • **Bake:** 1 hour + cooling
Makes: 12-16 servings

  2½ cups sugar
  1 cup canola oil
  3 large eggs
  3 cups all-purpose flour
  2 teaspoons baking soda
  1 teaspoon ground cinnamon
  1 teaspoon ground nutmeg
  ½ teaspoon salt
  ¼ teaspoon ground cloves
  1 can (15 ounces) solid-pack pumpkin
    Confectioners' sugar

1. Preheat oven to 350°. In a large bowl, combine sugar and oil until blended. Add eggs, one at a time, beating well after each addition. Combine flour, baking soda, cinnamon, nutmeg, salt and cloves; add to the egg mixture alternately with pumpkin, beating well after each addition.
2. Transfer to a greased 10-in. fluted tube pan. Bake 60-65 minutes or until toothpick inserted in the center comes out clean. Cool 10 minutes, then invert onto a wire rack, remove pan and cool completely. Dust with confectioners' sugar.

COOKIES & CANDIES

Just one cookie is never enough—and just one kind of cookie is never enough, either! Turn the page for a selection of delectable cookies and candies, each one as delicious and tempting as the last.

CHOCOLATE CHIP & COOKIE BUTTER THUMBPRINTS

I wanted to make a more festive version of chocolate chip cookies for the holidays. Since my mom's thumbprints are what I look forward to most, I decided to combine the two. We call the cookie spread "cookie butter"—which is how these got their name.
—**Crystal Schlueter** Babbitt, MN

Prep: 35 min.
Bake: 10 min./batch
Makes: about 2½ dozen

- ½ cup butter, softened
- ½ cup packed brown sugar
- ¼ teaspoon salt
- 1 large egg, separated
- 2 tablespoons 2% milk
- 1 teaspoon vanilla extract
- 1½ cups all-purpose flour
- ½ cup miniature semisweet chocolate chips
- 1 cup chopped pecans
- ⅔ cup Biscoff creamy cookie spread or Nutella
  Additional miniature semisweet chocolate chips, optional

1. Preheat oven to 350°. In a large bowl, cream butter, brown sugar and salt until light and fluffy. Beat in egg yolk, milk and vanilla. Gradually beat flour into the creamed mixture. Stir in chocolate chips. Cover and refrigerate for 1 hour or until firm enough to shape.
2. Shape tablespoons of dough into balls. Dip balls into egg white; then roll in pecans. Place balls 2 in. apart on lightly greased baking sheets. Press a deep indentation in center of each with your thumb. Bake until light golden brown, 12-14 minutes.
3. Remove from pans to wire racks to cool completely. Fill each with 1 teaspoon of cookie spread. If desired, sprinkle with additional chocolate chips.

ALMOND RASPBERRY STARS

The first Christmas I baked these, I ended up quickly making a second batch. The whole family enjoyed them.
—**Darlene Weaver** Lebanon, PA

Prep: 35 min. + chilling
Bake: 10 min./batch + cooling
Makes: about 1½ dozen

- ¾ cup butter, softened
- ½ cup confectioners' sugar
- 1 teaspoon vanilla extract
- ½ teaspoon almond extract
- 1¾ cups plus 2 tablespoons all-purpose flour
- 1 tablespoon finely chopped almonds
- 1 tablespoon granulated sugar
- ½ teaspoon ground cinnamon
- 1 large egg white, beaten
- ⅓ cup raspberry jam

1. Cream butter and confectioners' sugar until light and fluffy. Beat in the extracts. Gradually beat flour into the creamed mixture. Shape into a ball; refrigerate, covered, for 15 minutes.

2. Preheat oven to 350°. On a lightly floured surface, roll dough to ¼-in. thickness. With floured cookie cutters, cut dough into equal numbers of 2½-in. and 1½-in. stars. Combine almonds, sugar and cinnamon. Brush the small stars with egg white, then immediately sprinkle with almond mixture. Leave the large stars plain.

3. Place stars 1 in. apart on ungreased baking sheets. Bake just until the tips begin to brown, about 10 minutes for small stars and 12 minutes for large. Cool on wire racks.

4. To assemble, spread enough jam over large stars to cover centers. Top with the small stars; press lightly (jam should show around the edge of small stars). Let jam set before storing cookies in an airtight container.

CINNAMON CHIP CHAI-SPICED SNICKERDOODLES

I love cinnamon chips and am always looking for a way to use them. Make sure to stock up on them during the holiday season so you have plenty to last during the year.
—**Marietta Slater** Justin, TX

Prep: 30 min. + chilling • **Bake:** 15 min./batch
Makes: about 6 dozen

- ½ cup sugar
- 2 teaspoons ground cardamom
- 2 teaspoons ground cinnamon
- ½ teaspoon ground ginger
- ½ teaspoon ground cloves
- ¼ teaspoon ground nutmeg

DOUGH
- ½ cup butter, softened
- ½ cup shortening
- 1 cup sugar
- 2 large eggs
- 1 teaspoon vanilla extract
- 2¾ cups all-purpose flour
- 2 teaspoons cream of tartar
- 1 teaspoon baking soda
  Dash salt
- 1 package (10 ounces) cinnamon baking chips

1. For the spiced sugar, mix the first six ingredients.

2. In a large bowl, cream the butter, shortening, sugar and 2 tablespoons of the spiced sugar until light and fluffy. Beat in eggs and vanilla. In another bowl, whisk together flour, cream of tartar, baking soda and salt; gradually beat into the creamed mixture. Stir in baking chips. Refrigerate, covered, until firm enough to shape, about 1 hour.

3. Preheat oven to 350°. Shape dough into 1-in. balls; roll in the remaining spiced sugar. Place balls 2 in. apart on greased baking sheets.

4. Bake until set, 11-13 minutes. Remove from pans to wire racks to cool.

TEST KITCHEN TIP

When a recipe calls for greased baking sheets, use shortening or nonstick cooking spray. Avoid baking sheets with dark finishes; they may cause the cookies to become overly browned.

S'MOOKIES

S'mores are one of my favorite desserts. I wanted to create a cookie to replace the graham cracker—that's when my s'mookie was born. It's just as delicious as the classic!
—**Maria Davis** Hermosa Beach, CA

Prep: 15 min. + chilling
Bake: 10 min. + cooling
Makes: 10 cookies

- 1 cup all-purpose flour
- ½ cup old-fashioned or quick-cooking oats
- ⅓ cup packed brown sugar
- 2 teaspoons grated lemon peel
- ½ teaspoon grated whole nutmeg or 1 teaspoon ground nutmeg
- ½ teaspoon salt
- ¾ cup cold butter, cubed
- 2 tablespoons heavy cream
- 1 teaspoon vanilla extract
- ½ cup cinnamon baking chips
- 10 tablespoons Biscoff creamy cookie spread
- 20 large marshmallows

1. Place the first six ingredients in a food processor; process until blended. Add butter, cream and vanilla; pulse until dough comes together (do not overmix). Stir in cinnamon chips. Divide dough in half. Shape each into a disk; wrap in plastic. Refrigerate until firm enough to roll, about 30 minutes.

2. Preheat oven to 350°. On a lightly floured surface, roll each portion of dough to ¼-in. thickness. Cut with a floured 2½-in. square cookie cutter. Place 1 in. apart on ungreased baking sheets. Bake until cookies just begin to brown, 10-12 minutes (do not overbake). Remove from pans to wire racks to cool completely.

3. Preheat broiler. Spread 1 tablespoon cookie spread on bottoms of half of the cookies. Set aside. Place a marshmallow on bottoms of the remaining cookies; transfer to a baking sheet. Broil 5-6 in. from heat until marshmallows are golden brown, 30-45 seconds. Cover with cookie spread halves; press down gently.

(5) INGREDIENTS FAST FIX

CHOCOLATE PRETZEL RINGS

These easy snacks are positively delicious! You can switch them up for any season by choosing different colored M&M's.
—**Kim Scurio** Carol Stream, IL

Start to Finish: 30 min.
Makes: about 4 dozen

- 48 to 50 pretzel rings or squares
- 48 to 50 milk chocolate or striped chocolate kisses
- ¼ cup milk chocolate M&M's

1. Preheat oven to 275°. Place pretzels on greased baking sheets; place a chocolate kiss in the center of each pretzel. Bake until chocolate is softened, 2-3 minutes. Remove from the oven.

2. Place an M&M's candy on each; press down slightly so chocolate fills the pretzel holes. Refrigerate until chocolate is firm, 5-10 minutes. Store in an airtight container at room temperature.

FROSTED MALTED MILK COOKIES

My family loves anything made with malt or chocolate malted milk balls, so naturally these cookies are one of their favorites!
—**Nancy Foust** Stoneboro, PA

Prep: 40 min.
Bake: 10 min./batch + cooling
Makes: 4 dozen

- 1 cup butter, softened
- 2 cups packed brown sugar
- 2 large eggs
- ⅓ cup sour cream
- 2 teaspoons vanilla extract
- 4¾ cups all-purpose flour
- ¾ cup malted milk powder
- 2 teaspoons baking powder
- ½ teaspoon baking soda
- ½ teaspoon salt

FROSTING

- 3 cups confectioners' sugar
- ½ cup malted milk powder
- ⅓ cup butter, softened
- 1½ teaspoons vanilla extract
- 3 to 4 tablespoons 2% milk
- 2 cups coarsely chopped malted milk balls

1. Preheat oven to 350°. In a large bowl, cream butter and brown sugar until light and fluffy. Beat in eggs, sour cream and vanilla. In another bowl, whisk flour, malted milk powder, baking powder, baking soda and salt; gradually beat into the creamed mixture.
2. Divide dough into three portions. On a lightly floured surface, roll each portion to ¼-in. thickness. Cut with a floured 2½-in. round cookie cutter. Place 2 in. apart on parchment paper-lined baking sheets.
3. Bake until the edges are light brown, 10-12 minutes. Remove from pans to wire racks to cool completely.
4. For frosting, in a bowl, beat the confectioners' sugar, malted milk powder, butter, vanilla and enough milk to reach a spreading consistency. Spread over the cookies. Sprinkle with chopped candies.

BUTTER PECAN FUDGE

Toasted pecans add a nutty crunch to this creamy, buttery fudge. I have given this candy, with its wonderful caramel flavor, as gifts at Christmastime and people always rave about it!
—**Pam Smith** Alta Loma, CA

Prep: 10 min. • **Cook:** 10 min. + cooling
Makes: about 1½ pounds (64 pieces)

- 1 teaspoon plus ½ cup butter, cubed
- ½ cup granulated sugar
- ½ cup packed brown sugar
- ½ cup heavy whipping cream
- ⅛ teaspoon salt
- 1 teaspoon vanilla extract
- 2 cups sifted confectioners' sugar
- 1 cup coarsely chopped pecans, toasted

1. Line an 8x8-in. pan with foil; grease foil with 1 teaspoon butter.
2. In a large heavy saucepan, combine the remaining butter, granulated and brown sugars, cream and salt. Bring to a rapid boil over medium heat, stirring constantly. Cook, without stirring, until a candy thermometer reads 234° (soft-ball stage). Remove from heat. Add vanilla to pan (do not stir).
3. Cool, without stirring, to 110°, about 30 minutes. Beat with a spoon until fudge just begins to thicken. Gradually stir in confectioners' sugar until smooth; add nuts and continue stirring until fudge becomes very thick and just begins to lose its sheen. Immediately spread fudge into the prepared pan. Cool.
4. Using foil, lift fudge out of pan. Remove foil; cut fudge into 1-in. squares. Store between layers of waxed paper in an airtight container.
Note: To toast nuts, bake in a shallow pan in a 350° oven for 5-10 minutes or cook in a skillet over low heat until lightly browned, stirring occasionally.

HUNGARIAN WALNUT COOKIES

As a child, I always looked forward to eating these goodies at Christmastime. Now I make them for my own family.
—**Sharon Kurtz** Emmaus, PA

Prep: 50 min. + chilling
Bake: 10 min./batch + cooling
Makes: 4 dozen

- 1 cup butter, softened
- 1 package (8 ounces) cream cheese, softened
- 2½ cups all-purpose flour

FILLING

- 3 large egg whites
- ¾ teaspoon vanilla extract
- ⅓ cup sugar
- 3½ cups ground walnuts
- Confectioners' sugar

1. In a large bowl, cream butter and cream cheese until blended. Gradually beat flour into the creamed mixture. Divide dough into three portions. Shape each into a disk; wrap each disk in plastic. Refrigerate for 1 hour or until firm enough to roll.
2. Preheat oven to 375°. For filling, in a small bowl, beat egg whites and vanilla on medium speed until foamy. Gradually add sugar, 1 tablespoon at a time, beating on medium after each addition until well blended. Stir in walnuts.
3. Generously coat a work surface with confectioners' sugar. Roll one portion of dough into a 12-in. square about ⅛ in. thick, sprinkling with additional confectioners' sugar as necessary to coat well. Cut into sixteen 3-in. squares.
4. Shape 2 teaspoons filling into a small log about 2 in. long. Place diagonally onto a square. Overlap opposite corners of dough over filling; pinch tightly to seal. Place 2 in. apart on greased baking sheets. Repeat with remaining dough and filling.
5. Bake until bottoms are golden brown, 9-11 minutes. Remove from pans to wire racks to cool completely. Dust with confectioners' sugar.
To make ahead: Dough can be made 2 days in advance. Wrap in plastic and place in a resealable bag. Store in the refrigerator.
Freeze option: Freeze cookies in freezer containers. Thaw before serving. If desired, dust with additional confectioners' sugar.

MOUNTAIN COOKIES

I've been making these deliciously different cookies for more than 10 years. My kids especially like the creamy coconut filling. Wherever I take these cookies to share, people ask for the recipe. You'll be hard-pressed to eat just one!
—**Jeanne Adams** Richmond, VT

Prep: 30 min. • **Bake:** 10 min.
Makes: 4 dozen

- 1 cup butter, softened
- 1 cup confectioners' sugar
- 2 teaspoons vanilla extract
- 2 cups all-purpose flour
- ½ teaspoon salt

FILLING

- 3 ounces cream cheese, softened
- 1 cup confectioners' sugar
- 2 tablespoons all-purpose flour
- 1 teaspoon vanilla extract
- ½ cup finely chopped pecans
- ½ cup sweetened shredded coconut

TOPPING

- ½ cup semisweet chocolate chips
- 2 tablespoons butter
- 2 tablespoons water
- ½ cup confectioners' sugar

1. Preheat oven to 350°. In a large bowl, cream butter and sugar until light and fluffy. Beat in vanilla. Combine flour and salt; gradually add to the creamed mixture and mix well.
2. Shape into 1-in. balls; place 2 in. apart on ungreased baking sheets. Make a deep indentation in the center of each cookie. Bake until the edges just start to brown, 10-12 minutes. Remove to wire racks.
3. For the filling, in a large bowl, beat the cream cheese, sugar, flour and vanilla until smooth. Add pecans and coconut. Spoon ½ teaspoon of filling into each cool cookie.
4. For the topping, in a microwave-safe bowl, melt chocolate chips and butter with water; stir until smooth. Stir in sugar. Drizzle over cookies.

MOLE NEW MEXICAN WEDDING COOKIES

Heat and sweet is such an amazing combination. I added chili powder and chocolate chips to give a new twist to traditional Mexican cookies. They melt in your mouth, and then the spice hits you. I just love them.
—**Marla Clark** Albuquerque, NM

Prep: 30 min. • **Bake:** 15 min./batch
Makes: 2½ dozen

- ½ cup butter, softened
- ¾ cup confectioners' sugar, divided
- 1 teaspoon vanilla extract
- 1 cup all-purpose flour
- ½ cup ground pecans
- 1 teaspoon chili powder
- ¼ teaspoon ground cinnamon
- ¼ teaspoon ground cloves
- ¼ teaspoon ground allspice
- ½ cup miniature semisweet chocolate chips

1. Preheat oven to 350°. Cream butter and ⅓ cup confectioners' sugar until light and fluffy; beat in vanilla. In another bowl, whisk together the next six ingredients. Gradually beat into the creamed mixture. Fold in chocolate chips.

2. Shape dough into 1-in. balls. Place 1 in. apart on ungreased baking sheets. Bake until bottoms are lightly browned, 12-15 minutes. Remove from pans to wire racks to cool for 5 minutes. Roll in the remaining confectioners' sugar. Cool completely.

★★★★★ **READER REVIEW**

"I had the chance to make these cookies yesterday—I sampled one and it was delicious! Thank you for this recipe! It's a keeper!"

DELOWENSTEIN TASTEOFHOME.COM

FAST FIX

OATMEAL RAISIN COOKIES

A friend gave me the recipe for these cookies many years ago, and they're as delicious as the ones Mom used to make. The secret to the recipe is to measure exactly (no guessing on the amounts) and to not overbake.

—**Wendy Coalwell** Abbeville, GA

Start to Finish: 30 min.
Makes: about 3½ dozen

- 1 cup shortening
- 1 cup sugar
- 1 cup packed light brown sugar
- 3 large eggs
- 1 teaspoon vanilla extract
- 2½ cups all-purpose flour
- 2 teaspoons baking soda
- 1 teaspoon salt
- 1 teaspoon ground cinnamon
- 2 cups old-fashioned oats
- 1 cup raisins
- 1 cup coarsely chopped pecans, optional

1. Preheat oven to 350°. In a large bowl, cream the shortening and sugars until light and fluffy. Beat in eggs, one at a time, beating well after each addition. Beat in vanilla. Combine flour, baking soda, salt and cinnamon. Add to creamed mixture, stirring just until combined. Stir in the oats, raisins and, if desired, pecans.
2. Shape into 1-in. balls. Place 2 in. apart on ungreased baking sheets. Flatten with a greased glass bottom.
3. Bake until cookies are golden brown, 10-11 minutes. Do not overbake. Remove to a wire rack to cool.

SALTED CARAMEL COOKIE CUPS

When I brought these salty and sweet cookies to a potluck, I overheard people talking about how wonderful they were. I'm not sure whether it was the cookie, the caramel or the chocolate they loved best!

—**Priscilla Yee** Concord, CA

Prep: 30 min. • **Bake:** 10 min./batch + cooling
Makes: 3 dozen

- 1 package (17½ ounces) sugar cookie mix
- 2 tablespoons all-purpose flour
- ⅓ cup butter, softened
- 1 large egg

FILLING
- 6 ounces cream cheese, softened
- ½ cup semisweet chocolate chips, melted
- ⅓ cup confectioners' sugar
- 36 caramels
- 2 teaspoons coarse sea salt
- 36 pecan halves, toasted

1. Preheat oven to 375°. In a large bowl, combine cookie mix and flour. Beat in butter and egg until blended. Shape dough into 1¼-in. balls; press onto bottom and up sides of greased mini-muffin cups.
2. In a small bowl, combine cream cheese, chocolate chips and confectioners' sugar. Place a rounded teaspoon of filling in each cup. Press one caramel into the filling in each cup. Bake until the edges are golden brown and caramel is melted, 9-11 minutes. Sprinkle with sea salt; top each with a pecan half. Cool completely in the pan on wire racks.

RASPBERRY COCONUT BALLS

My family loves Hostess Zingers, especially the raspberry flavor coated with coconut. So we came up with this treat to make for school bake sales. We can make about four dozen in 30 minutes, and they sell out fast!

—**Pam Clark** Wheaton, IL

....

Prep: 30 min.
Makes: about 4 dozen

- 1 package (12 ounces) vanilla wafers, crushed
- 3⅓ cups sweetened shredded coconut, divided
- 1 can (14 ounces) sweetened condensed milk
- 3 teaspoons raspberry extract
- 1 teaspoon rum extract
- ¼ cup pink sanding sugar

Mix wafer crumbs and 1⅓ cups coconut. Stir in milk and extracts. In a shallow bowl, combine sugar and remaining coconut. Shape dough into 1-in. balls; roll in coconut mixture. Refrigerate in airtight containers.

CHOCOLATE-COVERED CHERRY THUMBPRINTS

When I dig out my best cookie recipes, they remind me of baking when my children were little. These thumbprints with cherries elicit sweet memories.

—**Deborah Puette** Lilburn, GA

....

Prep: 30 min. + chilling
Bake: 15 min. + cooling
Makes: 2 dozen

- ¼ cup butter, softened
- ¼ cup shortening
- ¼ cup packed brown sugar
- ¼ teaspoon salt
- 1 large egg, separated
- ½ teaspoon vanilla extract
- 1 cup all-purpose flour
- 1 cup finely chopped salted roasted almonds

FILLING

- ⅓ cup confectioners' sugar
- 1 tablespoon maraschino cherry juice
- 2 teaspoons butter, softened
- 1 teaspoon 2% milk

TOPPINGS

- 24 maraschino cherries
- 4 ounces milk chocolate candy coating, melted

1. In a large bowl, cream the butter, shortening, brown sugar and salt until light and fluffy. Beat in egg yolk and vanilla. Gradually beat flour into creamed mixture. Refrigerate, covered, until easy to handle, about 30 minutes.

2. Preheat oven to 350°. Shape dough into 1¼-in. balls. In a shallow bowl, whisk egg white until foamy. Place almonds in a separate shallow bowl. Dip balls in egg white, then roll in almonds.

3. Place 2 in. apart on ungreased baking sheets. Press a deep indentation in the center of each with your thumb. Bake until edges are light brown, 10-12 minutes. Remove from pans to wire racks.

4. In a small bowl, beat confectioners' sugar, cherry juice, butter and milk until smooth. Fill each cookie with ¼ tsp. of the filling; top with one cherry. Drizzle with candy coating. Let stand until set.

RAINBOW COOKIES

I always bake these two weeks ahead. That allows the cookies enough time to mellow, leaving them moist and full of almond flavor!
—**Mary Ann Lee** Clifton Park, NY

Prep: 50 min. + chilling
Bake: 10 min. + cooling
Makes: about 8 dozen

- 1 can (8 ounces) almond paste
- 1 cup butter, softened
- 1 cup sugar
- 4 large eggs, separated
- 2 cups all-purpose flour
- 6 to 8 drops red food coloring
- 6 to 8 drops green food coloring
- ¼ cup seedless red raspberry jam
- ¼ cup apricot preserves
- 1 cup (6 ounces) semisweet chocolate chips

1. Preheat oven to 350°. Grease bottoms of three matching 13x9-in. baking pans (or reuse one pan). Line the pans with waxed paper; grease the paper.
2. Place almond paste in a large bowl; break up with a fork. Cream with butter, sugar and egg yolks until light and fluffy. Stir in flour. In another bowl, beat egg whites until soft peaks form. Fold into the dough, mixing until thoroughly blended.
3. Divide the dough into three portions (about 1⅓ cups each). Color one portion with red food coloring and one with green; leave the remaining portion uncolored. Spread each portion of dough into one of the prepared pans. Bake until the edges are light golden brown, 10-12 minutes.
4. Invert onto wire racks; remove waxed paper. Place another wire rack on top and turn over. Cool completely.
5. Place the green layer on a large piece of plastic wrap. Spread evenly with raspberry jam. Top with the uncolored layer and spread with apricot jam. Top with the pink layer. Bring plastic wrap over layers. Slide onto a baking sheet and set a cutting board or heavy, flat pan on top to compress the layers. Refrigerate overnight.
6. The next day, melt the chocolate in a microwave; stir until smooth. Spread over the top layer; allow to harden. With a sharp knife, trim the edges. Cut into ½-in. strips across the width; then cut each strip into 4-5 pieces. Store in airtight containers.

(5) INGREDIENTS
COOKIES & CREAM FUDGE

I invented this confection for a bake sale at our children's school. Boy, was it a hit! The crunchy chunks of sandwich cookie soften a bit as the mixture mellows. It's so sweet that one panful serves a crowd.
—**Laura Lane** Richmond, VA

Prep: 25 min. + chilling
Makes: 3 dozen

- 16 Oreo cookies, broken into chunks, divided
- 1 can (14 ounces) sweetened condensed milk
- 2 tablespoons butter
- 2⅔ cups white baking chips
- 1 teaspoon vanilla extract
  Crushed peppermint candies, optional

1. Line an 8-in. square dish with aluminum foil; coat with cooking spray. Place half of the broken cookies in the pan.
2. In a heavy saucepan, combine the milk, butter and chips; cook and stir over low heat until the chips are melted. Remove from heat; stir in vanilla.
3. Pour mixture over cookies in pan. Sprinkle with the remaining cookies and, if desired, peppermint candies. Cover and refrigerate for at least 1 hour. Cut into small squares.

FROSTED BUTTER RUM BRICKLE BITES

The rum, real butter and toffee bits made these cookies my husband's new favorite. If you'd like them less sweet, skip the frosting and sprinkle the cookies with confectioners' sugar while still warm.

—Cindy Nerat Menominee, MI

Prep: 35 min. • **Bake:** 10 min./batch + cooling
Makes: about 4 dozen

- 1 cup butter, softened
- ¾ cup confectioners' sugar
- 2 teaspoons rum extract
- ½ teaspoon salt
- 2 cups all-purpose flour
- 1 package (8 ounces) brickle toffee bits

ICING

- ⅓ cup butter, cubed
- 2 cups confectioners' sugar
- ½ teaspoon rum extract
- 2 to 3 tablespoons 2% milk

1. Preheat oven to 375°. Beat the first four ingredients until blended. Beat in flour. Stir in toffee bits. Shape dough into 1-in. balls; place 2 in. apart on parchment paper-lined baking sheets.

2. Bake until edges are light brown and the toffee bits begin to melt, 8-10 minutes. Cool on pans 5 minutes. Remove to wire racks to cool completely.

3. In a small heavy saucepan, melt butter over medium heat. Heat until golden brown, about 5 minutes, stirring constantly. Remove from heat; stir in confectioners' sugar, rum extract and enough milk to reach desired consistency. Spread over cookies.

TEST KITCHEN TIP

You'll know these cookies are done when the toffee bits around the edges just start to melt and the edges of the cookies are lightly browned. The thick, buttery icing would also taste great on pecan shortbread or pumpkin cookies.

PEPPERMINT SWIRL FUDGE

Indulge your sweet tooth with these rich swirled squares. For Christmasy color, I add crushed peppermint candies and red food coloring.

—Suzette Jury Keene, CA

Prep: 15 min. + chilling
Makes: about 1½ pounds

- 1 teaspoon butter
- 1 package (10 to 12 ounces) white baking chips
- 1 can (16 ounces) vanilla frosting
- ½ teaspoon peppermint extract
- 8 drops red food coloring
- 2 tablespoons crushed peppermint candies

1. Line a 9-in. square pan with foil and grease the foil with butter; set aside.

2. In a small saucepan, melt chips; stir until smooth. Remove from heat. Stir in frosting and extract. Spread into the prepared pan. Randomly place drops of food coloring over the fudge; cut through the fudge with a knife to swirl. Sprinkle with candies. Refrigerate for 1 hour or until set.

3. Using foil, lift fudge out of pan. Gently peel off the foil; cut fudge into 1-in. squares. Store in an airtight container.

CHOCOLATE LEBKUCHEN

Having lived in Germany, I try to keep my German cooking and baking as authentic as possible. These lovely lebkuchen are a culinary Christmas custom.

—**Cathy Lemmon** Quinlan, TX

Prep: 1 hour + cooling
Bake: 15 min. + cooling
Makes: about 1½ dozen

- 1 cup plus 2 tablespoons all-purpose flour
- ¼ cup sugar
  Dash salt
- ⅓ cup cold butter, cubed
- 3 tablespoons water
- 1 teaspoon vanilla extract

TOPPING
- ¼ cup butter, softened
- ¼ cup sugar
- 1 large egg
- 1 tablespoon canola oil
- ⅔ cup quick-cooking oats
- ½ cup all-purpose flour
- ⅓ cup ground almonds
- ⅓ cup ground hazelnuts
- ¼ cup baking cocoa
- 1 teaspoon baking powder
- ½ teaspoon ground cinnamon
- ¼ teaspoon each ground cloves, cardamom and allspice
- ¼ cup finely chopped candied lemon peel
- ¼ cup finely chopped candied orange peel

GLAZE
- 6 ounces semisweet chocolate, chopped
- 2 ounces unsweetened chocolate, chopped
- ¼ cup butter, cubed

1. Preheat oven to 325°. In a small bowl, combine flour, sugar and salt; cut in butter until mixture resembles coarse crumbs. Combine water and vanilla; gradually add to the crumb mixture, tossing with a fork until the dough forms a ball.

2. On a lightly floured surface, roll out the dough to ¹⁄₁₆-in. thickness. Cut with a floured 2½-in. round cookie cutter. Place on ungreased baking sheets. Bake until set, 8-10 minutes. Remove from pans to wire racks to cool. Leave oven on.

3. For topping, in a small bowl, cream butter and sugar until light and fluffy. Beat in egg and oil. Combine the oats, flour, nuts, cocoa, baking powder and spices; gradually add to the creamed mixture and mix well. Fold in candied peels.

4. Drop a rounded tablespoonful of topping on each cookie; gently press down. Place 2 in. apart on ungreased baking sheets. Bake until cookies are set, 13-16 minutes. Remove from pans to wire racks to cool.

5. In a microwave-safe bowl, melt chocolate and butter; stir until smooth. Dip each cookie halfway in chocolate; allow excess to drip off. Place on waxed paper; let stand until set. Store in airtight containers.

⑤INGREDIENTS FAST FIX

TOFFEE PEANUT CLUSTERS

These are a favorite among all my family and friends. They come together quickly and the toffee adds a distinct twist.

—**Joy Dulaney** Highland Village, TX

Start to Finish: 30 min.
Makes: 5 dozen

- 1½ pounds milk chocolate candy coating, coarsely chopped
- 1 jar (16 ounces) dry roasted peanuts
- 1 package (8 ounces) milk chocolate English toffee bits

In a microwave, melt the candy coating; stir until smooth. Stir in peanuts and toffee bits. Drop by rounded tablespoonfuls onto waxed paper-lined baking sheets. Let stand until set. Store in an airtight container.

CRANBERRY OATMEAL COOKIES

Dotted with cranberries, orange peel and vanilla chips, these cookies are so colorful and fun to eat. They look lovely on a dessert tray and would be a great addition to your Christmas cookie lineup.
—**Pat Habiger** Spearville, KS

Prep: 15 min. • **Bake:** 10 min./batch
Makes: 6 dozen

- 1 cup butter, softened
- 1½ cups sugar
- 2 large eggs
- 1 teaspoon vanilla extract
- 2 cups all-purpose flour
- 1 teaspoon baking powder
- ½ teaspoon salt
- ¼ teaspoon baking soda
- 2 cups quick-cooking oats
- 1 cup raisins
- 1 cup coarsely chopped fresh or frozen cranberries
- 1 tablespoon grated orange peel
- 1 package (10 to 12 ounces) white baking chips

1. Preheat oven to 375°. In a large bowl, cream butter and sugar until light and fluffy. Add the eggs, one at a time, beating well after each addition. Beat in vanilla. Combine flour, baking powder, salt and baking soda; add to the creamed mixture. Stir in the oats, raisins, cranberries and orange peel. Stir in baking chips.
2. Drop by rounded teaspoonfuls 2 in. apart onto greased baking sheets. Bake until the edges are lightly browned, 10-12 minutes. Cool on wire racks.

DID YOU KNOW?

Quick-cooking oats and old-fashioned oats are interchangeable, but you must accommodate the differences between the two. Both have been flattened with large rollers, but quick-cooking oats are cut into smaller pieces first. As a result, quick-cooking oats cook faster, and they offer a more delicate texture to baked goods and desserts. For a heartier texture, use old-fashioned oats.

PEANUT PRETZEL TOFFEE BARK

My toffee has been a must-make treat for my family and friends for over 40 years. It was my dad's favorite candy and each time I make it, I think of him.
—**Barb Estabrook** Appleton, WI

Prep: 10 min. • **Cook:** 15 min. + chilling
Makes: 1½ pounds

- 2 teaspoons plus 1 cup butter, divided
- ⅔ cup honey-roasted peanuts, coarsely chopped
- ½ cup miniature pretzels, coarsely chopped
- 1 cup sugar
- 2 tablespoons water
- 2 tablespoons honey
- 1 cup (6 ounces) 60% cacao bittersweet chocolate baking chips
  Sea salt, optional

1. Line the bottom of a greased 9-in. square baking pan with foil; grease foil with 2 teaspoons butter. Sprinkle peanuts and pretzels onto foil.
2. In a large heavy saucepan, combine sugar, water, honey and the remaining butter; bring to a boil over medium-high heat, stirring constantly. Cook 4 minutes without stirring. Then, stirring constantly, cook 2-3 minutes longer or until mixture is caramel-colored (a candy thermometer should read 300° for hard-crack stage). Remove from heat. Immediately pour over the peanuts and pretzels.
3. Sprinkle with chocolate chips; let stand until the chocolate begins to melt. Spread evenly. If desired, sprinkle with salt. Cool for 15 minutes at room temperature. Refrigerate until set, about 30 minutes.
4. Break the toffee into pieces. Store between layers of waxed paper in an airtight container.

THREE-CHOCOLATE FUDGE

I make this fudge at Christmastime to give to friends and neighbors. That tradition started years ago when I made more candy than my husband, three sons and I could eat, so we shared it. It's a tasty tradition I'm glad to continue.

—**Betty Grantham** Hanceville, AL

Prep: 35 min. + chilling
Makes: about 5½ pounds

- 1 tablespoon butter
- 3⅓ cups sugar
- 1 cup packed dark brown sugar
- 1 can (12 ounces) evaporated milk
- 1 cup butter, cubed
- 32 large marshmallows, halved
- 1 teaspoon vanilla extract
- 2 cups (12 ounces) semisweet chocolate chips
- 14 ounces milk chocolate, chopped
- 2 ounces semisweet chocolate, chopped
- 2 cups chopped pecans, toasted

1. Line a 15x10x1-in. pan with foil; grease foil with 1 tablespoon butter.
2. In a heavy large saucepan, combine sugars, milk and cubed butter. Bring to a rapid boil over medium heat, stirring constantly; cook and stir for 5 minutes. Remove from heat. Stir in marshmallows and vanilla until blended.
3. Gradually stir in chocolate chips and chopped chocolate until melted. Fold in pecans. Immediately spread into the prepared pan. Refrigerate for 1 hour or until firm. Using foil, lift fudge out of pan. Remove foil; cut fudge into 1-in. squares. Store between layers of waxed paper in an airtight container.

TEST KITCHEN TIP

To achieve a smooth, shiny surface on your fudge, work quickly when spreading it into the pan, and touch it as little as possible. Gently tap and shake the pan to smooth out the top. When cutting the fudge, avoid ragged edges by cleaning your knife between cuts.

(5)INGREDIENTS

FIRST PLACE COCONUT MACAROONS

These cookies earned me a first-place ribbon at our county fair. They remain my husband's favorites—whenever I make them to give away, he always asks me where his batch is! I love that the recipe makes a small enough batch for the two of us to nibble on.

—**Penny Ann Habeck** Shawano, WI

Prep: 10 min. • **Bake:** 20 min. + cooling
Makes: about 1½ dozen

- 1⅓ cups sweetened shredded coconut
- ⅓ cup sugar
- 2 tablespoons all-purpose flour
- ⅛ teaspoon salt
- 2 large egg whites
- ½ teaspoon vanilla extract

1. Preheat oven to 325°. In a small bowl, combine the coconut, sugar, flour and salt. Add egg whites and vanilla; mix well.
2. Drop by rounded teaspoonfuls onto greased baking sheets. Bake until golden brown, 18-20 minutes. Cool on a wire rack.

GLAZED MAPLE SHORTBREAD COOKIES

Whever I visit friends in the United States, I make sure to buy maple syrup and maple sugar—it's the best I've ever had. These delicious cookies can be decorated with sprinkles but they're just fine as is.
—Lorraine Caland Shuniah, ON

Prep: 25 min. + chilling
Bake: 20 min. + cooling
Makes: 1½ dozen

- 1 **cup butter, softened**
- ¼ **cup sugar**
- 3 **tablespoons cornstarch**
- 1 **teaspoon maple flavoring**
- 1¾ **cups all-purpose flour**

GLAZE
- ¾ **cup plus 1 tablespoon confectioners' sugar**
- ⅓ **cup maple syrup**

1. In a large bowl, beat butter, sugar and cornstarch until blended. Beat in flavoring. Gradually beat in flour.
2. Shape dough into a disk; wrap disk in plastic. Refrigerate until firm enough to roll, about 45 minutes.
3. Preheat oven to 325°. On a lightly floured surface, roll the dough to ¼-in. thickness. Cut with a floured 2¾-in. leaf-shaped cookie cutter. Place 1 in. apart on parchment paper-lined baking sheets.
4. Bake until the edges are light brown, 20-25 minutes. Remove from pans to wire racks to cool completely.
5. In a small bowl, mix confectioners' sugar and maple syrup until smooth. Spread over cookies. Let stand until set.

SNOW-CAPPED MOCHA FUDGE DROPS

Everyone loves seeing chocolate on a cookie tray. My version is fudgy with a hint of mocha. If you're serving these at the holidays, add red and green colored sugar or sprinkles for a festive touch.
—**Patricia Harmon** Baden, PA

Prep: 40 min. • **Bake:** 10 min./batch + cooling
Makes: about 3½ dozen

- 1 cup (6 ounces) semisweet chocolate chips, divided
- ½ cup butter, cubed
- 1 tablespoon instant coffee granules or espresso powder
- ¾ cup sugar
- ¾ cup packed brown sugar
- 2 large eggs
- 2 teaspoons vanilla extract
- 2 cups all-purpose flour
- ¼ cup baking cocoa
- ½ teaspoon baking powder
- ¼ teaspoon salt
- ½ cup chopped pecans or walnuts
- 10 ounces white candy coating, melted
  White edible glitter and/or red and green colored sugar, optional

1. Preheat oven to 350°. In a large microwave-safe bowl, microwave ½ cup chocolate chips and the butter until butter is melted; stir until chocolate is melted. Stir in coffee granules; cool slightly.
2. Whisk in sugars. Whisk in eggs, one at a time, and vanilla until blended. In a small bowl, whisk the flour, cocoa, baking powder and salt; stir into the chocolate mixture. Stir in pecans and the remaining chocolate chips.
3. Drop dough by tablespoonfuls 1 in. apart onto ungreased baking sheets. Bake until set, 8-10 minutes. Cool on pans for 2 minutes. Remove to wire racks to cool completely.
4. Dip tops of cookies into melted candy coating; sprinkle with glitter and/or colored sugar if desired. Let stand until set.
Note: Edible glitter is available from Wilton Industries. Visit wilton.com or call 800-794-5866.

RASPBERRY RIBBONS

I make these attractive, buttery cookies to serve at our remote guest lodge, and all the cooks in the kitchen are addicted to them!
—**Patsy Wolfenden** Golden, BC

Prep: 20 min. • **Bake:** 20 min. + cooling
Makes: about 5 dozen

- 1 cup butter, softened
- ½ cup granulated sugar
- 1 large egg
- 1 teaspoon vanilla extract
- 2¼ cups all-purpose flour
- ½ teaspoon baking powder
- ¼ teaspoon salt
- ½ cup raspberry jam

GLAZE
- 1 cup confectioners' sugar
- 2 tablespoons evaporated milk
- ½ teaspoon vanilla extract

1. Preheat oven to 350°. In a large bowl, cream butter and granulated sugar until light and fluffy. Beat in egg and vanilla. Combine the flour, baking powder and salt; gradually add to the creamed mixture and mix well.
2. Divide the dough into four portions; shape each into a 10x2½-in. log. Place logs 4 in. apart on greased or foil-lined baking sheets. Make a ½-in. depression down the center of each log. Bake for 10 minutes.
3. Fill the depression in each log with jam. Bake until lightly browned, 10-15 minutes longer. Cool for 2 minutes. Remove to a cutting board; cut into ¾-in. slices. Place on wire racks.
4. In a small bowl, combine the glaze ingredients. Drizzle over warm cookies. Cool completely.

FROSTED CRANBERRY DROP COOKIES

After tasting a batch my friend whipped up, I immediately requested the recipe and have been baking these treats by the dozens ever since. The sweet icing beautifully complements the tart berries.
—**Shirley Kidd** New London, MN

Prep: 25 min. • **Bake:** 15 min./batch
Makes: about 5 dozen

- ½ cup butter, softened
- 1 cup sugar
- ¾ cup packed brown sugar
- ¼ cup whole milk
- 1 large egg
- 2 tablespoons orange juice
- 3 cups all-purpose flour
- 1 teaspoon baking powder
- ½ teaspoon salt
- ¼ teaspoon baking soda
- 2½ cups chopped fresh or frozen cranberries
- 1 cup chopped walnuts

FROSTING
- ⅓ cup butter
- 2 cups confectioners' sugar
- 1½ teaspoons vanilla extract
- 2 to 4 tablespoons hot water

1. Preheat oven to 350°. In a bowl, cream butter and sugars. Add milk, egg and orange juice; mix well. Combine the flour, baking powder, salt and baking soda; add to the creamed mixture and mix well. Stir in cranberries and nuts.

2. Drop by tablespoonfuls 2 in. apart onto greased baking sheets. Bake until golden brown, 12-15 minutes. Cool on wire racks.

3. For the frosting, heat the butter in a saucepan over low heat until golden brown, about 5 minutes. Cool mixture for 2 minutes; transfer to a small bowl. Add sugar and vanilla. Beat in water, 1 tablespoon at a time, until frosting reaches desired consistency. Frost the cookies.

⑤ INGREDIENTS
MOCHA TRUFFLES

Nothing compares to the melt-in-your-mouth flavor of these truffles...or to the simplicity of the recipe. Whenever I make them for my family or friends, they're quickly devoured. No one has to know how easy they are to prepare!
—**Stacy Abell** Olathe, KS

Prep: 25 min. + chilling
Makes: about 5½ dozen

- 2 packages (12 ounces each) semisweet chocolate chips
- 1 package (8 ounces) cream cheese, softened
- 3 tablespoons instant coffee granules
- 2 teaspoons water
- 1 pound dark chocolate candy coating, coarsely chopped
  White candy coating, optional

1. In a microwave-safe bowl, melt chocolate chips; stir until smooth. Beat in cream cheese. Dissolve coffee in water; add to cream cheese and beat until smooth.

2. Chill until firm enough to shape. Shape into 1-in. balls and place on waxed paper-lined baking sheet. Chill until firm, 1-2 hours.

3. In a microwave, melt chocolate coating; stir until smooth. Dip balls in chocolate; allow excess to drip off. Place on waxed paper; let stand until set. Melt white coating and drizzle over truffles if desired.

Note: Dark, white or milk chocolate confectionery coating is found in the baking section of most grocery stores. It is sometimes labeled almond bark or candy coating and is often sold in bulk packages (1-1½ pounds). It is the product used for dipping chocolate. A substitute for 6 ounces chocolate coating would be 1 cup (6 ounces) semisweet, dark or white chocolate chips and 1 tablespoon shortening melted together. Truffles can be frozen for several months before dipping in chocolate. Thaw in the refrigerator before dipping.

SEASONAL SPECIALTIES

Here you'll find some of our most popular recipes sure to impress guests during all kinds of festive celebrations. From summer's flame-broiled fare to winter's cozy comfort foods, the perfect dish is always at your fingertips.

CHOCOLATE-STRAWBERRY PRETZEL COOKIES

Every year I try to come up with a new recipe for my cookie tray, and this one has become a favorite. Who ever would guess how good pretzels are in cookies?
—**Isabel Minunni** Poughkeepsie, NY

Prep: 30 min. + chilling
Bake: 10 min./batch + cooling
Makes: about 1 dozen

- 1 cup unsalted butter, softened
- ½ cup sugar
- 2 large eggs
- 1½ cups finely ground pretzels (about 6 ounces)
- 1 cup all-purpose flour
- 1 teaspoon baking powder
- ⅔ cup semisweet chocolate chips, melted
- ⅓ cup seedless strawberry jam
  Confectioners' sugar

1. In a large bowl, cream the butter and sugar until light and fluffy. Add eggs, one at a time, beating well after each addition. In another bowl, mix the ground pretzels, flour and baking powder; gradually beat into creamed mixture. Divide dough in half. Shape each into a disk; wrap in plastic. Refrigerate until firm enough to roll, about 1 hour.
2. Preheat the oven to 350°. On a lightly floured surface, roll each portion of the dough to ¼-in. thickness. Cut it with a floured 3½-in. tree-shaped cookie cutter. Using a floured 1¾-in. tree-shaped cookie cutter, cut out the centers of half of the cookies. Place solid and window cookies 1 in. apart on ungreased baking sheets.
3. Bake 8-10 minutes or until edges are light brown. Remove from pans to wire racks to cool completely.
4. Spread the melted chocolate onto bottoms of solid cookies; let stand until firm. Spread jam over cooled chocolate; top with window cookies. Dust lightly with confectioners' sugar.
Freeze option: Freeze undecorated cookies in freezer containers. To use, thaw in covered containers and decorate as directed.

MARDI GRAS

PEPPERY HUSH PUPPIES

For our family, a good fish dinner just is not complete without these zesty hush puppies. You can also serve them alone as a spicy snack.
—**Carolyn Griffin** Macon, GA

Prep: 10 min. • **Cook:** 30 min.
Makes: 6 dozen

- 2 **cups cornmeal**
- 1 **cup plus 3 tablespoons all-purpose flour**
- 2 **teaspoons baking powder**
- 1½ **teaspoons sugar**
- 1 **teaspoon salt**
- ½ **teaspoon baking soda**
- 1 **large egg**
- ⅔ **cup water**
- ½ **cup buttermilk**
- ½ **cup butter, melted**
- 1 **cup grated onion**
- 2 **jalapeno peppers, seeded and chopped**
- 1 **small green pepper, chopped**
  Oil for deep-fat frying

1. In a large bowl, combine the cornmeal, flour, baking powder, sugar, salt and baking soda. In another bowl, whisk the egg, water, buttermilk and butter. Stir in the onion, jalapenos and green pepper. Stir into dry ingredients just until moistened.
2. In an electric skillet or deep-fat fryer, heat the oil to 375°. Drop the batter by teaspoonfuls, a few at a time, into hot oil. Fry it until golden brown on both sides. Drain on paper towels. Serve warm.
Note: Wear disposable gloves when cutting hot peppers; the oils can burn skin. Avoid touching your face.

SWEET CORN BEIGNETS WITH BACON-SUGAR DUST

Opposites attract deliciously in these irresistible beignets— crispy outside and soft and fluffy inside. Salty bacon sugar contrasts nicely with the sweet corn in the pastries.
—**Cheryl Perry** Hertford, NC

Prep: 25 min. + rising • **Cook:** 5 min./batch
Makes: 4 dozen

- 1 **package (¼ ounce) active dry yeast**
- 1 **cup warm 2% milk (110° to 115°)**
- 1¼ **cups fresh or frozen corn, thawed**
- ¼ **cup sugar**
- 2 **large eggs**
- ¼ **cup butter, melted**
- 1 **teaspoon salt**
- 1 **teaspoon vanilla extract**
- 4½ **to 5 cups all-purpose flour**
- 2 **cups confectioners' sugar**
- 6 **cooked bacon strips**
  Oil for deep-fat frying

1. In a large bowl, dissolve yeast in warm milk. Add the corn, sugar, eggs, butter, salt, vanilla and 4½ cups flour. Beat this until smooth. Stir in enough remaining flour to form a soft dough (dough will be sticky).
2. Turn onto a floured surface; knead until smooth and elastic, about 6-8 minutes. Place in a greased bowl, turning once to grease the top. Cover and let rise in a warm place until doubled, about 1 hour.
3. Meanwhile, in food processor, combine confectioners' sugar and bacon. Process until combined; set aside.
4. Punch dough down. Turn onto a lightly floured surface; roll it into a 16x12-in. rectangle. Cut into 2-in. squares.
5. In an electric skillet or deep-fat fryer, heat oil to 375°. Fry squares, a few at a time, until golden brown, about 1½ minutes on each side. Drain on paper towels. Dust with bacon-sugar mixture. Serve warm.
Note: These beignets are best served the day they're made.

SHRIMP GUMBO

A crisp green salad and crusty French bread complete this shrimp gumbo meal. I always have hot sauce available when I serve this, and have found that the instant microwave rice packages make the process a little easier.

—Jo Ann Graham Ovilla, TX

Prep: 30 min. • **Cook:** 1 hour
Makes: 11 servings

- ¼ cup all-purpose flour
- ¼ cup canola oil
- 3 celery ribs, chopped
- 1 medium green pepper, chopped
- 1 medium onion, chopped
- 1 carton (32 ounces) chicken broth
- 3 garlic cloves, minced
- 1 teaspoon salt
- 1 teaspoon pepper
- ½ teaspoon cayenne pepper
- 2 pounds uncooked large shrimp, peeled and deveined
- 1 package (16 ounces) frozen sliced okra
- 4 green onions, sliced
- 1 medium tomato, chopped
- 1½ teaspoons gumbo file powder
  Hot cooked rice

1. In a Dutch oven over medium heat, cook and stir flour and oil until caramel-colored, about 12 minutes (do not burn). Add the celery, green pepper and onion; cook and stir for 5-6 minutes or until tender. Stir in the broth, garlic, salt, pepper and cayenne; bring to a boil. Reduce heat; cover and simmer for 30 minutes.

2. Stir in the shrimp, okra, green onions and tomato. Return to a boil. Reduce heat; cover and simmer for 10 minutes or until shrimp turn pink. Stir in file powder. Serve with rice.

Note: Gumbo file powder, used to thicken and flavor Creole recipes, is available in spice shops. If you don't want to use gumbo file powder, combine 2 tablespoons each of cornstarch and water until smooth. Gradually stir into gumbo. Bring to a boil; cook and stir 2 minutes or until thickened.

TRADITIONAL NEW ORLEANS KING CAKE

Get in on the fun of the King Cake. Hide a little toy baby in the cake and whoever finds it has one year of good luck!

—Rebecca Baird Salt Lake Cty, UT

Prep: 40 min. + rising
Bake: 25 min. + cooling
Makes: 1 cake (12 slices)

- 2 packages (¼ ounce each) active dry yeast
- ½ cup warm water (110° to 115°)
- ¾ cup sugar, divided
- ½ cup butter, softened
- ½ cup warm 2% milk (110° to 115°)
- 2 large egg yolks
- 1¼ teaspoons salt
- 1 teaspoon grated lemon peel
- ¼ teaspoon ground nutmeg
- 3¼ to 3¾ cups all-purpose flour
- 1 teaspoon ground cinnamon
- 1 large egg, beaten

GLAZE
- 1½ cups confectioners' sugar
- 2 teaspoons lemon juice
- 2 to 3 tablespoons water
  Green, purple and yellow sugars

1. In a large bowl, dissolve yeast in warm water. Add ½ cup sugar, butter, milk, egg yolks, salt, lemon peel, nutmeg and 2 cups flour. Beat until smooth. Stir in enough remaining flour to form a soft dough (dough will be sticky).

2. Turn onto a floured surface; knead until smooth and elastic, about 6-8 minutes. Place in a greased bowl, turning once to grease the top. Cover and let rise in a warm place until doubled, about 1 hour.

3. Punch dough down. Turn onto a lightly floured surface. Roll into a 16x10-in. rectangle. Combine the cinnamon and remaining sugar; sprinkle over dough to within ½ in. of edges. Roll up jelly-roll style, starting with a long side; pinch seam to seal. Place seam side down on a greased baking sheet; pinch ends together to form a ring. Cover and let rise until doubled, about 1 hour. Brush with egg.

4. Bake at 375° for 25-30 minutes or until golden brown. Cool completely on a wire rack. For glaze, combine the confectioners' sugar, lemon juice and enough water to achieve desired consistency. Spread over cake. Sprinkle with colored sugars.

VALENTINE'S DAY

TRUE LOVE TRUFFLES

A few years ago, I began to hand out these smooth, minty truffles in tins as Christmas gifts. Now I can't go a year without sharing them. They also make a perfect Valentine's treat for someone dear.

—**Kim Weiesnbach** Claremore, OK

....

Prep: 50 min. + chilling
Makes: 8 dozen

- 1   tablespoon plus ¾ cup butter, divided
- 1½ cups sugar
- 1   can (5 ounces) evaporated milk
- 2   packages (4.67 ounces each) mint Andes candies
- 1   jar (7 ounces) marshmallow creme
- 1   teaspoon vanilla extract
- 22 ounces white baking chocolate, divided
- ½   cup semisweet chocolate chips
      Green food coloring, optional

1. Butter a 15x10x1-in. pan with 1 tablespoon butter; set aside. In a heavy saucepan, combine the sugar, milk and remaining butter. Bring it to a boil over medium heat, stirring constantly. Reduce the heat; cook and stir it until a candy thermometer reads 236° (soft-ball stage). Remove from the heat. Stir in candies until melted and mixture is well blended. Stir in the marshmallow creme and vanilla until smooth. Spread into prepared pan; cover and refrigerate for 1 hour.
2. Cut into 96 pieces; roll each into a ball (mixture will be soft). Place on a waxed paper-lined baking sheet.
3. In a heavy saucepan or microwave-safe bowl, melt 18 oz. of the white chocolate and chocolate chips. Dip balls in melted chocolate; place them on waxed paper to harden. Melt remaining white chocolate; add food coloring if desired. Drizzle over truffles. Store in an airtight container.
Note: We recommend you test your candy thermometer before each use by bringing water to a boil; the thermometer should read 212°. Adjust your recipe temperature up or down based on your test.

BUTTER COOKIES

These classic cookies will melt in your mouth. They're favorites of my nephews, who love the tender texture and creamy frosting. Kids can help decorate, too.

—**Ruth Griggs** South Hill, VA

....

Prep: 25 min. • **Bake:** 10 min./batch
Makes: about 6½ dozen

- 1   cup butter, softened
- ¾   cup sugar
- 1   large egg
- ½   teaspoon vanilla extract
- 2½ cups all-purpose flour
- 1   teaspoon baking powder
- ¼   teaspoon salt

FROSTING
- ½   cup butter, softened
- 4   cups confectioners' sugar
- 1   teaspoon vanilla extract
- 3   to 4 tablespoons 2% milk
      Red food coloring, optional

1. Preheat oven to 375°. Cream butter and sugar until light and fluffy. Beat in egg and vanilla. In another bowl, whisk flour, baking powder and salt; gradually beat into creamed mixture.
2. Using a cookie press fitted with a heart disk, press the dough 1 in. apart onto ungreased baking sheets. Bake until set but not brown, 6-8 minutes. Cool it on wire racks.
3. Beat the butter, confectioners' sugar, vanilla and enough milk to reach spreading consistency. If desired, tint it with food coloring. Decorate the cookies as desired.

BERRY-BEET SALAD

Here is a delightfully different salad that balances the earthy flavor of beets with the natural sweetness of berries. The ruby-red color makes it ideal for a special Valentine's Day dinner. If you like, substitute crumbled feta for the goat cheese.

—Amy Lyons Mounds View, MN

Prep: 20 min. • **Bake:** 30 min. + cooling
Makes: 4 servings

- 1 each fresh red and golden beets
- ¼ cup balsamic vinegar
- 2 tablespoons walnut oil
- 1 teaspoon honey
  Dash salt
  Dash pepper
- ½ cup sliced fresh strawberries
- ½ cup fresh raspberries
- ½ cup fresh blackberries
- 3 tablespoons chopped walnuts, toasted
- 1 shallot, thinly sliced
- 4 cups torn mixed salad greens
- 1 ounce fresh goat cheese, crumbled
- 1 tablespoon fresh basil, thinly sliced

1. Place beets in an 8-in. square baking dish; add 1 in. of water. Cover and bake at 400° for 30-40 minutes or until tender.

2. Meanwhile, in a bowl, whisk the vinegar, oil, honey, salt and pepper; set aside. Cool beets; peel and cut into thin slices.

3. In a large bowl, combine beets, berries, walnuts and shallot. Pour the dressing over the beet mixture and toss gently to coat. Divide the salad greens among four serving plates. Top with beet mixture; sprinkle with cheese and basil.

★ ★ ★ ★ ★ **READER REVIEW**

"This was my favorite summertime salad. I eat beets regularly with oil and vinegar. This recipe was a nice change! Makes a great presentation for a luncheon get-together. I served with homemade scones. So good!"

SUEFALK TASTEOFHOME.COM

TOASTED REUBENS

New Yorkers say my Reubens taste like those served in the famous delis there. Omit the horseradish for a milder flavor.

—**Patricia Kile** Elizabethtown, PA

Start to Finish: 20 min.
Makes: 4 servings

- 4 teaspoons prepared mustard
- 8 slices rye bread
- 4 slices Swiss cheese
- 1 pound thinly sliced deli corned beef
- 1 can (8 ounces) sauerkraut, rinsed and well drained
- ½ cup mayonnaise
- 3 tablespoons ketchup
- 2 tablespoons sweet pickle relish
- 1 tablespoon prepared horseradish
- 2 tablespoons butter

1. Spread mustard on four slices of bread. Layer with cheese, beef and sauerkraut. In a bowl, mix mayonnaise, ketchup, relish and horseradish; spread over remaining bread. Place over sauerkraut. Spread outsides of sandwiches with butter.

2. In a large skillet, toast sandwiches over medium heat 3-4 minutes on each side or until golden brown and cheese is melted.

FAVORITE IRISH STEW

Lamb is a great source of protein and adds a delicious flavor to this classic stew. If you can't find it at your grocery store, try using beef stew meat instead.

—*Taste of Home* Test Kitchen

Prep: 20 min. • **Cook:** 1¾ hours
Makes: 8 servings (2½ quarts)

- ⅓ cup plus 1 tablespoon all-purpose flour, divided
- 1½ pounds lamb stew meat, cut into 1-inch cubes
- 3 tablespoons olive oil, divided
- 3 medium onions, chopped
- 3 garlic cloves, minced
- 4 cups reduced-sodium beef broth
- 2 medium potatoes, peeled and cubed
- 4 medium carrots, cut into 1-inch pieces
- 1 cup frozen peas
- 1 teaspoon salt
- 1 teaspoon dried thyme
- ½ teaspoon pepper
- ½ teaspoon Worcestershire sauce
- 2 tablespoons water

1. Place ⅓ cup flour in a large resealable plastic bag. Add lamb, a few pieces at a time, and shake to coat.

2. In a Dutch oven, brown lamb in batches in 2 tablespoons oil. Remove and set aside. In the same pan, saute the onions in the remaining oil until tender. Add the garlic; cook 1 minute longer.

3. Add broth, stirring to loosen browned bits from pan. Return lamb to the pan. Bring to a boil. Reduce heat; cover and simmer for 1 hour or until meat is tender.

4. Add potatoes and carrots; cover and cook for 20 minutes. Stir in peas; cook 5-10 minutes longer or until vegetables are tender.

5. Add seasonings and Worcestershire sauce. Combine remaining flour with water until smooth; stir into stew. Bring to a boil; cook and stir 2 minutes or until thickened.

PADDY'S REUBEN DIP

This slow-cooked spread tastes just like the popular Reuben sandwich. Even when I double the recipe, I come home with an empty dish.

—Mary Jane Kimmes Hastings, MN

Prep: 5 min. • **Cook:** 2 hours
Makes: about 4 cups

 4 packages (2 ounces each) thinly sliced deli corned beef, finely chopped
 1 package (8 ounces) cream cheese, cubed
 1 can (8 ounces) sauerkraut, rinsed and drained
 1 cup (8 ounces) sour cream
 1 cup shredded Swiss cheese
   Rye bread or crackers

In a 1½-qt. slow cooker, combine the first five ingredients. Cover and cook on low for 2 hours or until the cheese is melted; stir until blended. Serve warm with bread or crackers.

FAST FIX
PEPPERMINT HOT CHOCOLATE

More than a hint of cool mint makes this rich sipper a special switch from traditional hot chocolate. A dollop of whipped cream studded with crushed candy lusciously tops each mug.

—Taste of Home Test Kitchen

Start to Finish: 15 min.
Makes: 6 servings

 3½ cups 2% milk
  8 ounces white baking chocolate, chopped
  ¼ to ½ teaspoon peppermint extract
  ½ cup heavy whipping cream
  8 spearmint or peppermint candies, crushed
   Additional crushed peppermint candies, optional

1. In a large saucepan, heat milk over medium heat until steaming. Add the chocolate; whisk until smooth. Stir in peppermint extract.
2. In a large bowl, beat cream until stiff peaks form. Fold in the crushed candies. Ladle hot chocolate into mugs; dollop with whipped cream. Sprinkle with additional candies if desired.

EASTER

MAMAW EMILY'S STRAWBERRY CAKE

My husband loved his Mamaw's strawberry cake. He thought no one could duplicate it. I gave it a try, and, luckily, this cake is just as scrumptious as the one he remembers.
—**Jennifer Bruce** Manitou, Kentucky

....

Prep: 15 min. • **Bake:** 25 min. + cooling
Makes: 12 servings

- 1 package white cake mix (regular size)
- 1 package (3 ounces) strawberry gelatin
- 3 tablespoons sugar
- 3 tablespoons all-purpose flour
- 1 cup water
- ½ cup canola oil
- 2 large eggs
- 1 cup finely chopped strawberries

FROSTING
- ½ cup butter, softened
- ½ cup crushed strawberries
- 4½ to 5 cups confectioners' sugar

1. Preheat the oven to 350°. Line the bottoms of two greased 8-in. round baking pans with parchment paper; grease paper.
2. In a large bowl, combine cake mix, gelatin, sugar and flour. Add water, oil and eggs; beat on low speed 30 seconds. Beat on medium 2 minutes. Fold in chopped strawberries. Transfer to prepared pans.
3. Bake 25-30 minutes or until a toothpick inserted in center comes out clean. Cool in pans 10 minutes before removing to wire racks; remove paper. Cool completely.
4. For frosting, in a small bowl, beat butter until creamy. Beat in crushed strawberries. Gradually beat in enough confectioners' sugar to reach desired consistency. Spread frosting between layers and over top and sides of cake.

TEST KITCHEN TIP
Wait to make the frosting until you are ready to ice the cake. Preparing it too early may cause the berries to release their juices, making the frosting runny.

⑤INGREDIENTS
BIRD NESTS

I found one more thing to love about Peeps, the perennial springtime favorite: They make perfect mother birds for these pretzel nests with candy eggs
—**Jessica Boivin** Nekoosa, WI

....

Prep: 40 min. • **Makes:** 2 dozen

- 2 packages (10 to 12 ounces each) white baking chips
- 1 package (10 ounces) pretzel sticks
- 24 yellow chicks Peeps candy
- 1 package (12 ounces) M&M's eggs or other egg-shaped candy

1. In a large metal bowl over simmering water, melt the baking chips; stir until smooth. Reserve ½ cup melted chips for decorations; keep warm.
2. Add pretzel sticks to remaining chips; stir to coat evenly. Drop mixture into 24 mounds on waxed paper; shape into bird nests using two forks.
3. Dip bottoms of Peeps in reserved chips; place in nests. Attach eggs with remaining chips. Let stand until set.

3 tablespoons mango chutney
3 tablespoons Dijon mustard
1 cup packed brown sugar

1. Place the ham on a rack in a shallow roasting pan. Score the surface of the ham, making diamond shapes ½ in. deep; insert a clove in each diamond. Pour cider into the pan.

2. In small saucepan, combine preserves, chutney and mustard. Cook and stir over medium heat until preserves are melted; brush over the ham. Press brown sugar onto the ham.

3. Bake, uncovered, at 325° for 2 to 2½ hours or until a thermometer reads 140°, basting occasionally with pan drippings. Cover loosely with foil if the ham browns too quickly. Let it stand for 10 minutes before slicing.

FAST FIX

TANGY POPPY SEED FRUIT SALAD

We combine berries and citrus with a honey lime dressing flecked with poppy seeds for a fruit salad that's refreshing, flavorful and full of nutrients.
—**Carrie Howell** Lehi, UT

Start to Finish: 20 min.
Makes: 10 servings

1 can (20 ounces) unsweetened pineapple chunks, drained
1 pound fresh strawberries, quartered
2 cups fresh blueberries
2 cups fresh raspberries
2 medium navel oranges, peeled and sectioned
2 medium kiwifruit, peeled, halved and sliced

DRESSING

2 to 4 tablespoons honey
½ teaspoon grated lime peel
2 tablespoons lime juice
2 teaspoons poppy seeds

Place all fruit in a large bowl. In a small bowl, whisk dressing ingredients. Drizzle over fruit; toss gently to combine.

FAST FIX

SPRING PEA & RADISH SALAD

Winters can be very long here in New Hampshire. I always look forward to the first veggies of spring and making some lighter dishes like this fresh salad.
—**Jolene Martinelli** Fremont, NH

Start to Finish: 20 min.
Makes: 6 servings

½ pound fresh wax or green beans
½ pound fresh sugar snap peas
2 cups water
6 large radishes, halved and thinly sliced
2 tablespoons honey
1 teaspoon dried tarragon
¼ teaspoon kosher salt
¼ teaspoon coarsely ground pepper

1. Snip ends off beans and sugar snap peas; remove strings from snap peas. In a large saucepan, bring water to a boil over high heat. Add the beans, reduce heat; simmer, covered, 4-5 minutes. Add sugar snap peas; simmer, covered, until both beans and peas are crisp-tender, another 2-3 minutes. Drain.

2. Toss beans and peas with radishes. Stir together honey, tarragon, salt and pepper. Drizzle over vegetables.

APRICOT & MANGO-GLAZED HAM

Chutney adds a nice sweetness to the glaze on this ham. The elegant entree is just perfect for festive occasions.
—**chinarose**, *Taste of Home* **Online Community**

Prep: 20 min. • **Bake:** 2 hours + standing
Makes: 18 servings

1 boneless fully cooked ham (6 pounds)
2 teaspoons whole cloves
2 cups apple cider or juice
¼ cup apricot preserves

CINCO DE MAYO

FAST FIX ▶
BLOODY MARIA

Tequila, lime and jalapenos give the brunch classic a fresh Mexican twist.
—***Taste of Home*** Test Kitchen

Start to Finish: 10 min.
Makes: 6 servings

- 4 cups tomato juice, chilled
- 8 ounces (1 cup) tequila
- ½ cup lime juice
- 4 to 8 teaspoons juice from pickled jalapeno slices
- 1 tablespoon Worcestershire sauce
- 2 to 4 teaspoons hot pepper sauce
- ¼ teaspoon celery salt
- ¼ teaspoon pepper
- 2 teaspoons prepared horseradish, optional
  Pickled jalapeno slices
  Pepper jack cheese, cubed
  Lime wedges

Mix first eight ingredients in a 2-qt. pitcher; stir in horseradish if desired. Pour over ice; serve with jalapenos, cheese cubes and lime wedges.

FAST FIX ▶
GRILLED CORN HUMMUS TOSTADAS

This recipe is a combo of both Mediterranean and Mexican cuisines, giving it a unique taste. Avocado and hummus may sound like an unusual mix, but they really go well together. Give it a try!
—Lauren Knoelke Milwaukee, WI

Start to Finish: 30 min.
Makes: 4 servings

- 4 medium ears sweet corn, husks removed
- 1 small red onion, cut crosswise into ½-inch slices
- 2 tablespoons olive oil, divided
- 8 corn tortillas (6 inches)
- 1 container (8 ounces) hummus
- ¼ teaspoon ground chipotle pepper
- 1 cup cherry tomatoes, halved
- ½ teaspoon salt
- 1 medium ripe avocado, peeled and sliced
- ½ cup crumbled feta cheese
- 1 jalapeno pepper, thinly sliced
  Lime wedges, optional
  Fresh cilantro leaves, optional
  Mexican hot pepper sauce, optional

1. Brush the corn and sliced onion with 1 tablespoon oil. Grill the corn and onion, covered, over medium-high heat until tender and lightly charred, 5-7 minutes, turning occasionally. Cool slightly.
2. Meanwhile, brush tortillas with the remaining oil. Grill, covered, until crisp and lightly browned, 2-3 minutes per side.
3. Cut corn from cobs. Process hummus, chipotle pepper and 2 cups of the cut corn in a food processor until almost smooth. Coarsely chop grilled onion; toss with tomatoes, salt and any remaining corn.
4. Spread hummus mixture over tortillas; top with onion mixture, avocado, cheese and jalapeno. If desired, serve with limes, cilantro and pepper sauce.
Note: Wear disposable gloves when cutting hot peppers; the oils can burn skin. Avoid touching your face.

MEXICAN CINNAMON COOKIES

My extended family shares a meal every Sunday. The aunts and uncles take turns bringing everything from main dishes to desserts like this traditional Mexican cinnamon cookie called Reganadas.
—Adan Franco *Milwaukee, WI*

Prep: 25 min. + standing
Bake: 10 min./batch
Makes: 12 dozen

- 1 large egg, separated
- 2 cups lard
- 4 cups all-purpose flour
- 3 teaspoons baking powder
- 1½ teaspoons ground cinnamon
  Dash salt
- ¾ cup sugar

COATING
- ⅔ cup sugar
- 4 teaspoons ground cinnamon
  Confectioners' sugar, optional

1. Place egg white in a small bowl; let stand at room temperature 30 minutes.
2. Preheat oven to 375°. In a large bowl, beat lard until creamy. In another bowl, whisk flour, baking powder, cinnamon and salt; gradually beat into lard.
3. Beat egg white on high speed until stiff peaks form. Gently whisk in sugar and egg yolk. Gradually beat into lard mixture. Turn onto a lightly floured surface; knead gently 8-10 times.
4. Divide dough into six portions. On a lightly floured surface, roll each portion into a 24-in.-long rope; cut diagonally into 1-in. pieces. Place 1 in. apart on ungreased baking sheets. Bake 8-10 minutes or until edges are light brown. Cool on the pans for 2 minutes.
5. In a small bowl, mix the sugar and cinnamon. Roll warm cookies in cinnamon sugar mixture or confectioners' sugar. Cool on wire racks.

MEXICAN STREET CORN BAKE

We discovered Mexican street corn at a festival. This easy one-pan version saves on prep and cleanup. Every August, I freeze an abundance of our own fresh sweet corn to use in this recipe. Store-bought corn works equally well.
—Erin Wright *Wallace, KS*

Prep: 10 min. • **Bake:** 35 min.
Makes: 6 servings

- 6 cups frozen corn (about 30 ounces), thawed and drained
- 1 cup mayonnaise
- 1 teaspoon ground chipotle pepper
- ¼ teaspoon salt
- ¼ teaspoon pepper
- 6 tablespoons chopped green onions, divided
- ½ cup grated Parmesan cheese
  Lime wedges, optional

1. Preheat oven to 350°. Mix first five ingredients and 4 tablespoons green onions; transfer to a greased 1½-qt. baking dish. Sprinkle with cheese.
2. Bake, covered, 20 minutes. Uncover; bake until bubbly and lightly browned, 15-20 minutes. Sprinkle with remaining green onions. If desired, serve with some lime wedges.

4TH OF JULY PICNIC

FAST FIX ▶

PAPA BURGER

When whipping up something for Father's Day or the Fourth of July, I go big and tall with this fully loaded, juicy yumburger.

—Chase Bailey Costa Mesa, CA

Start to Finish: 30 min.
Makes: 4 servings

- 1 pound ground beef or ground buffalo
- ⅓ cup finely chopped onion
- 1 slice whole-wheat or white bread, broken into small pieces
- 2 tablespoons red wine vinegar
- 1 tablespoon liquid smoke
- 2 teaspoons Worcestershire sauce
- 1 teaspoon hamburger or steak seasoning
- ¼ to ½ teaspoon garlic salt
- ¼ to ½ teaspoon pepper
- ¼ cup all-purpose flour
- 4 onion hamburger buns, split
- 4 Bibb or Boston lettuce leaves
- ⅓ cup prepared Thousand Island salad dressing
- 4 slices red onion
- 1 large heirloom tomato, sliced

1. Combine first nine ingredients; mix lightly. Shape into four ¾-in.-thick patties. Press patties into the flour to lightly coat both sides.

2. In a large nonstick skillet, cook burgers over medium heat until a thermometer reads 160°, about 4-5 minutes per side. Layer bun bottoms with lettuce, burgers, salad dressing, and onion and tomato slices. Replace bun tops.

FOURTH OF JULY BAKED BEANS

We always choose this family recipe for July Fourth or any picnic because it's a meaty twist on everyday baked beans and has a nice sweetness.

—Wendy Hodorowski Bellaire, OH

Prep: 10 min. • **Bake:** 55 min.
Makes: 8 servings

- ½ pound ground beef
- 1 large onion, finely chopped
- ½ cup sugar
- ½ cup packed brown sugar
- ½ cup ketchup
- ½ cup barbecue sauce
- 2 tablespoons yellow mustard
- 2 tablespoons molasses
- ½ teaspoon chili powder
- 2 cans (13.7 ounces each) beans with tomato sauce
- ½ pound bacon strips, cooked and crumbled

1. Preheat oven to 350°. In a large skillet, cook beef and onion over medium heat 6-8 minutes or until beef is no longer pink, breaking up beef into crumbles; drain. Stir in the sugars, ketchup, barbecue sauce, mustard, molasses and chili powder. Add beans and bacon.

2. Transfer to a greased 13x9-in. baking dish. Bake it, covered, 45 minutes. Bake, uncovered, 10-15 minutes longer or until heated through.

STAR-SPANGLED LEMON ICEBOX PIE

With a little chill time, my no-bake lemon pie turns into a potluck superstar. My kids like to arrange the berries in a star pattern.
—**Lauren Katz** Ashburn, VA

Prep: 35 min. + chilling
Makes: 8 servings

- 15 pecan shortbread cookies (about 8 ounces)
- 1 tablespoon sugar
- 3 tablespoons butter, melted

FILLING

- 8 ounces cream cheese, softened
- ½ cup mascarpone cheese
- 1 tablespoon grated lemon zest
- ½ cup lemon juice
- 1 can (14 ounces) sweetened condensed milk
- 1 cup sliced fresh strawberries
- 1 cup fresh blueberries

1. Preheat oven to 350°. Place cookies and sugar in a food processor; process until cookies are ground. Add melted butter; pulse just until combined. Press mixture onto bottom and up sides of an ungreased 9-in. pie plate. Bake 15-20 minutes or until lightly browned. Cool completely on a wire rack.

2. In a large bowl, beat cream cheese, mascarpone cheese, lemon zest and lemon juice until smooth; gradually beat in the milk.

3. Spread into prepared crust. Refrigerate, covered, at least 4 hours or until filling is set. Top with berries before serving.

⑤ INGREDIENTS
RED, WHITE & BLUE FROZEN LEMONADE

This patriotic drink is as pretty as it is delicious. With raspberries, blueberries and lemon juice, we created a striped lemonade that is perfect for your Fourth of July celebrations.
—**Shawn Carleton** San Diego, CA

Prep: 10 min.
Makes: 4 servings

- 1 cup lemon juice
- 1 cup sugar
- 4 cups ice cubes
- 1 cup fresh or frozen blueberries
  Maraschino cherries

Place lemon juice, sugar and ice in a blender; cover and process until slushy. Divide blueberries among four chilled glasses; muddle slightly. Add lemon slush; top with cherries.

SUMMER HARVEST

KHMER PICKLED VEGETABLE SALAD

I grew up as a missionary kid in Cambodia, and most of my favorite foods have a Southeast Asian background. Locals love eating this pickled salad for breakfast, but I enjoy it for lunch or dinner as a side with satay chicken.

—**Hannah Heavener** Belton, TX

Prep: 25 min. + chilling • **Cook:** 5 min.
Makes: 16 servings (¾ cup each)

- 2 medium daikon radishes (about 1¼ pounds each), peeled and thinly sliced
- 4 cups shredded cabbage (about ½ small)
- 1 large cucumber, thinly sliced
- 2 medium carrots, thinly sliced
- 1 cup cut fresh green beans (2 inch)
- ½ medium red onion, thinly sliced
- 1 piece fresh gingerroot (1 inch), thinly sliced
- 2 Thai chili or serrano peppers, halved lengthwise and seeded if desired
- 2 cups rice vinegar
- ¾ cup sugar
- 2 teaspoons salt
- 2 tablespoons chopped fresh cilantro

1. Place first eight ingredients in a large nonreactive bowl. Place the vinegar, sugar and salt in a 2-cup or larger glass measure; microwave until warm, 2-3 minutes. Stir until the sugar is dissolved. Stir into the vegetables. Refrigerate, covered, at least 1 hour before serving.

2. To serve, sprinkle with cilantro. Serve with a slotted spoon.

FAST FIX
GRILLED GARDEN PIZZA

Dazzle your family and friends with pizzas fresh off the grill. We top them with Asiago, Parmesan, veggies and fresh basil. Pile on the toppings you love.

—**Teri Rasey** Cadillac, MI

Start to Finish: 30 min.
Makes: 6 servings

- 2 plum tomatoes, thinly sliced
- ½ teaspoon sea salt or kosher salt
- 1 loaf (1 pound) frozen pizza dough, thawed
- 2 tablespoons olive oil, divided
- ½ cup shredded Parmesan or Asiago cheese
- ½ cup fresh or frozen corn, thawed
- ¼ cup thinly sliced red onion
- 8 ounces fresh mozzarella cheese, sliced
- ½ cup thinly sliced fresh spinach
- 3 tablespoons chopped fresh basil

1. Sprinkle tomatoes with salt; set aside. On a lightly floured surface, divide dough in half. Roll or press each of the halves to ¼-in. thickness; place each on a greased sheet of foil (about 10 in. square). Brush tops with 1 tablespoon oil.

2. Carefully invert crusts onto grill rack, removing foil. Brush tops with remaining oil. Grill, covered, over medium heat 2-3 minutes or until bottom is golden brown. Remove from the grill; reduce the grill temperature to low.

3. Top the grilled sides of the crusts with Parmesan or Asiago cheese, tomatoes, corn, onion and mozzarella cheese. Grill, covered, on low heat 4-6 minutes or until cheese is melted. Sprinkle with spinach and basil.

Health tip: Fresh mozzarella has about the same calories and fat as part-skim mozzarella; both are lighter than a lot of other cheeses like cheddar, Muenster and provolone.

END OF GARDEN RELISH

We dollop this tangy relish on burgers, hot dogs and salads. It's a cool way to use up garden produce and is always appreciated at picnics and potlucks.
—**Karen Stucky** Freeman, SD

Prep: 45 min. + standing • **Process:** 20 min.
Makes: 6 pints

- 7 large cucumbers, shredded
- 3 large onions, finely chopped
- 3 cups shredded carrots
- 2 medium sweet red peppers, finely chopped
- 5 tablespoons salt
- 5 cups sugar
- 3 cups white vinegar
- 1 tablespoon celery seed
- 1 tablespoon mustard seed

1. Toss first five ingredients; let stand for 3 hours. Drain; squeeze and blot dry with paper towels.
2. In a Dutch oven, mix sugar, vinegar, celery seed and mustard seed; bring to a boil. Reduce heat; simmer, uncovered, 5 minutes. Add vegetables; bring to a boil. Reduce the heat; simmer, uncovered, 20 minutes.
3. Ladle hot mixture into hot 1-pint jars, leaving ½-in. headspace. Remove the air bubbles and adjust the headspace, if necessary, by adding hot mixture. Wipe rims. Center lids on jars; screw on bands until fingertip tight.
4. Place jars into canner with simmering water, ensuring that they are completely covered with water. Bring to a boil; process for 20 minutes. Remove the jars and cool.
Note: The processing time listed applies to altitudes of 1,000 feet or less. For altitudes up to 3,000 feet, add 5 minutes; 6,000 feet, add 10 minutes; 8,000 feet, add 15 minutes; 10,000 feet, add 20 minutes.

TEST KITCHEN TIP

If you plan on preparing a lot of relish, make the chopping easier by using a food processor or a food grinder with a coarse grinding blade. Seed large zucchini or cucumbers before chopping.

GARDEN PESTO PASTA SALAD

My family and I live on a homestead in the Missouri Ozarks and produce much of our own food. In the summer, when the garden is bursting with fresh vegetables and it is too hot to cook, I enjoy using our seasonal veggies for pasta salads and other cool, refreshing meals.
—**Sarah Mathews** Ava, MO

Prep: 15 min. + chilling
Makes: 10 servings

- 3 cups uncooked spiral pasta (about 9 ounces)
- ½ cup prepared pesto
- 3 tablespoons white wine vinegar
- 1 tablespoon lemon juice
- ½ teaspoon salt
- ¼ teaspoon pepper
- ¼ cup olive oil
- 1 medium zucchini, halved and sliced
- 1 medium sweet red pepper, chopped
- 1 medium tomato, seeded and chopped
- 1 small red onion, halved and thinly sliced
- ½ cup grated Parmesan cheese

1. Cook pasta according to the package directions; drain. Rinse with cold water and drain well.
2. Meanwhile, whisk together pesto, vinegar, lemon juice and seasonings. Gradually whisk in oil until blended.
3. Combine the vegetables and pasta. Drizzle with pesto dressing; toss to coat. Refrigerate, covered, until cold, about 1 hour. Serve with Parmesan cheese.

CAMPFIRE CLASSICS

CAMPFIRE CHEESE HASH BROWN PACKETS

Dining by the campfire? This easy packet of potatoes, bacon and cheese makes a terrific hash. We like to serve it with eggs and fresh pico de gallo.
—**Gina Nistico** Denver, CO

Start to Finish: 30 min.
Makes: 4 servings

- 1 package (28 ounces) frozen O'Brien potatoes, thawed
- 1¼ cups shredded cheddar cheese, divided
- 8 bacon strips, cooked and chopped
- ½ teaspoon salt
- ¼ teaspoon pepper
  hard-boiled large eggs and pico de gallo, optional

1. Prepare campfire or grill for medium-high heat. Toss the potatoes with ¾ cup cheese, bacon, salt and pepper.
2. Divide mixture among four 18x12-in. pieces of heavy-duty nonstick foil, placing food on dull side of foil. Fold foil around potato mixture, sealing tightly.
3. Place packets over campfire or grill; cook 6-9 minutes on each side or until potatoes are tender. Open the packets carefully to allow steam to escape; sprinkle with remaining cheese. If desired, serve with eggs and pico de gallo.

BBQ HOT DOG & POTATO PACKS

The kids will have fun helping to assemble these nifty foil packs, then savoring the tasty results in short order. They're perfect for a camping or grilling in the backyard.
—**Kelly Westphal** Wind Lake, WI

Start to Finish: 20 min.
Makes: 4 servings

- 1 package (20 ounces) refrigerated red potato wedges
- 4 hot dogs
- 1 small onion, cut into wedges
- ¼ cup shredded cheddar cheese
- ½ cup barbecue sauce

1. Divide potato wedges among four pieces of heavy-duty foil (about 18 in. square). Top each with a hot dog, onion wedges and cheese. Drizzle with the barbecue sauce. Fold foil around the mixture, sealing tightly.
2. Grill, covered, over medium heat 10-15 minutes or until heated through. Open foil carefully to allow steam to escape.

LEMON-DILL SALMON PACKETS

Grilling salmon in foil is an easy technique. I often use this method with foods that cook quickly, like fish, shrimp, bite-sized meats and fresh veggies. The options are endless—and the cleanup is a breeze!
—**A.J. Weinhold** McArthur, CA

Start to Finish: 25 min.
Makes: 4 servings

- 1 tablespoon butter, softened
- 4 salmon fillets (6 ounces each)
- ½ teaspoon salt
- ¼ teaspoon pepper
- ½ medium onion, sliced
- 4 garlic cloves, sliced
- 4 fresh dill sprigs
- 1 tablespoon minced fresh basil
- 1 medium lemon, sliced

1. Prepare campfire or grill for medium heat. Spread butter in the center of each of four pieces of a double thickness of foil (about 12 in. square). Place one salmon fillet in the center of each; sprinkle with salt and pepper. Top with the onion, garlic, dill, basil and lemon. Fold foil around the fillets and seal.

2. Place packets on a grill grate over a campfire or grill. Cook 8-10 minutes or until fish just begins to flake easily with a fork. Open carefully to allow steam to escape.

★ ★ ★ ★ ★ **READER REVIEW**

"I love salmon, and this is a convenient way to prepare it. The only change I made was I used 1 tablespoon chopped lemon oregano from my garden instead of basil. The salmon was moist and flavorful; highly recommend."

KRISTINECHAYES TASTEOFHOME.COM

OKTOBERFEST

4. Sprinkle ¾ cup of bread crumbs over rectangle to within 1 in. of edges. Starting 3 in. from a short side, sprinkle 3 cups apples and ¼ cup raisins over a 3-in.-wide section of dough. Mix sugar and cinnamon; sprinkle half of the mixture over fruit. Drizzle with half of the melted butter.

5. Roll up jelly-roll style, starting at the fruit-covered end and lifting with the parchment; fold in sides of dough as you roll to contain filling. Using parchment, transfer strudel to a 15x10x1-in. baking pan; trim parchment to fit pan.

6. Bake on the lowest oven rack 45-55 minutes or until golden brown, brushing the top with sour cream two times while baking. Repeat with remaining ingredients.

7. Using the parchment paper, transfer to a wire rack to cool. Serve warm or at room temperature.

Note: To make fresh bread crumbs, tear the bread into pieces and place in a food processor; pulse until fine crumbs form. Two to three bread slices will yield about 1½ cups crumbs.

BAVARIAN PORK LOIN

I got the recipe for this tender pork roast from an aunt, who made it all the time. What a delicious taste sensation with sauerkraut, carrots, onions and apples.
—Edie DeSpain Logan, UT

Prep: 25 min. • **Cook:** 6 hours + standing
Makes: 10 servings

- 1 boneless pork loin roast (3 to 4 pounds)
- 1 can (14 ounces) Bavarian sauerkraut, rinsed and drained
- 1¾ cups chopped carrots
- 1 large onion, finely chopped
- ½ cup unsweetened apple juice
- 2 teaspoons dried parsley flakes
- 3 large tart apples, peeled and quartered

1. Cut the roast in half; place in a 5-qt. slow cooker. In a small bowl, combine the sauerkraut, carrots, onion, apple juice and parsley; spoon over roast. Cover and cook on low for 4 hours.

2. Add apples to slow cooker. Cover and cook 2-3 hours longer or until meat is tender. Remove roast; let stand for 10 minutes before slicing. Serve with the sauerkraut mixture.

GERMAN APPLE STRUDEL

This gorgeous strudel has just what you crave—thin layers of flaky crust and lots of chunky, juicy apples.
—Darlene Brenden Salem, OR

Prep: 1 hour + standing
Bake: 45 min./batch
Makes: 2 strudels (8 slices each)

- 3 cups all-purpose flour
- ½ cup canola oil, divided
- ¾ cup warm water (120°)
- 1 large egg, lightly beaten

FILLING

- 1½ cups fresh bread crumbs
- 6 cups chopped peeled apples (about 6 medium)
- ½ cup raisins
- 1 cup sugar
- 1½ teaspoons ground cinnamon
- ⅓ cup butter, melted
- 3 tablespoons sour cream

1. Place flour in a mixer bowl; beat in ¼ cup oil (mixture will be slightly crumbly). In a small bowl, slowly whisk warm water into beaten egg; add to flour mixture, mixing well. Beat in remaining oil until smooth. Transfer to a greased bowl, turning once to grease the top. Cover with plastic wrap and let rest in a warm place, about 30 minutes.

2. Preheat oven to 350°. Spread bread crumbs into an ungreased 15x10x1-in. baking pan. Bake 10-15 minutes or until they're golden brown, stirring occasionally. Cool completely.

3. Tape a 30x15-in. sheet of parchment paper onto a work surface; dust lightly with flour. Divide dough in half; place one portion on the parchment and roll to a very thin 24x15-in. rectangle. (Keep the remaining dough covered.) Remove the tape from parchment.

SLOW COOKER GERMAN POTATO SALAD

Here's the dish everyone looks for at our parties, so we always double the recipe. It was handed down from my mother-in-law and has been a family favorite for years.
—**Stacy Novak** Stafford, VA

Prep: 35 min. • **Cook:** 3 hours
Makes: 12 servings

- 3 **pounds red potatoes (about 8 medium)**
- 1 **pound bacon strips, chopped**
- 1 **large onion, chopped**
- 3 **tablespoons all-purpose flour**
- ⅔ **cup sugar**
- ⅓ **cup packed light brown sugar**
- 2½ **teaspoons salt**
- ½ **teaspoon pepper**
- ⅓ **cup cider vinegar**
- 2 **cups water**
  Minced fresh chives, optional

1. Place the potatoes in a 6-qt. stockpot; add water to cover. Bring to a boil. Reduce the heat; cook, uncovered, just until the potatoes are tender, about 15 minutes. Drain; cool slightly.

2. In a large skillet, cook the bacon over medium heat until it is crisp, stirring it occasionally. Using a slotted spoon, remove bacon to paper towels, reserving 3 tablespoons drippings.

3. For dressing, saute onion in drippings over medium-high heat until tender, 4-6 minutes. Stir in flour until blended. Stir in sugars, salt and pepper. Gradually stir in vinegar and water; bring to a boil, stirring constantly. Cook and stir until slightly thickened, 4-6 minutes.

4. Slice the potatoes; place in a greased 5- or 6-qt. slow cooker. Top with dressing; sprinkle with bacon. Cook, covered, on low until heated through, 3-4 hours. If desired, sprinkle with chives.

FAST FIX
OKTOBERFEST BRATS WITH MUSTARD SAUCE

I come from a town with a big German heritage, where we have a huge celebration each year for Oktoberfest. This recipe packs in all the traditional German flavors my whole family loves.
—**Deborah Pennington** Decatur, AL

Start to Finish: 20 min.
Makes: 4 servings

- ⅓ **cup half-and-half cream**
- 2 **tablespoons stone-ground mustard**
- ½ **teaspoon dried minced onion**
- ¼ **teaspoon pepper**
  Dash paprika
- 4 **fully cooked bratwurst links (about 12 ounces)**
- 1 **can (14 ounces) sauerkraut, rinsed and drained, warmed**

1. For sauce, mix the first five ingredients. Cut each bratwurst in thirds; thread onto four metal or soaked wooden skewers.

2. Grill brats, covered, over medium heat until golden brown and heated through, 7-10 minutes, turning occasionally. Serve with sauerkraut and sauce.

TEST KITCHEN TIP
Stone-ground mustard has more heat and a deeper flavor than yellow mustard. Other mustards can be substituted, too. Also, starting this recipe with cooked brats makes it speedy and convenient. If you decide to start with uncooked brats, grill them until fully cooked first, then cut into thirds and proceed with recipe.

HALLOWEEN

MUMMY POPPERS

I wrapped these spicy jalapeno poppers in puff pastry to look just like a mummy. You can tame the heat by adjusting the amount of chipotle peppers.
—**Nick Iverson** Denver, CO

Prep: 30 min. • **Bake:** 30 min.
Makes: 32 appetizers

- 1 package (8 ounces) cream cheese, softened
- 2 cups shredded cheddar cheese
- 2 green onions, finely chopped
- 1 to 2 chipotle peppers in adobo sauce, finely chopped
- 2 tablespoons lime juice
- 1 tablespoon honey
- ½ teaspoon salt
- ½ teaspoon ground cumin
- ¼ teaspoon pepper
- 16 jalapeno peppers, halved lengthwise and seeded
- 1 package (17.3 ounces) frozen puff pastry, thawed and cut lengthwise into 32 strips

1. Preheat oven to 400°. Beat first nine ingredients until blended. Spoon or pipe cheese mixture into pepper halves.
2. Wrap puff pastry strips around pepper halves. Transfer wrapped peppers to parchment paper-lined baking sheets. Bake until golden brown and cheese is melted, 30-40 minutes.

BROWNIE SPIDERS

Real spiders petrify me, but I can make an exception for these cute ones made from chocolate. They make deliciously fun Halloween treats.
—**Ali Ebright** Kansas City, MO

Prep: 20 min.
Bake: 30 min. + cooling
Makes: 9 brownie spiders

- 1 package (15.80 ounces) brownie mix
- ½ cup semisweet chocolate chips
- 2 cups crispy chow mein noodles
- 18 candy eyeballs

1. Prepare and bake brownies according to package directions using an 8-in. square baking pan lined with parchment paper. Cool completely in pan on a wire rack.
2. In a microwave, melt chocolate chips; stir until smooth. Remove 1 tablespoon melted chocolate to a small bowl; reserve for attaching eyes. Add the noodles to remaining chocolate; stir gently to coat. Spread onto a waxed paper-lined baking sheet, separating noodles slightly. Freeze until set.
3. Cut nine brownies with a 2¼-in. round cutter for spider bodies. Attach eyeballs using reserved melted chocolate. With a bamboo skewer or toothpick, poke eight holes in top of each spider for inserting legs. Insert a coated noodle into each hole. Store in an airtight container.

lightly floured surface, roll each half into a 12x9-in. rectangle. Transfer one rectangle to a greased baking sheet. Brush reserved marinade over rectangle to within ½ in. of edges. Top with the chicken, peppers and cheese. Sprinkle with salt. Place second dough rectangle over pizza and pinch the edges to seal. Using a kitchen scissors, cut out eyes and mouth. Cut bottom to form a jagged edge; pinch the edges of dough to reseal. Brush with remaining oil.

5. Bake for 10-15 minutes or until it is golden brown.

(5)INGREDIENTS FAST FIX

MAD SCIENTIST PUNCH

You can concoct this potion with convenience items such as juice concentrate, soft drink mix, soda and sherbet. It appeals to kids of all ages!
—*Taste of Home* **Test Kitchen**

Start to Finish: 15 min.
Makes: 16 servings (4 quarts)

- 2 cans (12 ounces each) frozen pineapple-orange juice concentrate, thawed
- 2 cups water
- 1 envelope unsweetened orange Kool-Aid mix
- 2 liters lemon-lime soda, chilled
- 1 pint orange sherbet, softened

In punch bowl, combine juice concentrate, water and Kool-Aid mix; stir in soda. Top with scoops of sherbet. Serve immediately.

GHOSTLY CHICKEN & PEPPER PIZZA

My friendly ghost pizza won't scare folks away from your dinner table. My family loves Halloween, so we like creating fun new recipes like this one. Fill it with whatever pizza toppings you like best.
—**Francine Boecher** Queensbury, NY

Prep: 50 min. + marinating. • **Bake:** 10 min.
Makes: 6 pieces

- ⅔ cup plus 2 tablespoons olive oil, divided
- ¼ cup lemon juice
- 4 garlic cloves, minced
- 1 tablespoon Dijon mustard
- 2 teaspoons dried oregano
- ¾ teaspoon dried thyme
- ¾ teaspoon pepper
- ½ pound boneless skinless chicken breasts
- ¾ cup chopped green pepper
- ¾ cup chopped sweet red pepper
- 1 loaf (1 pound) frozen pizza dough, thawed
- 1½ cups shredded part-skim mozzarella cheese
- ¼ teaspoon salt

1. Whisk together ⅔ cup oil with the next six ingredients. Reserve 3 tablespoons of marinade for pizza. Add the chicken to the remaining marinade; toss in a shallow dish to coat. Refrigerate, covered, 2 hours.
2. Preheat oven to 375°. Place chicken mixture in a greased 8-in. square baking dish. Bake until a thermometer reads 165°, 22-27 minutes. When chicken has cooled, cut into bite-size pieces.
3. Meanwhile, in a small skillet, heat 1 tablespoon oil over medium heat. Cook and stir peppers until tender, 4-6 minutes. Increase oven heat to 450°.
4. Divide the pizza dough in half. On a

ROASTED SAGE TURKEY WITH VEGETABLE GRAVY

This year, skip the stuffing and instead stuff the bird with fresh sage and sprigs of thyme for a delicous twist.
—**Beth Jacobson** Milwaukee, WI

Prep: 30 min. + chilling
Bake: 2 hours 10 min. + standing
Makes: 16 servings (3½ cups gravy)

- 1 turkey (14 to 16 pounds)
- 1 tablespoon kosher salt
- 1 teaspoon ground sage
- ½ teaspoon garlic powder
- 1 large onion, chopped
- 3 celery ribs, chopped
- 3 medium carrots, chopped
- 1¼ cups water, divided
- 3 tablespoons canola oil
- ½ teaspoon freshly ground pepper
- ¾ cup white wine
- 3 fresh sage sprigs
- 4 fresh thyme sprigs

GRAVY

- 1 to 1½ cups reduced-sodium chicken broth or homemade chicken stock
- ¼ cup all-purpose flour
- ¼ teaspoon minced fresh sage
- ¼ teaspoon freshly ground pepper

1. Remove giblets and neck from turkey. Reserve turkey neck; refrigerate, covered, overnight. Place turkey in a 15x10-in. baking pan, breast side up. Secure skin to underside of neck cavity with toothpicks. Mix salt, sage and garlic powder. Tuck wings under turkey; tie drumsticks together. Pat the turkey dry. Rub outside of turkey with salt mixture. Refrigerate turkey, loosely covered, overnight.
2. Preheat the oven to 475°. Place the onion, celery, carrots and reserved neck in bottom of a broiler pan; add ½ cup water. Place broiler pan rack over top; transfer turkey to rack. Rub outside of turkey with oil; sprinkle with pepper. Pour wine and remaining water into turkey cavity; add sage and thyme sprigs.
3. Place turkey in oven, legs facing back of oven. Roast, uncovered, 40 minutes.
4. Reduce oven setting to 350°. Cover breast tightly with a double thickness of foil. Roast 1½-2 hours longer or until a thermometer inserted in thickest part of thigh reads 170°-175°. (Thermometer should not touch bone or fat.)
5. Remove turkey from oven. Let stand, uncovered, 20 minutes before carving. Using a turkey baster, remove liquid from turkey cavity to a large measuring cup. Line strainer or colander with cheesecloth; place over measuring cup. With a slotted spoon, remove vegetables from bottom of broiler pan, reserving 1¼ cups. Discard turkey neck. Strain the cooking liquid into measuring cup. Skim fat, reserving ¼ cup fat. Add enough broth to the cooking liquid to measure 2 cups.
6. In a large saucepan, mix the flour and reserved fat until smooth; gradually whisk in the broth mixture. Bring to a boil over medium-high heat, stirring constantly; cook and stir for 1-2 minutes or until thickened. Add half of reserved vegetables. Puree gravy using an immersion blender; or, cool the gravy slightly and puree in a blender. Stir in the sage, pepper and remaining vegetables; heat it through. Serve with turkey.

COCONUT-PECAN SWEET POTATOES

These sweet potatoes cook effortlessly in the slow cooker so you can turn your attention to other holiday preparations. Coconut gives the classic dish new flavor.
—**Raquel Haggard** Edmond, OK

Prep: 15 min. • **Cook:** 4 hours
Makes: 12 servings (⅔ cup each)

- ½ cup chopped pecans
- ½ cup sweetened shredded coconut
- ⅓ cup sugar
- ⅓ cup packed brown sugar
- ½ teaspoon ground cinnamon
- ¼ teaspoon salt
- ¼ cup reduced-fat butter, melted
- 4 pounds sweet potatoes (about 6 medium), peeled and cut into 1-in. pieces
- ½ teaspoon coconut extract
- ½ teaspoon vanilla extract

1. In a small bowl, combine the first six ingredients; stir in melted butter. Place sweet potatoes in a 5-qt. slow cooker coated with cooking spray. Sprinkle with pecan mixture.
2. Cook, covered, on low 4 to 4½ hours or until potatoes are tender. Stir in extracts.
Note: This recipe was tested with Land O'Lakes light stick butter.

ELEGANT GREEN BEANS

Mushrooms and water chestnuts give new life to ordinary green bean casserole. Every time I make it for friends, I'm asked to share the recipe.
—Linda Poe Sandstone, MN

Prep: 20 min. • **Bake:** 50 min.
Makes: 8 servings

- 1 can (8 ounces) sliced water chestnuts, drained
- 1 small onion, chopped
- 1 jar (4½ ounces) sliced mushrooms, drained
- 6 tablespoons butter, divided
- ¼ cup all-purpose flour
- 1 cup 2% milk
- ½ cup chicken broth
- 1 teaspoon reduced-sodium soy sauce
- ⅛ teaspoon hot pepper sauce
  Dash salt
- 1 package (16 ounces) frozen French-style green beans, thawed
- ½ cup shredded cheddar cheese
- 1 cup crushed French-fried onions

1. Preheat oven to 350°. In a small skillet, saute the water chestnuts, onion and mushrooms in 2 tablespoons butter 4-5 minutes or until crisp-tender; set aside.
2. In large skillet, melt remaining butter; stir in flour until smooth. Stir in milk, broth, soy sauce, pepper sauce and salt. Bring to a boil; cook and stir 2 minutes or until thickened. Remove from heat; stir in the green beans and cheese.
3. Spoon half of the bean mixture into a greased 1½-qt. baking dish. Layer with water chestnut mixture and remaining bean mixture.
4. Bake it, uncovered, 45 minutes. Top with French-fried onions. Bake 5 minutes or until heated through.

(5) INGREDIENTS FAST FIX
TWO-BEAN HUMMUS

My children love this easy hummus and even like to help me make it. Hummus is a great way to sneak in some beans and important soluble fiber into their diets. I place this hummus in a bread bowl to serve as the body of a turkey for my vegetable platter at Thanksgiving.
—Kelly Andreas Eau Claire, WI

Start to Finish: 15 min.
Makes: 2 cups

- 1 can (15 ounces) garbanzo beans or chickpeas, rinsed and drained
- 1 can (15 ounces) white kidney or cannellini beans, rinsed and drained
- ¼ cup olive oil
- 2 tablespoons lemon juice
- 2 garlic cloves, minced
- ¼ teaspoon salt
  Assorted fresh vegetables

Process first six ingredients in a food processor until smooth. Transfer to a serving bowl; serve with vegetables.

HANUKKAH

PARSNIP LATKES WITH LOX & HORSERADISH CREME

A horseradish-flavored creme fraiche adds zip to these crispy homemade latkes, which draw a bit of sweetness from the parsnips. Add fresh dill sprigs for a garnish.
—Todd Schmeling Gurnee, IL

Prep: 30 min. • **Cook:** 5 min./batch
Makes: about 3 dozen

- 1 pound potatoes, peeled
- 1 pound parsnips, peeled
- ⅔ cup chopped green onions
- 2 large eggs, lightly beaten
- 1 teaspoon salt
- ½ teaspoon pepper
  Oil for deep-fat frying
- 1 package (3 ounces) smoked salmon or lox, cut into ½ inch wide strips
- 1 cup creme fraiche or sour cream
- 1 tablespoon snipped fresh dill
- 1 tablespoon prepared horseradish
- ¼ teaspoon salt
- ⅛ teaspoon white pepper
  Fresh dill sprigs

1. Coarsely grate potatoes and parsnips. Place the grated vegetables on a double thickness of cheesecloth; bring up corners and squeeze out any liquid. Transfer to a large bowl; stir in the onions, eggs, salt and pepper.
2. In an electric skillet, heat ⅛ in. of oil to 375°. Drop potato mixture by heaping tablespoonfuls into hot oil. Flatten to form patties. Fry until golden brown; turn and cook other side. Drain on paper towels.
3. Roll salmon to form rose shapes; set aside. Combine the creme fraiche, dill, horseradish, salt and pepper. Top latkes with a dollop of creme fraiche mixture and a salmon rose. Garnish with dill.

DID YOU KNOW?

Latkes, or potato pancakes fried in oil, are one of the most popular of all Jewish foods, especially during Hanukkah. They symbolize the ancient lamps that held only enough oil for one day but magically burned for eight. There are many tasty variations of latkes, which can be served as an appetizer or a side dish.

BRAISED HANUKKAH BRISKET

My mother, Enid, always used the most marbled cut of brisket she could find to so she'd get the most flavor. When she added carrots to the pan, she threw in some potatoes, too. The best thing about this dish is that it's even tastier the next day.
—Ellen Ruzinsky Yorktown Heights, NY

Prep: 25 min. • **Cook:** 2¾ hours
Makes: 12 servings (4 cups vegetables)

- 2 tablespoons canola oil
- 1 fresh beef brisket (4 to 5 pounds)
- 3 celery ribs, cut into 1-inch pieces
- 3 large carrots, cut into ¼-inch slices
- 2 large onions, sliced
- 1 pound medium fresh mushrooms
- ¾ cup cold water
- ¾ cup tomato sauce
- 3 tablespoons Worcestershire sauce
- 1 tablespoon prepared horseradish

1. In a Dutch oven, heat oil over medium heat. Brown brisket on both sides. Remove from pan.
2. Add celery, carrots and onions to same pan; cook and stir for 4-6 minutes or until crisp-tender. Stir in remaining ingredients.
3. Return brisket to pan, fat side up. Bring mixture to a boil. Reduce the heat; simmer, covered, 2½ to 3 hours or until the meat is tender. Remove beef and vegetables; keep warm. Skim fat from pan juices. If desired, thicken juices.
4. Cut brisket diagonally across the grain into thin slices. Serve with vegetables and pan juices.
Note: This is a fresh beef brisket, not corned beef.

HONEY CHALLAH

I use these shiny beautiful loaves as the centerpiece of my spread. I love the taste of honey, but you can also add chocolate chips, cinnamon, orange zest or almonds. Leftover slices work well in bread pudding or for French toast.

—**Jennifer Newfield** Los Angeles, CA

Prep: 45 min. + rising
Bake: 30 min. + cooling
Makes: 2 loaves (24 servings each)

- 2 packages (¼ ounce each) active dry yeast
- ½ teaspoon sugar
- 1½ cups warm water (110° to 115°), divided
- 5 large eggs
- ⅔ cup plus 1 teaspoon honey, divided
- ½ cup canola oil
- 2 teaspoons salt
- 6 to 7 cups bread flour
- 1 cup boiling water
- 2 cups golden raisins
- 1 tablespoon water
- 1 tablespoon sesame seeds

1. In a small bowl, dissolve yeast and sugar in 1 cup of warm water. Separate 2 eggs; refrigerate 2 egg whites. Place remaining egg yolks and eggs in a large bowl. Add ⅔ cup honey, oil, salt, yeast mixture, 3 cups of flour and the remaining water; beat on medium speed 3 minutes. Stir in enough of remaining flour to form a soft dough (dough will be sticky).

2. Pour boiling water over raisins in a small bowl; let stand 5 minutes. Drain and pat dry. Turn dough onto a floured surface; knead until it's smooth and elastic, about 6-8 minutes. Knead in the raisins. Place in a greased bowl, turning once to grease the top. Cover with plastic wrap and let rise in a warm place until almost doubled, about 1½ hours.

3. Punch down dough. Turn onto a lightly floured surface. Divide the dough in half. Divide one portion into six pieces. Roll each into a 16-in. rope. Place ropes parallel on a greased baking sheet; pinch ropes together at the top.

4. To braid, take the rope on the right and carry it over the two ropes beside it, then slip it under the middle rope and carry it over the last two ropes. Lay the rope down parallel to the other ropes; it is now on the far left side. Repeat these steps until you reach the end. As the braid moves to the left, you can pick up your loaf and recenter it on your work surface as needed. Pinch ends to seal and tuck under. For a fuller loaf, using your hands, push the ends of the loaf closer together. Repeat process with remaining dough. Cover with kitchen towels; let rise in a warm place until almost doubled, about 30 minutes.

5. Preheat oven to 350°. In a small bowl, whisk remaining egg whites and honey with water; brush over loaves. Sprinkle with sesame seeds. Bake 30-35 minutes or until golden brown and bread sounds hollow when tapped. Remove from pans to a wire rack to cool.

TZIMMES

I found this recipe a long time ago. It has become our traditional side dish for every Hanukkah and Passover feast and is a favorite of young and old alike. It also complements chicken and turkey well.

—**Cheri Bragg** Viola, DE

Prep: 20 min. • **Bake:** 1¾ hours
Makes: 12 servings

- 3 pounds sweet potatoes (about 4 large), peeled and cut into chunks
- 2 pounds medium carrots, cut into ½-inch chunks
- 1 package (12 ounces) pitted dried plums, halved
- 1 cup orange juice
- 1 cup water
- ¼ cup honey
- ¼ cup packed brown sugar
- 2 teaspoons ground cinnamon
- ¼ cup butter, cubed

1. In a greased 13x9-in. baking dish, combine the sweet potatoes, carrots and plums. Combine the orange juice, water, honey, brown sugar and cinnamon; pour over vegetables.

2. Cover and bake at 350° for 1 hour. Uncover; dot with butter. Bake 45-60 minutes longer, carefully stirring every 15 minutes, or until vegetables are tender and sauce is thickened.

PICKLED PEPPERONCINI DEVILED EGGS

It's hard to resist these adorable deviled trees on our holiday buffet table. The avocado filling has pepperoncini and cilantro for extra zip.

—**Carmell Childs** Clawson, UT

.....

Start to Finish: 30 min.
Makes: 1 dozen

- 6 hard-boiled large eggs
- 1 jar (16 ounces) garlic and dill pepperoncini
- 1 medium ripe avocado, peeled and pitted
- 1 tablespoon minced fresh cilantro, divided
- ¼ teaspoon salt
- ⅛ teaspoon pepper
- 1 tablespoon minced sweet red pepper
- ¼ teaspoon chili powder

1. Cut eggs lengthwise in half. Remove yolks, reserving whites. Mash yolks. Stir in 1 teaspoon of minced garlic from the pepperoncini jar and 2 teaspoons of pepperoncini juice. Add 3 tablespoons minced pepperoncini and the whole avocado; mash it with a fork until it is smooth. Stir in 2 teaspoons cilantro, salt and pepper.
2. Cut a small hole in the tip of a pastry bag or in a corner of a food-safe plastic bag; insert a medium star tip. Transfer avocado mixture to bag. Pipe into egg whites, swirling it upward to resemble Christmas trees. Sprinkle trees with minced red pepper, chili powder and remaining cilantro.
3. Cut open and seed one of the larger pepperoncini; slice into 12 small diamond shapes to top Christmas trees. Refrigerate, covered, until serving.

TEST KITCHEN TIP
Try this handy way to serve deviled eggs. Put them in paper or foil cupcake liners and set them in muffin tins for serving. The eggs stay upright and tidy in the cups, and they won't slide around on people's plates.

NANNY'S PARMESAN MASHED POTATOES

My grandsons rave over these creamy potatoes loaded with Parmesan. That's all the endorsement I need. Sometimes I use golden or red potatoes, with skins on.

—**Kallee Krong-Mccreery** Escondido, CA

Prep: 20 min. • **Cook:** 20 min.
Makes: 12 servings (¾ cup each)

- 5 pounds potatoes, peeled and cut into 1-inch pieces
- ¾ cup butter, softened
- ¾ cup sour cream
- ½ cup grated Parmesan cheese
- 1¼ teaspoons garlic salt
- 1 teaspoon salt
- ½ teaspoon pepper
- ¾ to 1 cup 2% milk, warmed
- 2 tablespoons minced fresh parsley

1. Place potatoes in a 6-qt. stockpot; add water to cover. Bring to a boil. Reduce heat; cook, uncovered, 10-15 minutes or until tender. Drain potatoes; return to pot and stir over low heat 1 minute to dry.
2. Coarsely mash potatoes, gradually adding butter, sour cream, cheese, seasonings and enough milk to reach desired consistency. Stir in parsley.

HERB-CRUSTED PRIME RIB

Prime rib always makes an impression on a holiday dinner table. But it's actually easy to prepare. This roast is wonderfully flavored with lots of fresh herbs.

—**Jennifer Dennis** Alhambra, CA

Prep: 20 min. • **Bake:** 1¾ hours + standing
Makes: 8 servings

- 1 large shallot, coarsely chopped
- 6 garlic cloves, quartered
- 3 tablespoons minced fresh rosemary or 1 tablespoon dried rosemary
- 2 tablespoons minced fresh oregano or 2 teaspoons dried oregano
- 2 tablespoons minced fresh thyme or 2 teaspoons dried thyme
- 2 tablespoons minced fresh sage or 2 teaspoons rubbed sage
- 2 tablespoons olive oil
- 3 teaspoons pepper
- 1 teaspoon salt
- 1 bone-in beef rib roast (4 pounds)

SAUCE
- 1½ cups reduced-sodium beef broth
- 1 cup dry red wine or additional reduced-sodium beef broth
- 1 teaspoon butter
- ½ teaspoon salt

1. Preheat oven to 350°. Place the first six ingredients in a food processor; cover and pulse until finely chopped. Add oil, pepper and salt; cover and process until blended. Rub over roast. Place on a rack in a large roasting pan.
2. Bake, uncovered, 1¾ to 2¼ hours or until meat reaches desired doneness (for medium-rare, a thermometer should read 145°; medium, 160°; well-done, 170°).
3. Remove the roast to a serving platter and keep warm; let it stand 15 minutes before slicing.
4. Meanwhile, in a small saucepan, bring broth and wine to a boil; cook until liquid is reduced to 1 cup. Remove from heat; stir in butter and salt. Slice roast; serve with sauce.

HOLIDAY TREATS

SNOW ANGEL COOKIES

Why not enjoy a little snow at the holidays, no matter where you are. Head to the kitchen and bake a batch of angel cookies swirled with heavenly frosting.
—**Carolyn Moseley** Dayton, OH

Prep: 40 min. + chilling
Bake: 15 min./batch + cooling
Makes: about 5 dozen

- 1 cup butter, softened
- 1 cup granulated sugar
- 1½ teaspoons vanilla extract
- 2 large eggs
- 3½ cups all-purpose flour
- 1 teaspoon ground cinnamon
- ½ teaspoon baking powder
- ½ teaspoon salt
- ¼ teaspoon ground nutmeg
- ¼ teaspoon ground cloves

FROSTING
- 9 cups confectioners' sugar
- ¾ cup shortening
- ½ cup lemon juice
- 4 to 6 tablespoons water
  Coarse sugar, optional

1. In a large bowl, beat the butter, sugar and vanilla until blended. Beat in the eggs, one at a time. In another bowl, whisk the flour, cinnamon, baking powder, salt, nutmeg and cloves; gradually beat into creamed mixture.

2. Divide dough in half. Shape each into a disk; wrap in plastic. Refrigerate 1 hour or until firm enough to roll.

3. Preheat the oven to 350°. On a lightly floured surface, roll each portion of dough to ⅛-in. thickness. Cut with a floured 4-in. angel-shaped cookie cutter. Place 1 in. apart on ungreased baking sheets.

4. Bake 12-14 minutes or until the edges begin to brown. Remove from pans to wire racks to cool completely.

5. For frosting, in a large bowl, beat the confectioners' sugar, shortening, lemon juice and enough of the water to reach a spreading consistency. Spread or pipe over cookies; sprinkle with coarse sugar.

RED VELVET PEPPERMINT THUMBPRINTS

Red velvet cookies and cakes are so pretty, but I always wish they had a bigger flavor. So I infused these thumbprints with a peppermint pop.
—**Priscilla Yee** Concord, CA

Prep: 30 min. • **Bake:** 10 min./batch + cooling
Makes: about 4 dozen

- 1 cup butter, softened
- 1 cup sugar
- 1 large egg
- 4 teaspoons red food coloring
- 1 teaspoon peppermint extract
- 2½ cups all-purpose flour
- 3 tablespoons baking cocoa
- 1 teaspoon baking powder
- ¼ teaspoon salt
- 2 cups white baking chips
- 2 teaspoons canola oil
- ¼ cup crushed peppermint candies

1. Preheat oven to 350°. In a large bowl, cream the butter and sugar until light and fluffy. Beat in the egg, food coloring and extract. In another bowl, whisk the flour, cocoa, baking powder and salt; gradually beat into creamed mixture.

2. Shape dough into 1-in. balls. Place 1 in. apart on ungreased baking sheets. Press a deep indentation in the center of each with the end of a wooden spoon handle.

3. Bake 9-11 minutes or until set. Remove from pans to wire racks to cool.

4. In a microwave, melt baking chips with the oil; stir until smooth. Spoon a scant teaspoon filling into each cookie. Drizzle tops with remaining mixture. Sprinkle with peppermint candies. Let stand until set.

RASPBERRY RED BAKEWELL TART

I fell for this British dessert while stationed in Dubai. Jam with almond filling is traditional, but red velvet makes it a holiday dazzler. The recipe makes enough icing to cover the top.

—Crystal Schlueter Babbitt, MN

Prep: 30 min. + freezing
Bake: 30 min. + cooling
Makes: 12 servings

- 1 sheet refrigerated pie pastry
- 1 large egg white, lightly beaten

FILLING
- ¼ cup seedless raspberry jam
- ⅔ cup butter, softened
- ¾ cup sugar
- 3 large eggs
- 1 large egg yolk
- 1 tablespoon baking cocoa
- 2 teaspoons red paste food coloring
- 1 cup ground almonds

ICING
- 2½ cups confectioners' sugar
- 3 tablespoons water
- ¼ teaspoon almond extract

1. Preheat oven to 350°. Unroll pastry sheet into a 9-in. fluted tart pan with removable bottom; trim even with rim. Freeze 10 minutes.
2. Line unpricked pastry with a double thickness of foil. Fill with pie weights, dried beans or uncooked rice. Bake for 12-15 minutes or until edges are golden brown.
3. Remove foil and weights; brush bottom of crust with egg white. Bake 6-8 minutes longer or until golden brown. Cool on a wire rack.
4. Spread jam over bottom of crust. In a bowl, cream butter and sugar until light and fluffy. Gradually beat in eggs, egg yolk, cocoa and food coloring. Fold in ground almonds. Spread over jam.
5. Bake 30-35 minutes or until filling is set. Cool completely on a wire rack.
6. In a small bowl, mix confectioners' sugar, water and extract until smooth; drizzle or pipe over the tart. Refrigerate the leftovers.

Note: Let pie weights cool before storing. Beans and rice may be reused for pie weights, but not for cooking.

HOLIDAY DANISH PUFFS

It's worth the extra effort to make this delightful candy cane-shaped dessert. Best of all, the recipe makes two pastries, so it's perfect for gift-giving.

—Susan Garoutte Georgetown, TX

Prep: 45 min. • **Bake:** 1 hour + cooling
Makes: 2 pastries (8 servings each)

- 1 cup all-purpose flour
- ½ cup cold butter, cubed
- 2 to 3 tablespoons cold water

TOPPING
- 1 cup water
- ½ cup butter, cubed
- ¼ teaspoon salt
- 1 cup all-purpose flour
- 3 large eggs
- ½ teaspoon almond extract

FROSTING
- 1½ cups confectioners' sugar
- 2 tablespoons butter, softened
- 2 tablespoons water
- 1½ teaspoons vanilla extract
- ½ cup sliced almonds, toasted

1. Place flour in a small bowl; cut in butter until crumbly. Gradually add water, tossing with a fork until the dough holds together when pressed. Divide dough in half. On a lightly floured surface, roll each into a 14x2½-in. rectangle. Transfer to an ungreased baking sheet; curve one end of each pastry to form tops of canes. Refrigerate while preparing topping.
2. Preheat the oven to 350°. In a large saucepan, combine water, butter and salt; bring to a rolling boil. Add flour all at once and beat until blended. Cook over medium heat, stirring vigorously until mixture pulls away from sides of pan and forms a ball. Remove from heat; let stand 5 minutes.
3. Add the eggs, one at a time, beating well after each addition until smooth. Add the extract; continue beating until mixture is smooth and shiny. Spread it over the pastry dough.
4. Bake 60-70 minutes or until puffed and golden brown. Cool on pans 10 minutes before removing to a wire rack; cool it completely.
5. In a small bowl, beat confectioners' sugar, butter, water and extract until smooth. Spread over pastries; sprinkle with almonds. Refrigerate leftovers.

Note: To toast nuts, bake in a shallow pan in a 350° oven for 5-10 minutes or cook in a skillet over low heat until lightly browned, stirring occasionally.

ALPHABETICAL INDEX

SUBSTITUTIONS & EQUIVALENTS

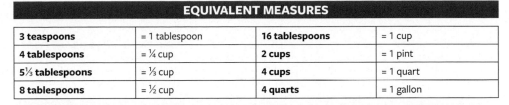

EQUIVALENT MEASURES

3 teaspoons	= 1 tablespoon	16 tablespoons	= 1 cup
4 tablespoons	= ¼ cup	2 cups	= 1 pint
5⅓ tablespoons	= ⅓ cup	4 cups	= 1 quart
8 tablespoons	= ½ cup	4 quarts	= 1 gallon

FOOD EQUIVALENTS

Macaroni	1 cup (3½ ounces) uncooked	= 2½ cups cooked
Noodles, Medium	3 cups (4 ounces) uncooked	= 4 cups cooked
Popcorn	⅓-½ cup unpopped	= 8 cups popped
Rice, Long Grain	1 cup uncooked	= 3 cups cooked
Rice, Quick-Cooking	1 cup uncooked	= 2 cups cooked
Spaghetti	8 ounces uncooked	= 4 cups cooked

Bread	1 slice	= ¾ cup soft crumbs, ¼ cup fine dry crumbs
Graham Crackers	7 squares	= ½ cup finely crushed
Buttery Round Crackers	12 crackers	= ½ cup finely crushed
Saltine Crackers	14 crackers	= ½ cup finely crushed

Bananas	1 medium	= ⅓ cup mashed
Lemons	1 medium	= 3 tablespoons juice, 2 teaspoons grated peel
Limes	1 medium	= 2 tablespoons juice, 1½ teaspoons grated peel
Oranges	1 medium	= ¼-⅓ cup juice, 4 teaspoons grated peel

Cabbage	1 head = 5 cups shredded	Green Pepper	1 large = 1 cup chopped
Carrots	1 pound = 3 cups shredded	Mushrooms	½ pound = 3 cups sliced
Celery	1 rib = ½ cup chopped	Onions	1 medium = ½ cup chopped
Corn	1 ear fresh = ⅔ cup kernels	Potatoes	3 medium = 2 cups cubed

Almonds	1 pound = 3 cups chopped	Pecan Halves	1 pound = 4½ cups chopped
Ground Nuts	3¾ ounces = 1 cup	Walnuts	1 pound = 3¾ cups chopped

EASY SUBSTITUTIONS

WHEN YOU NEED...		USE...
Baking Powder	1 teaspoon	½ teaspoon cream of tartar + ¼ teaspoon baking soda
Buttermilk	1 cup	1 tablespoon lemon juice or vinegar + enough milk to measure 1 cup (let stand 5 minutes before using)
Cornstarch	1 tablespoon	2 tablespoons all-purpose flour
Honey	1 cup	1¼ cups sugar + ¼ cup water
Half-and-Half Cream	1 cup	1 tablespoon melted butter + enough whole milk to measure 1 cup
Onion	1 small, chopped (⅓ cup)	1 teaspoon onion powder or 1 tablespoon dried minced onion
Tomato Juice	1 cup	½ cup tomato sauce + ½ cup water
Tomato Sauce	2 cups	¾ cup tomato paste + 1 cup water
Unsweetened Chocolate	1 square (1 ounce)	3 tablespoons baking cocoa + 1 tablespoon shortening or oil
Whole Milk	1 cup	½ cup evaporated milk + ½ cup water

GET COOKING WITH A WELL-STOCKED KITCHEN

In a perfect world, you would plan weekly or even monthly menus and have all the ingredients on hand to make each night's dinner. The reality, however, is that you likely haven't thought about dinner until you've walked through the door.

With a reasonably stocked pantry, refrigerator and freezer, you'll still be able to serve a satisfying meal in short order. Consider these tips:

QUICK-COOKING MEATS—such as boneless chicken breasts, chicken thighs, pork tenderloin, pork chops, ground meats, Italian sausage, sirloin and flank steaks, fish fillets and shrimp—should be stocked in the freezer. Wrap them individually (except shrimp), so you can remove only the amount you need. For the quickest defrosting, wrap meats for freezing in small, thin packages.

FROZEN VEGETABLES packaged in plastic bags are a real time-saver. Simply pour out the amount needed—no additional preparation is required.

PASTAS, RICE, RICE MIXES AND COUSCOUS are great staples to have in the pantry—and they generally have a long shelf life. Remember that thinner pastas, such as angel hair, cook faster than thicker pastas, and fresh (refrigerated) pasta cooks faster than dried.

DAIRY PRODUCTS like milk, sour cream, cheeses (shredded, cubed or crumbled), eggs, yogurt, butter and margarine are perishable, so check the use-by date on packages and replace as needed.

CONDIMENTS like ketchup, mustard, mayonnaise, salad dressings, salsa, taco sauce, soy sauce, stir-fry sauce, hot sauce, lemon juice and lime juice add flavor to many dishes. Personalize the list to suit your family's tastes.

FRESH FRUIT AND VEGETABLES can make a satisfying pre-dinner snack. Oranges and apples are not as perishable as bananas. Ready-to-use salad greens are perfect for an instant salad.

DRIED HERBS, SPICES, VINEGARS and seasoning mixes add lots of flavor and keep for months.

PASTA SAUCES, OLIVES, BEANS, broths, canned tomatoes, canned vegetables and canned or dried soups are ideal to have on hand for a quick meal—and many of these items are common recipe ingredients.

GET YOUR FAMILY INTO THE HABIT of posting a grocery list. When an item is used up or is almost gone, just add it to the list for your next shopping trip. This way you're less likely to run completely out of an item, and you'll also save time when writing your grocery list.

MAKE THE MOST OF YOUR TIME EVERY NIGHT

With recipes in hand and the kitchen stocked, you're well on the way to a relaxing family meal. Here are some pointers to help get dinner on the table fast:

PREHEAT THE OVEN OR GRILL before starting on the recipe.

PULL OUT THE REQUIRED INGREDIENTS, mixing tools and cooking tools before beginning any prep work.

USE CONVENIENCE ITEMS whenever possible. Think pre-chopped garlic, onion and peppers, shredded or cubed cheese, seasoning mixes and jarred sauces.

MULTITASK! While the meat is simmering for a main dish, toss a salad together, cook a side dish or start on dessert.

ENCOURAGE HELPERS. Have younger children set the table. Older ones can help with ingredient preparation or can even assemble the recipes themselves.

TAKE CARE OF TWO MEALS IN ONE NIGHT by planning main-dish leftovers or making a double batch of favorite sides.

TRICKS TO TAME HUNGER WHEN IT STRIKES

Are the kids begging for a pre-supper snack? Calm their rumbling tummies with nutritious, not-too-filling noshes.

START WITH A SMALL TOSSED SALAD. Try a ready-to-serve salad mix, and add their favorite salad dressing and a little protein, like cubed cheese or julienned slices of deli meat.

CUT UP AN APPLE and smear a little peanut butter on each slice, or offer other fruits such as seedless grapes, cantaloupe, oranges or bananas. For variety, give kids vanilla yogurt or reduced-fat ranch dressing as a dipper, or combine a little reduced-fat sour cream with a sprinkling of brown sugar. Too busy to cut up the fruit? A fruit snack cup will also do the trick.

DURING THE COLD MONTHS, a small mug of soup with a few oyster crackers on top can really hit the spot.

RAW VEGGIES such as carrots, cucumbers, mushrooms, broccoli and cauliflower are tasty treats, especially when served with a little hummus for dipping. Many of these vegetables can be purchased already cut.

OFFER A SMALL SERVING of cheese and crackers. Look for sliced cheese, and cut the slices into smaller squares to fit the crackers. Choose a cracker that's made from whole wheat, such as an all-natural seven-grain cracker.